From *Verismo* to Experimentalism

Essays on the Modern Italian Novel

From *Verismo* to Experimentalism

Essays on the Modern Italian Novel

Edited by Sergio Pacifici

Indiana University Press

BLOOMINGTON   LONDON

Published in Canada by Fitzhenry & Whiteside Limited,
Don Mills, Ontario

Library of Congress catalog card number: 74–98980
SBN: 253–32515–3 [CL.]
     253–20134–9 [PA.]

Manufactured in the United States of America

To Professor Giuseppe Cardillo

Contributors

SERGIO PACIFICI, the editor of this volume, is Professor of Romance Languages at Queens College of the City University of New York. A contributing editor to the *Grolier International Encyclopedia*, the *Encyclopedia Americana*, and *Books Abroad*, he is the author of *A Guide to Contemporary Italian Literature: From Futurism to Neorealism* (New York, 1962) and *The Modern Italian Novel: From Manzoni to Svevo* (Carbondale, Ill., 1967).

JOHN FRECCERO received his Ph.D. at the Johns Hopkins University and is now Professor of Italian at Yale University. He is the editor of *Dante: A Collection of Critical Essays* (Englewood Cliffs, N. J., 1965) and of numerous scholarly essays on Dante and contemporary Italian writers, which have appeared in *Italica*, *Italian Quarterly*, the *PMLA*, and *Dante Studies*.

E. ALLEN McCORMICK, Professor of German and Director of Comparative Literature at Queens College of the City University of New York, is the author of several monographs, translations, and critical studies, among which are *Theodor Storm's Novellen: Essays on Literary Technique* (Chapel Hill, N. C., 1964) and *Johann Elias Schlegel, on Imitation and Other Writings*, translated, with an Introduction (New York, 1965). His *History of German Literary Criticism* will appear in the near future.

G. SINGH was educated at the Universities of Rajasthan (India), London, Milan, and Bologna, achieving his degrees in English and Italian. His publications include a study of *Leo-*

pardi and the Theory of Poetry (Lexington, Ky., 1964) and numerous translations and critical essays on major English and Italian writers. Dr. Singh is at present a Reader in Italian at Queen's University at Belfast, Ireland.

GIACOMO DEBENEDETTI, a brilliant editor, translator, and critic of European and American literature, was a Lecturer in Italian at the University of Rome until his death in 1966. His critical essays have been brought out in three volumes, *Saggi critici* (Milan, 1929, 1945, and 1963). A complete edition of his work (which includes narrative as well as criticism) is being readied for publication by Signora Renata Debenedetti.

IRVING HOWE is Professor of English and Comparative Literature at Hunter College of the City University of New York. He is a Fellow at Indiana University School of Letters, Editor of *Dissent,* and a recipient of numerous honors and awards, including a Guggenheim fellowship. His writings have appeared in many leading publications. His recent books include *Politics and the Novel* (New York, 1958), *The Radical Papers* (New York, 1966), and *Steady Work: Essays in the Politics of a Democratic Radicalism* (New York, 1966).

R. W. B. LEWIS, Master of Calhoun College and Director of American Studies at Yale University, is a well-known critic and perceptive commentator of American and continental literature. His work includes *The American Adam* (Chicago, 1956), *The Picaresque Saint* (New York, 1958), *Trials of the World* (New Haven, 1965), and *The Poetry of Hart Crane* (Princeton, 1967). He held the Kenyon Review Fellowship in 1954 and a Guggenheim fellowship in 1966.

DONALD HEINEY, a California-born critic, novelist, and translator, has spent considerable periods of his life in Italy, in Bologna and Venice, as a Fulbright Fellow in 1959–60, and in Rome, as a grantee of the American Council of Learned

Societies and the American Philosophical Society, in 1962–1963. He is the author of *America in Modern Italian Literature* (New Brunswick, 1964), and *Three Italian Novelists* (Ann Arbor, 1968). At present, he is Professor of English and Director of the Program in Comparative Literature, University of California, Irvine.

GIAN-PAOLO BIASIN received his Ph.D. at the Johns Hopkins University. He is Associate Professor of Italian in the Department of Romance Studies at Cornell University and Associate Editor of the *Italian Quarterly*. His book on Cesare Pavese, the first full-length study in English of the novelist, was published by Cornell University Press in 1968 with the title *The Smile of the Gods*. Mr. Biasin has published in *Modern Language Notes, Belfagor, La Comunità internazionale,* and other journals.

FRANK ROSENGARTEN has taught at Columbia University, Case Western Reserve, and Queens College of City University of New York, where he is now Associate Professor of Italian. His study of *Vasco Pratolini* was published in 1965 by Southern Illinois University Press. Case Western Reserve University Press recently brought out his second work, *The Italian Anti-Fascist Press (1919–1945)*. Mr. Rosengarten is the recipient of a Junior Fellowship from the National Endowment Foundation for the Humanities.

OLGA RAGUSA, Professor of Italian at Columbia University, is a critic and translator of continental European literature and editor of *Italica*, the journal of the American Association of Teachers of Italian. Her numerous publications include *Mallarmé in Italy: Literary Influences and Critical Responses* (New York, 1957), *Verga's Milanese Tales* (New York, 1964), and *Luigi Pirandello*, in the "Columbia Essays on Modern Writers" series (1968).

Contents

Preface

This volume does not propose to offer a detailed history of the modern novel in Italy, for such an ambitious project requires a far different orientation and methodology. Regrettably, only a very small number of writers could be included in this anthology, but we trust that the depth of sustained analyses is to be preferred to coverage and inclusiveness. Choices, as editors surely know, are difficult to make, especially in a project that spans several decades of a country's literary history. Decisions of what to exclude are often as agonizing as decisions of what to include, and all choices are destined to be questioned, indeed challenged, by the informed reader with his own table of preferences. Nonetheless, it is hoped that the essays in this volume will make possible a better understanding of their subjects by addressing themselves to those issues that illustrate the diversity as well as the continuity and development of the Italian novel.

The fact that this collection—the first of its kind in English—would even be published demonstrates the breadth and the seriousness of American interest in Italy. I believe I speak for all contributors when I express my opinion that this volume will amply justify its publication if it sharpens the curiosity of the general reader and prods other scholars to offer their own views of a sector of Italian letters that has still to receive the attention it justly deserves.

S. P.

Larchmont, N. Y.
July 25, 1969

Introduction

It is, or it should be, a well-known fact that, unlike England and France, Italy did not produce her first great novel until 1827, when Alessandro Manzoni published *I promessi sposi (The Betrothed)** in the first of two strikingly different versions of the work. A detailed analysis of the factors that delayed the birth of the novel in a country boasting a rich and influential narrative tradition dating back to the thirteenth century and Giovanni Boccaccio remains to be made. As I have suggested elsewhere,[1] our understanding of the problem before us will be enlarged once we grasp the fact that Italy was simply not blessed with those special conditions that made possible elsewhere in Europe the practice and acceptance of a new genre. Thus, for example, the great social and economic upheavals that transformed England and France into modern nations did not begin to reach Italy in any meaningful way until the beginning of the 1800's. Similarly, the centuries-old political fragmentation she endured, her lack of linguistic unity, the absence of a stable, well-defined social life, the weakness of her middle class, the preferential status traditionally enjoyed by poetry, a backward economy coupled with an archaic system of education that kept books out of the reach and understanding of the people—all these and still other factors played a decisively negative role in the emergence of a new literary genre in Italy.

It is precisely in the light of what has been said thus far that Manzoni's *The Betrothed* justly occupies a central position

---

* Italian works mentioned for the first time are followed by their English titles, which are in italic type if the English translation has been published and in roman type if it has not.

in the history of Italian literature. Thanks to a combination of fortuitous circumstances and sheer genius, Manzoni succeeded in transforming what had been a much disparaged mode of expression into an art form capable of expressing the entire spectrum of human emotions. Like Dante's *Comedy*, Manzoni's work was at once the product of a profound spiritual crisis and the reflection of a growing political awareness. It is no mere accident that the publication of *The Betrothed* should coincide with the birth of several clandestine political movements whose goal was the liberation of Italy from foreign tyranny.

From the perspective of quantity, if not of quality, the historical novel had a rather successful run in Italy and underwent its own special evolution. Thus, after the unification of the nation had been achieved, the novel moved toward a reinterpretation of the dramatic events of the *Risorgimento*—as in Ippolito Nievo's sprawling novel *Le confessioni di un italiano* (*The Castle of Fratta*, New York, 1951) or Antonio Fogazzaro's *Piccolo mondo antico* (*The World of the Past*, New York, 1962) or toward a personal and highly critical presentation of how the lofty ideals and the lives of thousands of young men who had fought to make unity possible had been betrayed by the political powerhouses—a view dramatically offered by Federico De Roberto's *I Vicerè* (*The Viceroys*, New York, 1962).

The historical novel had succeeded in satisfying artistic and intellectual needs. The realistic novel, which was being written in Italy during the second half of the century, was partly the result of the end of the romantic imagination and of the widespread European tendency to offer more accurate, objective, and impersonal accounts of the human experience. The fact that realism should reach Italy somewhat late (Balzac and Flaubert, the two acknowledged masters of this trend had completed their major work around 1850) constitutes another persuasive evidence that, by and large, literary movements are born and gain momentum only when certain social, cultural, and political-economic conditions are ready for them. The ad-

vanced social conditions and the sophistication of scientific
discoveries in France, for example, proved to be the major
factors in the development of the novel in that country. The
resulting "realism" and "naturalism" were simply new ways
to express the new reality of the times—a reality that, as the
artist understood, was too complex to be expressed by old
approaches and outmoded techniques. While both movements
were basically committed to the depiction of contemporary
society, its ills and flaws, the latter proposed, after Emile Zola,
to follow methods similar to, or patterned after, those used in
scientific laboratories. Italian *verismo* (closeness to "truth"
and "reality") had its own special qualities in its emphasis on
the passions (often sensual in a rather primitive way) and problems (usually economic) of the exploited peasantry and working class of the provinces and the Mezzogiorno. The achievements of the *veristi* were many, if not always startling: they
helped acquaint the national audience with little-known aspects
of rural life, thus indirectly improving the fabric of national
life, and contributed to fashioning a new language, which, for
all its closeness to the rhythm and structure of local speech,
never slipped into an outright use of dialects.

Realism, however, was more than a mere series of technical
innovations aiming at bridging the gap between what happens
in life and the re-creation of it through the modalities of literature. It signified an unparalleled freedom for the artist to treat
any aspect of contemporary life and manners—however sordid
it might seem, however unjustifiable as fitting ground of artistic
expression, however offensive to the cultural Establishment.
No two writers made use of identical methods to achieve their
goal. Yet, all realists were convinced that an objective, faithful
reproduction of reality or any part of it could never be accomplished without eliminating the exaggerations, the vagaries and
distortions, of romanticism, which viewed the world with the
heart and not with the intellect. Fortunately, in practice,
Italian realism seldom allowed itself to be lured by the possi-

bility of following semiscientific methods in order to arrive at a rendition of reality incontrovertible only because it was supported by documentary evidence. Beyond all issues raised by realism as a method, there loomed yet another substantial question begging an answer: could the writer seeking to understand himself and illuminate particular facets of the human condition achieve his goal by focusing exclusively on a world of things, material interests, and factual props? Those writers who considered realism as an end in itself enjoyed brief popularity and were soon forgotten, as they deserved to be. Those who realized that no tradition can be self-perpetuating endured. For them, the "happy few," innovations and experimentation remained ultimately justifiable in terms of what they contributed to giving the novel greater flexibility, scope, range, and depth. They understood that when an artist is faced with new experiences, he is forced by his creative impulse to invent new techniques of expression adequate to represent life as *he* sees it—something that accounts for the diversity of writers who subscribe to common assumptions.

Like any other literary tradition, realism was destined to change with time. Yet, its vitality and importance can be neither denied nor underestimated, for it is to realism that most contemporary writers owe their largest debt. It is fitting, therefore, that this volume should begin with a broad examination of the world of Giovanni Verga, who (as the essay in this volume will try to show) epitomizes those practices and innovations that served as models for the generations of writers who followed him.

Verga was by no means the first modern writer to depict the vicissitudes of poor, semi-forgotten men and women living in hamlets almost completely cut off from the pulsating centers of national life. The history of Italian literature has a rich tradition embedded in reality and supremely concerned with the plights of the plebe. However, he was unquestionably the first modern Italian novelist to achieve that perfect fusion of content and form that characterizes all significant works of imaginative writing. The reader of today will no doubt find odd the notions Verga expressed in the Preface to his masterpiece, *I Malavoglia* (*The House by the Medlar Tree*), particularly since we have been conditioned, especially in our country, to believe in human perfectibility achieved through competition and "self-improvement." But it should be clear that what Verga in the last analysis tells us is that without myths (call them the myth of home and the family or, as Verga's recent translator has it, "the meaning of work and the dignity of human striving and suffering"), man does not have the strength to cope with, let alone survive, the difficulties of life. There is, in his major works, a message particularly relevant to our own affluent society: the security that comes with the acquisition or possession of material values is an illusion bound to be shattered, with a force proportioned to one's wealth, when man confronts—psychologically, philosophically, and humanly—the universal condition of death.

It will not be a shocking surprise for the reader to find a master realist followed by a master psychological writer. The end of the last century is characterized by a concern not with externals, but internals, not with man's surroundings but his consciousness, not with what he does but what he thinks, even if his thoughts often prove to be completely at odds with his actions. "By the end of the century," writes Harry Levin, "the novel was more concerned with man's place in nature rather than man's place in history, and no man could be a hero to the naturalist."[2] The statement has excellent application to the work of Italo Svevo (1861–1928), the strangest "outsider" Italy has produced in modern times. Svevo's first novel, *Una vita*, 1892 (*A Life*, New York, 1963), firmly rooted in naturalism, already contains the seeds of the estrangement of the individual from his society and that lack of "heroism" that characterizes much contemporary fiction. *Senilità*, 1895 (*As a Man Grows Older*, New York, 1932), exhibits a further movement toward introspection fully realized in *La coscienza di Zeno*, 1923 (*The Confessions of Zeno*, New York, 1930). Gradually Svevo was able to do away with many trappings of the novel as it had been known: the eye of the narrator is turned inward, rather than outward; and chronology and history are displaced by psychology. Reality is no longer observed and re-created in a sociological or pathological manner, but as a mirror, however distorted, of the drives, the flaws, the anxieties of the protagonist himself. The central figure of his books is the probing, meditative hero, or, better still, the doubting, guilt-ridden, and insecure antihero. Indeed, as represented in his work, man is no arbiter of his destiny, no pilot of his course, no hero of a gigantic drama that takes place with unending regularity on the stage of life. He can only be a creature who acts instinctively and impulsively, groping for happiness but achieving only misery, knowing himself to be fundamentally insincere and incompetent, yet striving, or at least pretending, to achieve worthy goals in his private and public life. The irony is all in that contrast—in what he *is* and what he *longs* to be (if only in his imagination), in the pleasures and victories he seeks, and in the anguish and defeats he is doomed to suffer, more because of his ineptitude than because of fate.

To express his special world, Svevo needed a language that could effectively express the grayness and dullness of a provincial middle class. He found "his" style in the Triestino dialect, which is contaminated by German syntax but tempered by conventional Italian. The result, as someone recently remarked, is a kind of "merchants' Esperanto," which, in its own particular way, continued the gradual rejection of a conventional literary Italian (modeled on Manzoni's prose) begun by Giovanni Verga and continued by many major and minor novelists after him.

Luigi Pirandello (1867–1936) is Svevo's kin, at least insofar as their background and vision, not to say anything about their posture toward writing, are concerned. Both were born in cities

that were in the periphery of Italian cultural life—Svevo in
Trieste, Pirandello in Girgenti, Sicily; both spent several of
their formative years away from their native city or country—
Svevo in an Austrian school at Steignitz, Pirandello in Rome
and then at Bonn, where he received his degree with a thesis
on the dialect of Girgenti; finally, both were victims of family
personal and financial misfortunes that forced them to take
different directions than they had anticipated. Although I do
not subscribe fully to the theory that everything an artist con-
signs to the written page is shaped, and even determined by his
personal disasters, neuroses, or insignificant events, it is certain
that the prolonged mental illness of Pirandello's wife (whose
paranoiac jealousy caused him untold anguish) and Svevo's
frustrations at not achieving recognition had a great deal to do
with shaping their sensitivity and therefore the ways they
chose to look at life.

This notwithstanding, the differences between the two are
as deep as they are numerous. Where Svevo's humor evokes
our laughter by placing us in the enviable position of con-
templating serenely the follies of mankind, Pirandello's brand
of humor springs from what he defined, in a little-read essay
"On Humor," "the feeling of contrast," the smile of the on-
looker who sees something on the surface quite funny, only to
realize, when the intellectual process begins, the pathos, or
paradox, or downright tragedy of existence. Irony is Svevo's
chief weapon; sarcasm, Pirandello's. Svevo looks bemusedly
at the world; Pirandello identifies with its tragic condition.
Pirandello exploits the "explosion" of personality and is always
intent on identifying and analyzing the perennial conflict
between reality and illusion; Svevo continuously pokes fun at
the myth of personality by showing how lack of assertiveness
produces a salutary kind of "inaction" that brings success and
even happiness to his characters. Compromises and deceits are
viewed by Pirandello as necessary evils to avoid estrangement,
while Svevo considers them basic ingredients of human con-

tentment. If Svevo gave us the dimension of human failure with a smile on his lips, Pirandello could offer us only the tragic dimensions of the consciousness of "living." As Irving Howe perceptively notes, "Pirandello is a skeptic. His best work is characterized by unqualified doubt, at times by an extreme relativism of perspective that can be said to approach epistemological panic."[3] All certainties steadily crumble in his work, and everywhere we find disquieting signs of the difficulty or incapacity—of the individual and of society—to organize, devise, or invent a life that may be, in some ways, meaningful.

In an age dominated by introspection, it seems hard to imagine the existence of an artist like Aldo Palazzeschi (b. 1888). Yet, exist he does—acclaimed by his critics, who revere him as a superb narrator and a graceful stylist, and loved by an audience that has been reading him for well over half a century. My own assessment of him is less enthusiastic than that of his critics in Italy, who invariably praise him as the preserver of a great narrative tradition that is as old as their literature. But if Palazzeschi lacks that depth and range we have come to expect of great novelists, he is certainly a careful and astute craftsman. Light, invariably a bit mischievous, gifted with a wry sense of humor, he represents the best a provincial culture (the term is not used disparagingly here) could produce. A poet turned novelist, his fable-like, amusing novels deserve consideration in a volume that seeks to present the development of the novel in Italy: the quality of his canvases of his native Tuscany are memorable less for their profundity than for the light pastel colors that are bound to recall the paintings of Ottone Rosati.

Federigo Tozzi (1883–1920), born in the Tuscan city of Siena, has traditionally been an enigma, if not an embarrassment, to his critics. All his serious readers readily confess that they are impressed by the forceful way in which he creates characters sufficiently compelling to move us and shock us.

Nonetheless, they often add, no positive statement on his work can be made, either on stylistic grounds, or on structural ones—much less, on the manner in which he developed as a spinner of provincial tales. To these and other damaging comments, the late Luigi Russo adds, in his volume *I Narratori*: "... we must say with excessive simplicity that neither *Tre croci* nor *Il podere* (The Farm) seem to us masterpieces; and we cannot even speak [of them as] minor works of art, because Tozzi's art lacks, in order to be granted such a characterization, unity and cohesion of themes."[4] There is, to be sure, a great deal of substance in these contentions. Tozzi does lack that lyrical quality so pivotal to any Italian writer seeking recognition in his country; his provincialism is obvious, although it has been misinterpreted as a narrow outlook rather than a kind of liberating experience; and structurally his novels are nothing if not traditional. If Italian critics have been unresponsive to him, despite the publication of an increasing number of studies on his work that have appeared since his death in 1920, the outlook is distinctly more encouraging elsewhere. In this country he has been called "one of the three masters of Italian narrative writing since the unification of Italy,"[5] a judgment reinforced by his inclusion (by reason of his influence "upon contemporary Italian writers, particularly the young"[6]) in a recent anthology of modern Italian fiction. The fact that recognition of his worth should come from foreign critics is ironical, to be sure, but not surprising, since geographical distance is frequently helpful in formulating an objective assessment of a writer.

The inclusion of such a controversial artist as Tozzi in this volume was dictated by critical, rather than polemical reasons. Whatever his flaws may be—and they are undeniable—Tozzi belongs to that small group of artists who, with varying success, revolutionized the traditional concept of the novel in one way or another. Like Verga, Tozzi was unafraid to create characters speaking the only language they knew, an unliterary

Sienese incapable of unusual literary effects; like Verga, Tozzi
felt, biographically and artistically, that no amount of heroism
could change the basic condition of man at the mercy of the
mysterious, incomprehensible forces of Nature, man destined
to mistake the fleeting taste of honey (or, as in his books, the
taste of refined foods) as evidence of his permanency in the
world. Finally, like so many impelling writers, he sought to
reconstruct the meaning of the absurdity of existence not
through heroic gestures, but through a studied observation and
a highly controlled depiction of the most casual elements in
the ordinary lives of his characters.

The "case" of Ignazio Silone (b. 1900), as Italians call it, is
in every way exceptional. In 1929, in order to avoid being
imprisoned by the Fascists, by then in full control of all so-
called law enforcement agencies, Silone fled from his native
country to a self-imposed exile that was to last until 1945. A
good deal of his work—and quite likely the most enduring part
of it—was composed in Switzerland, where he had taken
refuge, and appeared in several translations before being published in the original. The reception accorded to his books,
particularly *Fontamara*, 1930 (New York, 1960) and *Pane e
vino*, 1937 (*Bread and Wine*, New York, 1962), was exceedingly enthusiastic and was instrumental in making him famous
everywhere except in his own country. Although he is not the
first writer of political novels Italy has produced in modern
times (one thinks here of Fogazzaro, Pirandello, and Alvaro,
among others), he is by far the most effective and most moving.
Irving Howe has offered an accurate definition of the political
novel as one in which *"we take to be dominant* political ideas
or the political milieu, a novel which permits this assumption
without thereby suffering any radical distortion and, it follows,
with the possibility of some analytical profit."[7] The point is
highly relevant to our understanding of Silone; but we will do
fuller justice to his art when we admit that the political element, seemingly the central preoccupation of his books, is al-

ways and persuasively fused with, if not subjugated to, the human needs of Silone's world. The "right" political order can ultimately be justified only in terms of its capacity to respond most completely to the fundamental concept of the worth of Man and his dignity, to the fulfillment of his hopes and expectations.

There are many remarkable sides to Silone: the character of his style, at once colloquial and genuinely poetic in its simplicity and understatements; the modest and yet perceptive manner in which the large questions of good and evil are discussed by his *cafoni* (the underdogs anywhere), who, incapable of organized resistance against the political Establishment, are forced to accept its legacy of exploitation and shame; the conflict between the cities and the country, a topical and irksome problem of our own time. But there is more to Silone. It is a quality Albert Camus singled out when he remarked that "Silone speaks to the whole of Europe." "The reason I feel myself so close to him," he continued, "is that he is at the same time so incredibly rooted in his national, even provincial, tradition."[8] A master of the understatement—a rare quality among the Italians—Silone is a novelist gifted with a compassionate understanding of life and with a humor rooted in the simple life of the disenfranchised *contadini*, who, although aware that life is fundamentally unjust, never allow themselves to become preys of despair and hopelessness. His is a humor which, to quote R. W. B. Lewis, "consists . . . of an inexhaustible awareness of the droll and the grotesque in human conduct, even in superhuman conduct."[9]

It would be problematic to find, among contemporary Italian writers, one who has so successfully reached as wide an international audience as Alberto Moravia. A prolific and industrious novelist, he has worked in many forms with varying degrees of success: from the novel to the novella, from the essay to the short story, from the play to cinema criticism, from high-level reportages to the short short story, the latter a genre capable of yielding as much fun as the sonnets of Giuseppe G. Belli, the Roman poet whose work has received Moravia's attention and praise. Literary diversity notwithstanding, the problems that recur in Moravia's books are relatively few and easily identifiable. Indeed, thematically at least, Moravia is a monotonous artist, a judgment with which he concurred when he remarked that, like good music composers, literary artists are rarely capable of too many tunes, as "their truth is self-repeating."[10]

Born in Rome in 1907, Moravia began his literary career in the Twenties when, after writing a couple of short stories, he published *Gli indifferenti*, 1929 (*The Time of Indifference*, New York, 1953), a book that overnight became one of the most controversial novels of our time. Since 1929, Moravia has busied himself with dramatizing the substance of bourgeois life—desiccated, as in T. S. Eliot's *Wasteland*, by affluence, insensitive, and downright vulgar. In an era of political conformity and hostility toward the novel (a genre whose critical stance fascism could neither view sympathetically nor tolerate), writing about the shabby values of a morally corrupt society must be regarded as a bold act, one for which Moravia had to pay a stiff price in that he was forced to write under a pseudonym in order to be published. All this is hardly designed to make a moralist out of Moravia, a role he would not accept and much less wish to assume, disinterested as he is in proposing viable alternatives to the morbid, "sick" world he depicts in his *oeuvre*, a world we should not have trouble recognizing as a monster of our own making. Moravia's books elicit our interest not only because they tell intriguing stories, but because they dramatize how sex and money are the two dominating forces of modern life as well as effective and valid instruments of power and "knowledge." It may be argued, with ample justification that the concern with sex and money is as old as literature itself and occupies a prominent place in the books of such diverse writers as Boccaccio and Machiavelli,

Flaubert and Stendhal, Hemingway and Faulkner. But in the fiction of Moravia sex and money permit the characters to establish and define a special relation with one another as well as with the world they live in, much in the same way as, say, Manzoni used the Roman Catholic religion or Verga used respect toward the tradition of the house or Silone used political action.

Elio Vittorini (1908–1966) belongs to the generation of writers who grew up and matured during the Fascist years. His work can best be understood by touching upon certain aspirations rooted in his private life and intellectual preparation. The son of an employee of the state railway, Vittorini left his native Syracuse (Sicily) at seventeen and headed for the urban north, the "mainland," and its opportunities. He worked with a construction gang in the northern city of Udine, then in Florence as a proofreader for a daily paper. A self-educated man, he came to understand his own literature by coming to grips with American and continental fiction, as a translator and as a critic. In the early Thirties he joined other intellectuals who had become disenchanted with the Fascist revolution and its false promises and turned to the political and literary left. This move implied, on the one hand, a kind of conspiratorial friendship with artists sharing similar views and, on the other hand, a commitment to keep in close contact with European and American literatures, a commitment which was disparaged by Fascist culture. One way to accomplish these objectives was to publish in such liberal, avant-garde literary magazines as *Solaria* and *Letteratura* and make the best foreign literary texts known in Italy. Later on, during World War II, Vittorini found it natural to become actively engaged in the struggle against the Fascist dictatorship by joining the Partisans.

For a good many years, from 1934 onward, Vittorini earned his livelihood by translating from American and English literature. He learned English painfully, and in an unorthodox manner to say the least—by translating *Robinson Crusoe* by consulting each word in a dictionary. Having mastered the language, he proceeded to present versions from the work of E. A. Poe, William Saroyan, William Faulkner, John Steinbeck, and D. H. Lawrence, among others. It is hazardous to state categorically how deeply his translations affected his own work, although it would be impossible to deny that, to some extent, they enabled Vittorini to find the style that was eventually to become the trademark of his genius. By the same token, his readings and his own experiences undoubtedly shaped his sensitivity and no doubt taught him how to look at the world. His best novel, and certainly one of the finest works of fiction of our century, is his most typical and his most lyrical. Entitled *Conversazione in Sicilia*, 1941 (*Conversation in Sicily*, New York, 1949), it is the record of a journey, at once literal and allegorical, of a young Linotype operator named Silvestro to his native Sicily in search of his identity and roots. *Conversation in Sicily*, aside from its being the most intriguing book Vittorini wrote, is the one that represents his most complete answer to a specifically structural and stylistic question of the first order:

> Can the modern novel, contaminated by other literary genres and other disciplines, still express the whole spectrum of human feelings without having to rely on the conventional ingredients of storytelling, plot, character development, and so forth? Can the novel manage to articulate something eternal and meaningful without pretending to be, as it were, "close to life"? In short, can the novel be like poetry, or, better still, like the opera, which effectively conveys feelings and moods without ever intending to reproduce life on the stage?

These and other points of immediate concern to the student of the novel as an art form and to the student of Italian literature were raised in an essay Vittorini prepared on the occasion of the 1949 publication of *Il garofano rosso* (*The Red Carnation*, New York, 1952), originally composed between 1932 and 1933 and brought out in several installments in *Solaria*. Regrettably, the problem haunting Vittorini until his death in

1966 was never resolved to his, and our, satisfaction. But the reader with more than a casual acquaintance with postwar continental European fiction is aware that that problem may well be one of the chief causes of the crises the novel has experienced since the demise of neorealism in the Fifties.

Were we to look for the connecting link between Elio Vittorini and Cesare Pavese, so different and yet so much alike, we would find it, first of all, in the work they cut out for themselves, with different reasons and motivations, as translators and critics of American literature. Beyond this common commitment, there is also a common extraordinary effort to chart new directions for imaginative writing, taking it beyond the frontiers of realism and of the psychological novel. In the novels of Vittorini, the movement is toward symbolism and allegory: things, people, actions are always what they obviously appear to be, fully recognizable by the attentive reader, but also, at times at any rate, something at once larger and more significant than their historical or literary meaning. In Pavese, the process is substantially different even if it is rooted in a concept to which Vittorini could have subscribed: "The art of the nineteenth century," Pavese noted in his sensitive diary, *Il mestiere di vivere*, 1952 (*The Burning Brand*, New York, 1961), "was centered on the development of situations . . . the art of the twentieth century, on static essentials. In the first, the hero was not the same at the beginning of the story as he was at the end; now he remains the same." Pavese began thinking about the problems of his craft early in his career, and once confessed to an interviewer that when writing a novel his point of departure was "an indistinct rhythm, a play of events that, more than anything else, are sensations and feelings."[11] After his creative vein had undergone an unusually complicated metamorphosis, Pavese ultimately found the answer to his creative problem by mythologizing his tales. Myth, in his words, has "a language of its own, an instrument of expression." "When we retell an old myth," he continued, "—a

proper name, an action, a heroic feat—we are expressing, with
the utmost economy of means, a general and comprehensive
fact, a core of reality which quickens and feeds a whole organic
growth of passion and human existence, an entire conceptual
complex."[12]

Born at Santo Stefano Belbo, in Piedmont, in 1908, Pavese
took his degree in American literature with a thesis on Walt
Whitman. Pavese began his literary career in 1938 by publishing a volume of poems, *Lavorare stanca* (Work Is Wearying),
which contain the seeds of all the novels he was to write. As
a writer and as one of the managing editors of the liberal,
leftist publishing house of Giulio Einaudi, he led an unusually
rewarding, intellectually productive, and exciting existence. But
there is little evidence that his achievements ever made up for
the loneliness he experienced, even when he was among his
friends. Paradoxically enough, he seemed to taste the pleasure
of contentment shortly before he took his life, in 1950.

Pavese's incapacity to find a measure of happiness, however
illusory, is reflected in the morose, brooding characters that
people his books. As in the case of his long-time friend Vittorini, Cesare Pavese's contribution to modern fiction in Italy
is less technical than stylistic. From the formal point of view,
his books are traditional; but their language, with its restrained
lyricism, is a unique blend of Piedmontese dialect with literary
Italian, and the result is an evocative style that has a special,
distinct rhythm. The result, as his most recent translator remarks, "is a terse, pungently oblique new domestic language
of 'small' people, apparently living small lives, the inflection of
whose speech, however, carry the full weight of time."[13] Just
as Vittorini remained committed to creating a novel of feelings
without exploiting traditional narrative modes and structures,
so Pavese strove to give his readers the *sense* of reality by
transforming what could otherwise be banal action into my-
thologized re-creations of life. "The surest, and the quickest,
way for us to arouse the sense of wonder," he stated in his

Dialoghi con Leucò, 1945–1946 (*Dialogues with Leucò*)—a work he called his best—"is to stare, unafraid, at a single object. Suddenly—miraculously—it will look like something we have never seen before."[14]

No panorama of representative modern Italian novelists can avoid coming to grips with two aspects that distinguish the literary scene: the impressive number of writers who, from the Forties through the Fifties, have dealt with, or have been inspired by, the Resistance movement; and the experimental work that characterizes a rather large share of the writings of such an oldtimer as Carlo Emilio Gadda (b. 1893) and of the young, dynamic Pier Paolo Pasolini (b. 1922). The purpose of the two essays that complete this volume is to place in their proper context a number of writers who have played a definite role in extending, modifying, and renovating—thematically or stylistically or both—a novelistic tradition that begins with Alessandro Manzoni.

Most critics agree that from the Forties to the Fifties the socio-political situation in Italy served as a source of inspiration—possibly the richest one—for poets and novelists alike. Although it is perhaps hazardous, as in the case of France, to speak of a Resistance novel, the critic can no longer avoid coming to grips with the immediate questions posed by those works of fiction depicting a special moment of Italian literary history: What is the worth and significance of the novels of the Resistance qua novels? What did they contribute to the development of the genre and to the illumination of the human condition?

Our historical perspective is, to be sure, still too limited to permit answers that may claim to be definitive. But some general reflections about the significance—thematic, stylistic, and structural, not to say "moral"—and the impact such novels have had upon the younger generation of writers are in order. First, with few exceptions, under scrutiny the novels of the period (I am thinking primarily of Vittorini's *Conversazione in Sicilia* and *Uomini e no*) are notable less for their technical experimentations than for the courage and compassion with which they deal with certain issues avoided, for obvious political reasons, during fascism. Second, it is now clear that the traumatic experience of the Fascist era and the chaos, anguish, and devastation of World War II did not leave the sensibilities of writers old and young alike unscarred. After the terror of Nazi concentration camps and Hiroshima, the world could never be the same. Third, the revulsion toward the entire Fascist experience was so intense that the majority of writers (particularly those belonging to the generation of 1910) fell under the short-lived illusion that an engaged stance would balance the indolence and intellectual timidity of the Thirties. For the first time in his life, the writer faced a nation militarily, politically, and physically bankrupt; and for the first time he realized that he was free to depict things as they were. It is no wonder that in depicting humanity attempting to retrieve something it had lost—that special order of man in his world—he should turn to *verismo,* a school *sui generis* that had emerged at the end of the *Risorgimento.* In its orientation toward a candid representation of some of the ills plaguing the working class and the bourgeoisie and in its unadorned, colloquial manner of telling, the postwar Italian writer found an example he could follow, and a tradition he could extend.

A period of cultural parochialism, if not downright repression, was followed by one of sufficient freedom to permit a thorough, if at times oblique, criticism of all social institutions. What matters, I think, is not just what the climate permitted the writer to produce, but the new feelings it created. Possibly, as Frank Rosengarten points out in his essay, through its dramatization of the ideals that had sustained anti-Fascist writers, the so-called Resistance novel proved to be a kind of liberating experience, whose impact on the novels yet to be composed was to prove more radical than had been suspected.

The general disappointment with the political situation experienced by many intellectuals, beginning with 1950 or thereabouts, and their awareness of the practical difficulties of translating their ideals into reality, coupled with the problems brought about by the industrialization of life and culture in Italy, were to produce a climate ready for a new type of novel. What distinguishes the new or, as some would call it, the "anti" novel, is explored in the final essay of this volume by Olga Ragusa. The original handling of local dialects, often intelligently interwoven into the more literary style of the author; the looseness of the plot; the open-ended character of the novel; and the artist's dramatic rejection of many ground rules of his narrative tradition are the first qualities of the contemporary novel that strike us. Interestingly enough, the new avant-garde looks not to the young and vibrant Pier Paolo Pasolini (born in 1922), but to the much older Carlo Emilio Gadda (born in 1893) as its "authentic forerunner." It is Gadda, in fact, who throughout his long and unusual artistic activity (he is the author of what must surely rank as the largest number of unfinished novels by a contemporary writer), has been in the forefront of linguistic experimentations. Unlike the postwar neorealists, who opted for a mimetic solution as the most appropriate way to reestablish contact with reality, Gadda employs a wide assortment of Italian dialects—particularly the Roman, the Milanese, and the Neapolitan—and several classical and modern languages (all of them carefully subjected to a special process of distortion) in order to allow his characters to express themselves more convincingly, or to allow his sensibility to enjoy one of its usual lyrical and hilarious bursts of impatience.

The varied responses to the old and thorny "problem of the language" together with the richness of themes of postwar fiction have made possible, in the words of Angelo Guglielmi, "a liberation of substance." But all liberations carry along with them certain dangers, such as, in the present case, the impossibility of writing what Warren Beach defined "the well-made novel." In his anthology, *Vent'anni d'impazienza*, 1965 (Two Decades of Impatience) Guglielmi attributes this situation to "the human incapacity to entertain with the world of objects a relation other than one of usefulness."

> The thoughts and actions of contemporary man do not survive themselves and perish when the objectives for which they had been predisposed are achieved. . . . It is in this sense that we are accustomed to say that human life of today succeeds at best to thrive in terms of [its] functionality, certainly not [in terms] of [its] value. . . . value is not what dies, but rather what survives its end."

The contemporary reader, brought up on easier and more digestable fare, realizes no doubt that the links between today's and yesterday's novels are tenuous at best. But a conspicuous part of the radical difference between them is due to the artist's conception and understanding of the role imaginative literature must assume today, particularly in terms of depicting what Guglielmi elsewhere calls "an unconquerable center of disorder." To be sure, there are numerous difficulties preventing the reader from grasping easily a novelist's intention and meaning. Nevertheless, as Umberto Eco remarked at the 1965 meeting of the self-styled Gruppo 63, "it would be crazy for an author of the avant-garde to write in order to be never, never, never understood; on the contrary, he writes to break a situation, to communicate something different."

To examine the work of such bold, unorthodox novelists, as, say, Sanguineti and Leonetti, and to come to terms with their writings, is a task no observer of the Italian literary scene of today can refuse to undertake. Only a sensitive, sympathetic reading of the newest texts can give him a sense of the manner in which the novel is developing as an art form. Comparisons with the work of Gadda and Pasolini or with that of such established, traditional writers as Moravia, Cassola, and Bassani (all of whom have been engaged in bitter polemics with the younger novelists) are ultimately valuable and justifiable in any attempt to gain new insights into the character of the novel of the neo-avant-garde, and perceive the flaws, be they technical or ideological, frequently marring all experimental writing. Even in a moment of flux, as the present, one observation can be made: the crisis the novel seems to be experiencing is certainly due not to the drying-up of the creative intelligence, but to the formidable obstacles confronting the artist in his efforts to seize the meaning of a "political" unrest which, as recent events indicate, transcends all national boundaries. The involvement of today's artist in international causes, his awareness of other literatures, point to the likelihood that the time is fast approaching when he will be entirely free to draw from transnationalized traditions and techniques. Perhaps the future historian of literature may even conclude that the writings of today's neo-avant-garde are less important *per se* as aesthetic achievements than as precious documents of the artist's struggle to find the appropriate form to recreate and illuminate paradoxes of a "brave new world" of technology and nuclear *angst*.

NOTES

1. For a somewhat ampler treatment of this problem, see my study, *The Modern Italian Novel, from Manzoni to Svevo* (Carbondale, Southern Illinois University Press, 1967), pp. 3–26.

2. *The Gates of Horn: A Study of Five French Realists* (New York, Oxford University Press, 1963), p. 59.

3. "Forword" to *The Merry-Go-Round of Love* (New York, The American Library, 1964), p. 8.

4. *I Narratori: 1850–1957* (Milan, Principato, 1958), p. 274.

5. Ben Johnson, ed., *Stories of Modern Italy* (New York, Random House, 1960), p. xviii.

6. William Arrowsmith, ed., *Six Modern Italian Novellas* (New York, Pocket Book, 1964), p. vii.

7. *Politics and the Novel* (New York, World Publishing Co., 1957), p. 17.

8. Quoted by R. W. B. Lewis in his *The Picaresque Saint* (London, Gollancz, 1960), p. 179.

9. *Ibid.*, p. 144.

10. Interview in *The New Yorker*, May 7, 1955.

11. *La Letteratura Americana e altri saggi* (Turin, Einaudi, 1953), p. 249.

12. *Dialogues with Leucò*, trans. William Arrowsmith and D. S. Carne-Ross (Ann Arbor, University of Michigan Press, 1965), n.p.

13. *The Selected Works of Cesare Pavese*, translated, with an Introduction by R. W. Flint (New York, Farrar, Straus and Giroux, 1968), p. ix.

14. *Dialogues with Leucò*, n.p.

From *Verismo* to Experimentalism

Essays on the Modern Italian Novel

1

THE TRAGIC WORLD
OF VERGA'S PRIMITIVES

Sergio Pacifici

After Alessandro Manzoni, it is Giovanni Verga who is accorded the honored second place in modern Italian fiction. Dubbed by the critics "the greatest novelist Italy has produced after Manzoni," Verga has long been consigned to the group of classical writers who enjoy the dismal fate of being frequently mentioned, rarely understood, and almost never closely read, except by the happy few. Ever since the publication, in 1919, of Luigi Russo's ground-breaking work that put Verga's achievement and importance in proper perspective, many monographs and countless articles on him have made their appearance. By and large, however, a positive critical estimate has done little to change the taste of the large reading public, for which the stark, tragic world of Verga's better novels has held far less fascination than that of his lesser, conventional, and trivial works, such as *Tigre reale* (*Royal Tigress*) and *Eros*. Only in recent months was this deplorable trend suddenly and inexplicably reversed. An edition of almost 200,000 paperback copies of *I Malavoglia* (New

York, 1964; *The House by the Medlar Tree*) and another edition of *Mastro-don Gesualdo* (New York, 1955) were sold out in less than a fortnight.

From many angles, Verga's figure looms large on the literary scene of modern Italy. The magnitude and meaning of his lesson, the significance of his presence in the world of the novel can be perceived only through the practice of the novelists who have emerged in the last two decades. The objectivity he recommended and practiced during the most important phase of his career, the difficult operation he performed on the aulic, literary language of his country, his deep compassion for the plight of a suffering humanity, his vision of a society whose structure, drives, and goals can largely be measured by irresistible economic laws and by a persistent human hunger for material improvement, constitute but a small part of the rich legacy of ideas, insights, and technical-linguistic innovations he brought to the art of the novel. For the writers who have followed him, the problems of life and literature that concerned him persist in haunting their imagination.

Giovanni Verga was born in Catania in 1840. He was educated first at the private school of Antonino Abate, and then at the University of Catania. During the better part of his productive years he traveled extensively, living in such exciting cultural centers as Florence and Milan, where he made many friends among writers and critics. Personally and intellectually, Verga led a life immersed in the doings of his era. Yet, he founded no school, had no disciples and, although he did commit his artistic credo to the printed page, he never permitted himself to become embroiled in literary controversies.

By comparison with many writers, Verga's career spans a rather extended period of time; his first work was published in 1861, his last one, in 1902. Nonetheless, the best of his fiction —consisting of a respectable number of short stories and two novels—was produced within a single decade, 1878–88. After that, although he remained active, publishing numerous stories, novels, and a handful of undistinguished plays, he lived in a state of semiretirement. In 1893 he left Milan, where he had resided for several years, abandoned the cultural circles in which he had assiduously participated, and withdrew to his native city. There he spent the remaining years of his life meditating on his past experiences, planning the continuation of a five-novel cycle that never went beyond the first chapter of the third book, and simply watching the world go by. In 1920 the Italian Government honored him by naming him Senator; two years later he died.

There are at least two sides of Verga's personality that must be considered in a study of his work, and so strikingly do they differ that it is hard to conceive that they were parts of a man who could write, on the one hand, such a novel as *Una peccatrice* (A *Sinner*), 1866, and, on the other, *The House by the Medlar Tree*. Indeed, one is tempted to say that Verga had not one but two different careers, each with its own zenith and declining stage. First, of course, there is the youthful production, consisting of several historical novels Verga composed when he was still an adolescent or a law student at the university, the unpublished "Amore e patria" ("Love and Motherland"), *I Carbonari della Montagna*, 1861, and *Sulle laguna* (*On the Lagunas*), 1863. These works were followed by a number of novels in the romantic tradition, mostly stories of illicit or sensual love, composed during his sojourns in Florence and Milan. Such books, written during the first decade and a half of his literary career, present a world that only seemingly bears little or no relation with his other world, the grim, deterministic, harsh world of *la roba* in *The House by the Medlar Tree*, and *Mastro-don Gesualdo*. Actually, everything Verga wrote seems to be characterized by the same pessimism, the same frustrated yearning for happiness and well-being, the same tragic fate to which most, if indeed not all, of his characters are doomed.

As a rule, his early heroes are drawn from the aristocracy and the middle class. They are pseudo-intellectuals, would-be artists, spineless human beings Verga must have studied at close range when he frequented the fashionable salons of Mesdames Ciaffei and Greppi. Generally speaking, the typical hero of the early Verga is always falling in love with a woman older than himself, invariably attracted by her magnetic personality and power of seduction. The attraction, at first seemingly innocent, becomes a sentimental tie and soon blossoms into a full-fledged love affair, complete with the inevitable sexual fulfillment and the equally inevitable boredom that follows the consummation of such love. At times, the relationship proves to be too much for one of the lovers, one of whom (usually the heroine) dies of tuberculosis or of a mysterious malady; less frequently we have a suicide. The plot is standard, and the technique shows little diversity from one novel to the other. Characters and events change to be sure, but after a while they become practically indistinguishable from the personages and events of the previous books. The feminine characters seem to be regularly stronger than the heroes, and certainly appear to know what they want out of life and how they intend to achieve their objectives. Their major weapon is their voluptuousness, which they use effectively to trap and enslave their unsophisticated suitors.

In *Storia di una capinera* (*Story of a Linnet*), 1870, for example, we find a young novice falling in love with a young man who eventually marries her stepsister. The heroine joins a religious order, but unable to cope with her disappointment and frustration, succumbs to madness and dies. *A Sinner* revolves around the love nourished by a law student by the name of Pietro Busio for the attractive Narcisa Valderi Countess of Prato. The heroine first rejects her suitor, then falls in love with him—by this time Pietro has become a famous playwright and poet—only to become aware that their relationship is rapidly becoming meaningless. She then takes her life, while Pietro, wishing to forget the past, withdraws to a small provincial town and earns his bread by composing occasional poetry. *Royal Tigress* is only slightly different from the pattern, as it is modeled on the traditional love triangle. Here we have Giorgio La Ferlita, a weakling, who falls in love with Nata, a wealthy Russian incurably ill with tuberculosis. Before returning to her motherland with her husband, Nata promises Giorgio that she will return to Italy to die. She does indeed return, only to discover that during her absence Giorgio has married and is now a father. Upon learning of Nata's return, Giorgio rushes to her and at last their love is consummated. Nata's death and the hero's realization that the world will not be the same provide a fitting conclusion to the story. Not much different is the case of *Eva*, 1873, justly called the best and most typical of Verga's minor works. Here we have the hero, an aspiring painter by the name of Enrico Lanti, falling in love with a dancer, Eva, who leads a carefree, amoral existence. His love is returned for a while; but eventually, the two decide to part. One day Enrico, who has become a famous artist, asks Eva to return to live with him. To attain his wish, he even challenges Eva's lover to a duel, but his attempts to reconquer her heart fail miserably. He then goes back to his native town, where he dies of consumption amidst depressingly abject conditions.

It would be interesting to pursue further a study of Verga's early novels, but it is doubtful whether it would produce any startling discovery. Ultimately, we must simply admit that his first literary efforts were frankly autobiographical, and their interest is limited to a disclosure of the books the author himself must have been reading in that period, the life he was leading, the people who befriended him, and the places in which he lived. What one invariably finds striking about the early heroes of Verga is their incredible mediocrity, their inability to react to anything that is not a sensual desire. They are weak, immoral, empty; they neither hold any values, nor are they restrained or inspired by religious, civil, or intellectual beliefs. They move in a world that is the civilized world of Verga himself, a world of inane talk, trite events, ridiculous passions, exaggerated mannerisms, immature behavior. It is also a world where people do not work to earn their bread, seem to fear nothing except their eventual sexual desiccation, and engage in such diversions as travel less because this is what they *want* to do than because this is the *thing* to do, the fashionable element that provides distraction and a mild degree of amusement to an otherwise empty, boring, shabby existence.

The year 1874, barely a few months before the completion of *Eros,* marks an important turning point in Verga's career, for it signals the beginning of his second moment of creativity. It was in that year that the Sicilian composed "Nedda: A Sicilian Sketch." It is in this brief work of barely twenty pages that we find the first concrete evidence that something in the creative spirit of Verga was prodding him to return to a world he knew so well in the depth of his subconsciousness. Strikingly different from anything the novelist had written up to that time, the *bozzetto* does not yet represent a complete, sharp break with his earlier work. It may be compared to a new, tenuously stated theme that appears for the first time in a musical composition to be realized fully and satisfactorily only in a subsequent opus. In other words, "Nedda" is the first concrete evidence of Verga's realization that his earlier narrative had largely dealt with an acquired experience, not one necessarily close to the center of his sensibility. If his Florentine and Milanese experiences had been invaluable to him in enabling him to become socially and intellectually known and accepted, they had not revealed what his commitments as an artist should be, or how he might legitimately renew the genre he had chosen for himself.

From the purely stylistic point of view, "Nedda" is easily classifiable as a story in the tradition of clear, unpretentious short narratives. Thematically the story does represent a bold break with the previous novels. Gone are the bejeweled women, the aspiring intellectuals, the affluent northern bourgeois life, the decadent passions of the flesh. In "Nedda" we find ourselves suddenly thrust into the world of the peasants exploited by the rich landowners, infinitely oppressed by what Verga's world view will ultimately recognize as one of mankind's greatest evils: poverty. We smell not the delicious perfumes of the ladies, but the pungent odor of onions, black bread and minestra; we see not the delicate, elegant, and alluring gowns but the dirty, miserable rags of the olive pickers. We are placed not in the busy, hurried cities of the north, but in the hard landscape of the island of Sicily. We have no time to know either pleasure or boredom, only pain and work. The greatest human joy is experienced when people can find work and earn enough money to overcome the immediate needs of food and shelter.

The short tale recounts the story of three deaths, all perhaps avoidable in a different social order, and of the loneliness and hopelessness of the poor. Nedda's mother, gravely ill and unable to receive adequate medical attention, dies, leaving her daughter alone in the world. Her only relative, Zio Giovanni, is too selfish to care either about her well-being or her fate. Nedda is proud to earn her own bread working on a farm; there she meets and falls in love with Janu, a young man who, like Nedda, is an olive picker. Out of their brief, intense love, a baby is born. One day Janu, ill with malaria, falls from an olive tree and dies; shortly afterwards, their baby dies of malnutrition. Nedda, who has sold the few meager things she had put together for a marriage which never took place, is left alone once more, destitute, blessing the dead that suffer no more.

It is, as can be imagined, a terse story, and one told with considerable restraint and economy of means: Nedda's bewilderment and anguish are depicted in a few, somber words; her love affair is barely hinted. The pivotal incidents of the story—

first, the mother's death, then Nedda's own sense of loss, her willingness to take on any hard job so that she may support herself, her affair with Janu, her baby's death—are given no special prominence. They are registered almost casually, as though they were matters of simple fact. The story is not perfect; there is the artificial device of the story being told within a story, and there is a certain unevenness of tone. Verga shifts from the condescension of an urbane, humanitarian gentleman to the disinterestedness of a casual observer. This notwithstanding, we are moved by the sense of fatalism that pervades the whole tale, by Nedda's thoughtful conclusion that death is preferable to life. It is with Nedda that we enter the world of Verga's special primitives, capable of enormous sacrifices and unusual stoicism. His people appear from the outset as vanquished, defeated by the brute force of nature and by an egotism that respects no human values or principles. Their heroism is in their striving to find the strength to endure a life that offers little joy but imposes continual toil and suffering. Theirs is the heroism which in their most desperate and bleak moments permits them to find a stature and dignity possible to the characters of Greek tragedies.

Like "Nedda," the stories that Verga wrote during the following years, *Primavera* (*Primavera and Other Tales*), 1877, and *Vita dei campi* (*Life in the Fields*), 1880, are notable for their rare simplicity. Invariably, they revolve around the hardships or passions endured or experienced by Sicilians—laborers, farmhands, shepherds—all equally proud yet resigned to a wretched existence, wishing merely to live simply and quietly, enjoying whatever little satisfaction life can offer them. Their existence could hardly be more precarious: they live from day to day, constantly faced by a harsh nature, unforgiving and indifferent to the plight of humankind in a manner bound to recall the work of Giacomo Leopardi. The elements become more prominent in the stories; we become aware of how important the weather is since, as Thomas G. Bergin notes, "the *contadini* depend for their existence on the whim of the weather. . . . If the *annata* is good, all is well; if not, then those on the margin of society pay the price." Similarly, the role played by the animals becomes more important—the animals that are valuable assets, to be sure, but that also poignantly and silently reenact the unbelievably hopeless activity of Verga's peasants. They live like dogs, work like donkeys (which, in Italy, occupy the last place in the animal hierarchy); like horses, they exist purely to work the land, and like the sheep they take to pasture, day in and day out they must exhibit meekness of spirit and restrained behavior. At times, as Pina (in the story "The She-Wolf"), they are nicknamed after animals, and appropriately so in Pina's case, since the wolf is a treacherous, proud animal whose only allegiance is to itself. "The horses," Verga writes at one point, "are made to be sold; similarly, the lambs are born to go to the slaughterhouse, and the clouds bring rain with them."

The world of Verga's primitives is distinguished by its simple feelings, its modest aspirations, where people, as Lia remarks in "Ieli" "act like animals . . . that scratch each other's neck," and where man, with no opportunity to educate himself, confesses, with Ieli, "I'm poor . . . I don't know anything."

A life of deprivations and poverty, of exploitation and betrayals can only produce, in the fiction of Verga at any rate, unhappiness and violence. The stories of *Life in the Fields* are replete with deaths, of violent deaths that represent the culmination of a heroic but unbearable despair. There is Alfio who kills his rival Turiddu in the famous "Cavalleria rusticana"; Ieli the shepherd who murders his boyhood pal, Don Alfonso, who has seduced Ieli's wife, Maria, and thus ruined his dream of a tranquil home; there is Nanni Lasca who slaughters the she-wolf with an ax and curses her afterward. Thus violence, murder, and fighting provide a dramatic contrast to the peace of mind Verga's heroes seek in vain. In a way, Rosso Malpelo, the protagonist of the story by the same title, presents the philosophy of the novelist's special world in no uncertain terms. Rosso, "a little brat whom nobody wanted around" in the stone quarry where his father lost his life for a handful of miserable tari, grows accustomed to the beatings his master and even his friends regularly administer upon his back. "In fact, he took the beatings without complaining, just like the donkeys that arch their backs, but go on doing things their own way." Rosso understands very well the reality of his condition. Speaking to his friend Frog, he says, "The donkey must be beaten, because he can't beat us; if he could, he'd smash us under his hoofs and rip our flesh apart." With Rosso Malpelo, we become aware that we are confronting a world of dog-eat-dog, ruled by a combination of power, personal interests, and crude egotism.

Thematically and stylistically, *Life in the Fields* is obviously an important work, whose significance is this time also theoretical. In the case of two short stories, "Fantasticheria" ("Reverie") and "L'amante di Gramigna" ("Gramigna's Mistress"), the novelist makes several revealing points about his poetics and, at the same time, announces the first novel of a cycle of five he had undertaken to write, a series he would eventually title "The Vanquished."

> When in the novel the affinity and the cohesion of its every part will be so complete that the process of creation remains a mystery like the development of human passions themselves, and the harmony of its forms will be so perfect, the sincerity of its reality so evident, its mode and reason for being so necessary that the hand of the artist will remain absolutely invisible, then it will have the stamp of a real happening and the work of art will seem to have produced itself, to have matured and to have grown spontaneously like a fact of nature, without maintaining any point of contact with its author, without the blemish of the sin of creation.

The statement has a familiar ring, for it echoes some of the programs and theories of French realists, particularly Flaubert.

Much has been made of Verga's theory of impersonality, and justly so. In the history of the novel in Italy, his declaration is a true milestone. Today we are likely to be less impressed by theoretical pronouncements than by the discovery of a technique that succeeds in making a work of fiction truly original as well as believable and compelling. No matter how desperately the author may try to disappear from his fiction, he is always retraceable in the very people, landscapes, and actions his imagination has created. Perhaps Verga did not at all intend to formulate an ideal technique but rather to underscore the fact, which seems incontrovertible to us born and raised in a post-Henry James era, that, in order to sound authentic, real, *lived*, the novelist would have to do away with his customary clumsy treatments that made his characters puppets rather than independent creatures. We need not assume that this practice was limited to Italy, as it was, as has been pointed out by many critics in the past, a European trend. As Joseph Warren Beach put it in his admirable study of *Fiction in the Twentieth Century,*

> The one thing that will impress you more than any other [in the modern novel] is the disappearance of the author. In Fielding and Scott, in Thackeray and George Eliot, the author is everywhere present in person to see that you are properly informed on all circumstances of the action, to explain the characters to you and to insure your forming the right opinion of them, to scatter nuggets of wisdom and good feeling along the course of the story, and to point out how, from the failures and successes of the characters, you may form a sane and right philosophy of conduct.

Verga's position was one strikingly modern, for he believed that only by disappearing from his work would the novelist make his tale believable without question and give it a spontaneity and a truthfulness unattainable by conventional narrative techniques. Whether or not such worthy goals can really be attained by an objective, or impersonal kind of narrative, has become after Wayne C. Booth's brilliant book, *The Rhet-*

oric of Fiction, debatable to say the least. Nonetheless, it is
difficult to deny that the obtrusive, moralizing role traditionally played by the author-narrator in the bulk of fiction up to
that time was anything if not damaging to the illusion of reality
each artist seeks to create in his work. Furthermore, the intru-
sions of the author were frequently but poor surrogates for
an experience that, to ring true for the reader, needed to be
dramatically presented. To quote Mr. Beach once more, "if the
author succeeds in presenting his theme effectively . . . we shall
not quarrel with his personal appearances. . . . Our main quarrel
is with the author who makes his personal appearance a *substitute* for the artistic presentation of his subject, thinking that
talking about it is equivalent to presenting it."

Verga's approach to fiction was to undergo some changes
in the years that followed his Sicilian stories, and eventually
blossomed in the Preface to *The House by the Medlar Tree*
where he takes up his points from where the letter to Salvatore
Farina (in "Reverie") had left off. The basic scheme of the
cycle was contained in a single, illuminating sentence of the
story just quoted. "Whenever one of those small, or weaker,
or less cautious, or egotistical plebian actors decides to cut himself off from his own folk because of his yearning for the
unknown, or his desire to better himself, or his curiosity to
know the world, the world—voracious fish that it is—swallows
him and all those nearest to him." This vision of man's fate
was to be dramatically presented in *The House by the Medlar
Tree* and in the four novels that were to be its sequel.

Verga himself gave a first account of his ambitious plan in
a letter written to his friend Salvatore Paola, on April 21, 1878,
defining his project a "fantasmagory of life's struggle, extending from the ragpicker to the minister of state and the artist,
assuming all forms from ambition to avidity of profit, and lend-
ing itself to a thousand representations of the great, grotesque
play of mankind, the providential struggle guiding humanity
through all appetites, high and low, to its conquest of truth!"

Each of the novels planned was to have its own special physiognomy, and each was to be self-contained. It took several years before Verga completed *The House by the Medlar Tree* and readied the manuscript for press. He saw it in print in 1881.

The reception accorded the novel was to be a grave disappointment to the Sicilian. Aside from a few favorable reviews—written for the most part by his friends—the publication of one of the finest novels of the century, and one of the most revolutionary works of fiction produced by the modern Italian imagination, was to pass practically unnoticed.

The conceptual framework of "The Vanquished" is tersely outlined in the Preface that accompanied *The House by the Medlar Tree*. Any reader wishing to gain some insights into Verga's quasi-Balzacian project must inevitably turn to such statements as the piece offers for his enlightenment.

"This story," Verga writes, "is the genuine and dispassionate study of how the first aspirations for well-being probably originate and develop in the humblest classes. It is the study of the perturbations brought into a family, that up to that point had lived a relative happy existence." The artist's intention was "to give a representation of reality as it actually was, or as it should have been," and to analyze "the mechanism of human passions." The range of his observation was to be all-inclusive, moving progressively from the lowest social class (a family of poor fishermen), to the bourgeoisie and ultimately to the aristocracy. The additional volumes that were to follow *I Malavoglia* were to bear the following titles: *Mastro-don Gesualdo, La Duchessa de Leyra* (*The Duchess of Leyra*), *L'onorevole Scipioni* (*The Honorable Scipioni*), and finally *L'uomo di lusso* (*The Man of Wealth*). Each social class, with its unique aspirations and ambitions, its diverse life and ensuing world view, was to be depicted through the use of a narrative style wholly consonant with the social condition and the sophistication of its characters. A similarly tragic fate would constitute their common denominator, since the author envisioned the world as the same ground of battle, where today's winners would end up being tomorrow's losers. Notwithstanding the pseudo-scientific pretensions of such a plan, Verga succeeded admirably in creating two novels that are not in the least contrived.

Few stories could actually be simpler than the one told with consummate skill by Verga in *The House by the Medlar Tree*. It is a tale revolving around the many vicissitudes that strike a family of fishermen, the Malavoglia. In the course of the story, the heroes discover the meaning of death, defeat, moral degradation, fear, misery, and love. Somehow, thanks to the force that pulls them close to one another, they manage to survive the large and small crises regularly disrupting the rugged course of their existence, and rediscover and reassert the precious values inherited from their ancestors. Indeed, without such values, their universe would prove to be meaningless. Such a characterization of the essence of the novel is but a mere approximation to what it ultimately says. So rich and different are its meanings that it lends itself to a variety of interpretations, many of which are perfectly justified by the text. It can be called the drama of a brave family, buffeted by misfortunes and doomed to much suffering before it can once more experience the tranquillity for which it yearns; it can be read as an absorbing representation of what life must have been in many parts of the *Mezzogiorno* during the last century (or in ours for that matter); it is also a tale of the misery and trouble life brings to the human kind, and how they are accepted, endured, and occasionally overcome by brave men. But the novel, because it is a great work of art, manages to be all these things and many more. Its manifold meanings can be uncovered not by the insights of a single critic, or several critics, but by the sensitivity of a reader capable of discerning and recognizing in the events of the book's plot a reflection and an illumination of the destiny of man. Thus, the novel lends itself to be read as a depiction of the perennial conflicts be-

tween the new and the old generations; or of the restlessness
every young person experiences when he faces life on his own
and grows disillusioned with a social, political, and moral system and an order of values he can no longer comprehend,
because they fail to fill his needs and respond to his aspirations.

Grand and powerful, though by no means unusual, as the
themes of the book may be, it must be acknowledged that
what makes the novel an unusually fine work is its style and
technique; or, better stated, the manner in which the form of
the tale is one with its content. The problem of style is one that
has historically occupied every great writer; hardly a poet or
novelist has avoided a confrontation with this vital issue. It
is clear (but, I hasten to add, only to the reader capable of
handling the novel in the original), that Verga must have been
faced by a number of alternatives when he first thought of his
cycle, and in particular in the case of *The House by the Medlar
Tree*. The major choices no doubt were three: to use the literary
language he had inherited from his tradition (the language of
Manzoni's *The Betrothed*); or to deviate slightly from such a
choice by injecting into the novel expressions, sayings, or isolated worlds drawn from the Sicilian dialect; or to write his
book entirely in dialect. Of these alternatives, the last he
considered the least desirable, as it would restrict his public to
those possessing a mastery of the dialect. Moreover, neither
of the other two possibilities satisfied him, although in some of
his short stories he had indeed resorted to employing dialect
words or local sayings whenever he felt that Italian was simply
incapable of recapturing the nuances and force of the Sicilian
expression.

Dissatisfied with the available linguistic options, he decided
to embark on the road that was to lead him to the outright
invention of a language capable of expressing the thoughts,
feelings, and utterances of his Sicilian heroes in a manner that
would be comprehensible to the reader untrained in the dialect.
The course chosen was not without difficulties and special

problems, for it demanded a thorough preparation of his part
not unlike that necessary to Joyce in writing *Ulysses*. Verga
was not only obliged to study anew the traditions, beliefs, and
customs of the people he intended to fictionalize, but indeed
the psychology of their language. In short, the speeches and
thoughts of the characters had to be filtered by the author and
translated, so to speak, into a language understandable to the
general reader without losing the special flavor and cadence
of their native dialect or of their personality. Ultimately, this
operation was clearly one that required a reshaping of the literary language, cleansing it of its pomposity and artificiality,
transforming it into the aptest expressive tool of characters
who are ignorant peasants. Moreover, as Luigi Russo perceptively noted, he "gave a provincial coloring to the language of
The House by the Medlar Tree through the images and proverbs of the town [of Aci Trezza], [and] through a choral
syntax."

The problem of "how" the characters might speak or the
novel be told was obviously intimately connected with a problem of structure. Up to that moment, the traditional novel in
Italy was generally narrated by an omniscient author, (frequently occupying the role of the protagonist as well) who
looked on the events from the outside, remaining a kind of
special, partial observer. Another technique frequently used,
especially in France, was that of the epistolary novel of the
type Verga himself had practiced in his early *Story of a Linnet*.
With *The House by the Medlar Tree* Verga took a different
path. He rejected both the role of the omniscient narrator and
the possibility of identifying himself with one of the principal
characters. The story he chose to tell is narrated from the
inside, not by one but indirectly by *all* the personages of the
novel. Every character is thus magically transformed into a
narrator, each contributing something, with his unmistakable
voice, to the description of the Malavoglia's woes. As Verga's
most recent translator points out, "It is their voice that we hear

telling the story; the entire novel is, so to speak, dialogued."
Verga's technique is one based on direct and indirect discourse;
we either hear the characters speak or we are told, by one of
the characters, the essence of what has taken place. Indeed,
what the characters say is often reported indirectly in a way
that mirrors the spoken rather than written speech. The so-
called minor characters often act as a chorus, whose function,
much like a Greek tragedy, is to comment upon the dramatic
events of the story.

Nowhere does Verga attempt to make a direct comment on,
or judgment of, the action he describes, and much less does he
try to influence the opinion of the reader. The method he
selects is that of a novelist whose function must be deceptively
limited to providing the information in as vivid and complete
a manner as possible so the reader may see and judge for himself. In addition, in the novel seeing is combined with hearing.
What we *hear* a character say, or what is said about him, enables us to recognize him by his personal idiosyncrasies, by his
speech and action. Our insights into their quality as human
beings are extended by frequent opinions and gossip offered
by friends and relatives, whose conversations reveal an intimate, but never offensive, concern for life in the community.
The unusual feat is accomplished by transporting us into the
town of Aci Trezza, where we are forced to mingle with its
inhabitants, learning about them from their own words. Their
language is real and believable not because it flows effortlessly
but because it remains highly consistent with their personality,
their experience of life, their background—making use of a
vocabulary that is drawn not from literature but from life
itself, their occupation and interests.

The relatively few descriptive passages of *The House by
the Medlar Tree*—such as the beautiful and lyrical opening of
Chapter III or the melancholy paragraphs that close the book—
are written as though they were in fact spoken by an unidentified villager whose manner of speech follows a pattern familiar

to us since we have encountered it many times in the unfolding of the tale.

The novel's setting is kept purposely narrow: practically the entire story takes place in the town of Aci Trezza. Conversely, the cast of characters that meet at the house of the Malavoglia, at the town watershed, at the local inn, or just in the streets is comparatively large. Their heated, at times humorous, political conversations, their constant commentaries on the events of the day, their small business deals take place not in the intimacy of their homes but out in the open, on the landings, and in the streets. Everything in the novel helps create the illusion that we are in a small town: the small talk we hear, the provincial attitude of the peasants, the petty jealousies and nagging grievances, the unobtrusive manner in which some of the extraordinary or important happenings that take place in the mainland reach the town as faint echoes. Thus, for example, when word reaches them at Luca Malavoglia has died in the war, the news stuns the friends of the family, who express their disbelief and surprise by flatly affirming that the whole affair "is a lot of talk, just to sell newspapers." We are truly cut off not only from the continent but from history itself. We live a drama with many self-repeating acts, a drama whose heroes change their names but not their roles for they are all equally involved in the endless struggle for survival and furtherance of their own selfish interests. We are thrust into a world where misery is rampant and greed is frequently out of proportion with what is at stake; a world of hard work and sorrow accepted with resignation as the lot of man. In such a world there is little awareness of the tragic fact that, sooner or later, everyone will be overcome by the vicissitudes of life.

Religion, which permeates the whole of Manzoni's novel, is conspicuously absent here, except in the most perfunctory way. Left to their wits for centuries, the people of Aci Trezza have replaced a traditional faith in God with a stubborn confidence in their capacity to resolve the daily obstacles confronting them. The town's vicar, Gianmaria, is depicted as an observer equaly unconcerned with the Malavoglia's troubles and the day-to-day hardships endured by the townsfolk. He performs his religious duties in a most perfunctory manner, with a minimum of faith in what he does and a maximum of speed. The ultimate reality, which for Manzoni had been a boundless faith in the Love and Justice of the Maker, is transformed, in the world of Verga, into a purely economic fact, a question of money and circumstances. This explains the frequent laconic comments of its people, or young 'Ntoni's compulsion to leave town in search of fortune after his family has repeatedly been struck by disaster.

The fate of the Malavoglia is a tragic one: one by one, it seems, they must bow their heads to an unpredictable destiny. Bastianazzo is the first to die in the first shipwreck of the family's boat, *La Provvidenza;* Luca loses his life while serving his country and fighting a war which few can believe is taking place; Lia becomes a woman of the streets and leaves town; *Comare* Maruzza dies of cholera during a frightening epidemic; and old 'Ntoni ends his life in a lonely hospital, after an existence marked by incredible toil.

Why is it that they must go down to their death or ruin so unjustly or so unnecessarily? The temptation is great to take the essence of the Preface literally, and explain their tragic end through their obstinate drive to improve their material lot. As it actually turns out, the family's speculation in a cargo of lupins proves to be the least serious offense to the Verghian code of life, and, as such, the element only remotely responsible for their subsequent woes. Their defeat is rooted not in their economic disasters, but in their betrayal of the religion of the home, as it has been called, in their having broken the tradition of steadfastness to an ancestral code. They have failed to abide by what the novelist elsewhere (in the story "Reverie") had defined as "the ideal of the oyster." Only the members of the family who truly believe in such an honor-

able ideal find the strength necessary to bear their heavy burden of grief. What gives Mastro 'Ntoni, Alessi, and Mena—
the three people whose strength of character and allegiance to
the code enables them to survive their ordeal—an unusual
amount of vitality, fortitude, and resilience is their strong commitment to enduring human values: their unshakeable belief
in the necessity of working hard, and above all honorably;
their indestructible faith in the dignity of man; their joy of
working as a unit; and their deep affection for the house by the
medlar tree, which throughout the novel remains the center of
family life, the most overt symbol of their attachment to life.
When the house is lost to repay a debt, it becomes the ideal
point of return for the Malavoglia.

The nature of Verga's impersonal technique excludes the
presence of the customary portraits of characters we find so
admirably done in Manzoni's novel. While the Milanese writer's method calls for a historical-moral approach to the problem of character presentation and analysis (can anyone forget
the masterful, three-dimensional portraits of Don Abbondio,
Fra Cristoforo, or the Nun of Monza?) Verga relies exclusively
on a few bold strokes and details to give his heroes a quality
and dimension we are not likely to forget. It is his economy
of means coupled with the adroit device of allowing his characters to define themselves through their acts and utterances,
complemented by the comments made by the other personages
of the book, that constitutes one of the fresh and vital aspects
of the work. Master 'Ntoni's first words in the story denote
clearly what kind of an individual he is. He speaks frequently
by way of proverbs and maxims, almost as a kind of oracle,
and through his terse words, which in wisdom and an unflag-
ging belief in the validity of human experience, we get a distinct feeling of what will prove to be the key issues of the
story. "To pull an oar, the five fingers must work together";
or "Be satisfied with what your father made you, if nothing

else you won't be a rascal." The other characters of the story are presented in very quick succession, in a manner that echoes a spoken rather than a literary style. There is old 'Ntoni's son, Bastianazzo, "who was big and burly" but "he'd put about directly when ordered and wouldn't blow his nose without his father's say-so"; then comes his wife Maruzza, called La Longa, a "tiny woman who kept busy weaving, salting anchovies and bearing children, like a good housewife." Then come their five children: 'Ntoni, "a big loafer of twenty"; Luca, "who . . . had more sense than his older brother"; Alessi, "a little snot nose, who was the spitting image of his grandfather"; and Lia, "who was not yet fish, flesh or fowl." Just a few words are sufficient to introduce, and in several profound ways anticipate, the character of the heroes, what they are capable of doing and how they will eventually turn out as human beings.

For generations the Malavoglia have lived in the same town, leading a modest but dignified existence, esteemed by the community as hard-working and industrious people. Theirs is a patriarchical family with the old grandfather, the respected leader, entrusted with the responsibility of making major deci sions that will affect the course of their lives. It is he who holds the family together with his strength and wisdom, giving it a direction and a sense of purpose and stability, guiding its route as an experienced shipmaster. His wisdom, however, is not acquired through book learning but from life itself—from the understanding he has attained of the kind of duties and obligations he must exercise both with respect to himself and to his dear ones. Master 'Ntoni clings with rare tenacity to the moral relevance—the ethics, as it were—of the tenets guiding his life. In this sense, too, the proverbs and maxims through which he speaks serve to convey the meaning and intimate reasons for his actions. It is for the good of the family that he has contracted a debt with Uncle Crocefisso, known as Dumbbell, buying a cargo of lupins which he plans to take to the nearby town of Riposto. From there, a larger ship will transport it to the northern port of Trieste. But, during a storm, the family's boat is severely damaged, Bastianazzo and a helper Monico lose their lives, and the lupins are lost in the sea.

Soon, the credit extended by Uncle Crocefisso runs out. When the unpaid debt threatens to stain the family's good name, Master 'Ntoni first thinks of the possibility of resorting to legal maneuverings to invalidate the transaction (especially since the lupins were said to be spoiled), then sets himself to do whatever must be done to pay back the money he owes. But he suffers still more setbacks, and, after having exhausted all honest avenues open to him, he consents to give up his beloved house by the medlar tree and make good on his word.

Once the house is lost, Master 'Ntoni's goal becomes that of regaining possession of what has always been for the family the supreme symbol of unity and security. As Russo perceptively writes, "the house is not a harbor of peace and well-being; it is not a tranquil refuge of small egotism, but the small brown anthill to which the ants go back and onto which they cling, after the anguish of the comings and goings of their dispersion and storm." Gradually, the book becomes less a tale of a debt that honor demands be repaid, but a story of personal heroism, the account of enormous sacrifices each member of the family willingly makes to retrieve a vital part of his way of life. The technique of Verga's narration is such that we remain only dimly aware of the passing of time—a thoroughly effective way to remind us that there is a larger dimension to the Malavoglia story, since their fate is but a continual cycle of disasters that only infrequently alternate with imperceptible gains. Suffering is, in the world of the Sicilian novelist, an ever-present condition no one can avoid. "The world," so comments at one point the impersonal voice of the narrator, "is packed with trouble: some get half, some get double, and the people who were outside in the yard kept looking at the sky for another bit of rain that would have been as welcome as bread."

Those who depart from the world of the living seem to be the most fortunate of the lot, for they will not have to confront the dread of moral or economic ruin. A bitter fate, charged with infinite toil and endless suffering, awaits those who live on. It is a fate that must be accepted, for the alternative is perhaps even gloomier. Thus, young 'Ntoni is thoroughly corrupted by the glamour and glitter of city life during his military tour of duty; back in his native town, he realizes that he has become estranged to its values and way of life. He rejects the possibility of working like the other members of the family, especially since he is convinced of the futility of the human struggle for survival by honest means. He takes up with the town's worst people, gets into trouble and is sentenced to jail for having stabbed the local customs official Don Michele (with whom he has a long standing grievance) who caught him smuggling coffee, sugar, and silk kerchiefs. As a result of seeing his oldest grandson brought to trial as a criminal, old 'Ntoni suffers a stroke and, at his insistence, is brought to the city hospital. There he dies a lonely death, shortly after Alessi has brought him the good news that the house by the medlar tree is once again about to be theirs. Alessi is the one who is destined to carry on the name and the tradition of the family; he is also the only one to experience the happiness of a good marriage. Mena, promised to Brasi Cipolla, sees her plans go up in smoke after the first setback of the boat. Later, she accepts to bear the brunt of the shame brought to the family by Lia's dishonorable behavior and turns down Alfio Mosca's request to marry him, despite the fact that she has always loved him. "I'm twenty-six and the time when I could get married has passed," she confesses sadly. She goes back to living in the old family house, where she takes up an attic room "waiting for Nunziata's children so she could mother them." The story will see young 'Ntoni back to his town after having completed his sentence. The single night he spends there, however, is sufficient to persuade him that it is impossible for any man to remain in a place full of bitter, haunting memories.

The novel's events are sparse and modest almost to the point of seeming trivial. It is one of the many achievements of the book, however, to show us that what it presents is no inconsequential struggle, but a dramatic battle that takes place, in a larger scale and on a vastly more complicated stage, in life as we know it. Only by viewing the book from a distance are we able to study its architecture and begin to discover the perfection of its design. There is both progress and continuity in the story. Whatever happens to its heroes manages to keep us in a continual state of suspense, even though we expect that our feelings will not be betrayed. In the world so starkly created by the imagination of Verga, man is resigned to his lot, even though he never gives up at least the hope of a material improvement of his condition. We are carefuly led to the final climax through a series of ups and downs; by the time old 'Ntoni dies, we have been through events that have changed, in one way or another, every member of his family. The misfortunes that strike the Malavoglias are never sufficiently serious to destroy their dogged attachment to life, or their stubborn hope that there may still be something good in store for them. By the same token, their recoveries from their setbacks are never great enough to enable them to resolve their problems in any substantial way.

Tragic and comic touches alternate in the novel, for this is no bleak account of the numerous disasters that have hit the family and have destroyed its confidence in life itself, but a tale of the irony and humor of life. There is, to begin with, irony in the very name the Malavoglia bear, for far from their being full of ill-will as their nickname implies, they are conscientious and hard-working, and there is irony, too, in the name of their boat, which brings them not good luck or abundance but hardships and troubles. There is still another kind of irony in the fact that Don Michele, who is partly responsible for saving the life of Master 'Ntoni when he is brought back, seriously hurt, from the second shipwreck of the boat, is also the one who seduces Lia and is eventually responsible for sending young 'Ntoni to jail, thus contributing materially to the misery of the family. There is also a well-measured humor in Brasi Cipolla's falling prey to Mangicarubbe, a no-good woman with whom he takes up when his engagement with Mena is dissolved, and there is humor in Uncle Crocefisso's marriage with La Vespa, who delights in squandering the money he has painfully accumulated after years of speculations and usury.

Humor and irony successfully establish and enhance contrasts and vary the tone of the narrative; they do not decrease its fatalism, the inescapable absurdity of all its events. The question that faces us, and cannot be adequately answered, is: Why should the Malavoglias, upright, honest, hard-working and God-fearing, be so repeatedly and mercilessly struck by Fate? Is God, or nature, or another incomprehensible force responsible for their misery and misfortunes? Perhaps, as someone recently remarked, we transcend in the novel even a Leopardian type of pessimism, for we find ourselves in a universe where, discern as we do the difference between good and evil, no differentiation between them can actually be made. Who is better off: Master 'Ntoni, always striving but invariably defeated, or Rocco Spatu, the town's best specimen of the good-for-nothing who lives off the fat of the land, taking from it but never contributing anything in return? Prodded by his grandfather to work hard and to be thankful for what he has, young 'Ntoni puts his problem into perspective by answering

> But are you people living any better than I am, with all your working and useless struggling? It's our cursed lot, that's what it is! You see how worn out you are, you look like a fiddle bow, and you've grown old always liking the same life! And now, what have you got? You people don't know the world, you're like kittens with their eyes still closed. Do you eat the fish you

catch? Do you know for whom you work, from Monday to Saturday, and for whom you've worn yourself out so that they wouldn't even take you in at the hospital? For the people who never do a lick of work, and have piles of money. That's who you're working for. . . . Ah, by the book of the thieving Judas, what a miserable fate!

'Ntoni's rebellion, which climaxes in his eventual downfall, and Lia's placid surrender to her sexual instincts represent an answer of sorts, however inconclusive and ultimately damaging to their well-being, to the wretchedness humans are asked to accept without protest as an inescapable part of their condition. Unconsciously, both 'Ntoni and Lia aspire to joining the ranks of those who, like Piedipapera and Uncle Crocefisso, have succeeded in scoring a victory in the harsh struggle of existence. What they have neglected to comprehend is that in life no victory is ever total or permanent, and in Verga's scheme of life today's winners will turn out to be tomorrow's vanquished. In the novel, only the losers elicit our sympathy, less because they are the underdogs than because they go down to defeat—or barely manage to survive their ordeal—without surrendering their obstinate faith in those moral values that have always given a measure of coherence and meaning to what would otherwise be a senseless affair.

Unlike Manzoni, Verga offers no answers to the eternal riddle of existence, no program of action, no staunch commitment to a religious faith. In some ways, Verga has something in common with Albert Camus in indirectly asserting that only a genuine solidarity with other human beings is ultimately capable of alleviating, and rendering more bearable, the suffering and tragedy that mankind has to endure.

Mastro-don Gesualdo, the second and last novel completed by Verga as part of his projected cycle, is infinitely more complex than *The House by the Medlar Tree* but less successful and satisfying, despite its many fine pages and excellent episodes. It is, from the point of view of scheme, the attempt to carry on to a higher social class the same basic struggle we find in the tale of the Malavoglias—a struggle we know must end in defeat, for an inimical fate sternly denies man any possibility of trespassing the boundaries of his inherited condition. The hero of the novel is a contractor, Mastro-don Gesualdo Motta, who, by the sweat of his brow, has been able to free himself from the shackles of his humble origin, achieving an enviably comfortable economic status. The sacrifices he has made are as numerous as the calculating deals that have enabled him to become a wealthy man. Yet, the material success he has achieved at such a hard price does not prevent his ultimate failure, for the scheme must be fulfilled; the victories of today beget the defeats of tomorrow.

From a proletarian, humble, primitive milieu, Verga moves in the second novel to a bourgeois society, the world of businessmen, and *nouveaux riches*. Such a world obviously requires a new language in order that its yearnings, aspirations, and quality might be expressed and studied in a manner consonant with its character. But the style Verga employs in the book is disappointing for it lacks the freshness, inventiveness, and vitality of his earlier novel.

Much like *The House by the Medlar Tree*, the great theme of *Mastro-don Gesualdo*—the struggle for property and the consequences of wealth—is adumbrated in a short piece titled "La roba." The narrative, barely six pages long, can hardly be classified as a short story, since it does not revolve around an unusual event, but merely gives us a brief glimpse of its protagonist, Don Mazzarò, and his incredible appetite for possessions through which he believes he can achieve not only a secure position but happiness as well. *Mastro-don Gesualdo* repeats, in a larger and more involved social context, much the same struggle of Don Mazzarò. He incarnates the same human greed and drive for material possessions, his acceptance of a system of values that, devoid as they are of any real need of human solidarity, ultimately contribute to his psychological,

financial, and physical ruin. In some ways Mastro-don Gesualdo might be seen as an extension of sorts of Lia and
'Ntoni Malavoglia, and their yearnings to improve their lot
even at the cost of becoming corrupt or leaving the beloved
house by the medlar tree. Unlike them, Gesualdo has indeed
managed to amass a veritable fortune; yet his fate is not
different from theirs. Gesualdo is a temporary winner in the
human struggle to conquer his environment and overcome the
restrictions of his social class, and yet he ends a defeated man.
His life of toil and loneliness, amidst people he mistrusts and
does not love, ends in a humiliating failure after he realizes
that the wealth so painfully accumulated brings him no comfort whatever. Indeed, his money far from giving him the
tranquillity, respect, and contentment he had hoped for, causes
him misery and discontent compounded by the scorn heaped
upon him when his health takes a severe turn for the worse and
he approaches death. He ends his days in a house he abhors,
without proper medical attention, cheated by his own family,
who patiently waits for his death to squander the property he
has accumulated—a true alienated man.

Unlike *The House by the Medlar Tree,* where the entire
community of Aci Trezza is skillfully used by the novelist to
tell his tale, and plays a vital role in the illusion that the drama
is actually being lived and recounted by several people, in
Mastro-don Gesualdo we have a hero and a cast of characters
that are clearly defined and fully developed. Through four successive stages encompassing a period of approximately two
and one-half decades (the story is set between 1820 and 1846),
we are shown the rise and fall of a man in search of a false
god: money. "Property," Luigi Russo writes, "is no longer
idolized for its own sake, but as a complex symbol of life, as a
sentiment of labor, as a complacency of a constructive astuteness, as a sensuality of possession, an indiscriminate desire of
survival and immortality." "You are good and beautiful!"
shouts Don Gesualdo to his wife during his wedding night,

"Fine stuff . . . fine stuff you are!" The English translation cannot help its failing us at this point, however, for it hardly conveys the materialistic, almost vulgar connotations of the word *roba*, whose meaning is often property, goods, possessions ostentatiously displayed or enviously desired. Verga's choice is very apt here and elsewhere, and after repeated usage, it becomes a leitmotiv of the novel that might well be called a hymn to real estate, to man's greed for things, yet another meaning of *la roba*. So intense is the impelling necessity to accumulate property—more specifically, land and grains—and so thoroughly does it pervade every one of the episodes in the story that the values of society can no longer be comprehended except in the coarsest material terms. If, as Harry Levin has reminded us in his study *The Gates of Horn*, realism etymologically means "thing-ism," then *Mastro-don Gesualdo* must be considered the realistic Italian novel par excellence. It is understandable that business transactions should be made for the sake of monetary gains, since this is an ancient practice and cornerstone of commerce since time immemorial. But in Verga's novel, every human action, from the most personal and delicate arrangement for matrimony to the most trivial family relationship is solely determined by money. "Whoever has money is right," proclaims the canon priest Lupi; and Baron Zacco, in another context, dryly observes: "Everyone is out for his own interest. . . . Nowadays interests come before family relations."

Mastro-don Gesualdo's failure cannot be attributed to his miscalculations or bad judgment in his business any more than the plight of the Malavoglia family may be explained by its drive to improve its lot. In both novels, Verga is in essence repeating the same theme, restating his view in different words, a view simply synthesized in the expression "You can't graft peaches on an olive tree." If Mastro-don Gesualdo has done anything wrong, his major sin is that he has betrayed, by his actions and by his strivings, the goodness, simplicity, and worth of that background he has fiercely fought to eradicate from his personal history. His entire existence has been planned to insert himself into a social class to which he aspires but that would hardly tolerate him under other circumstances. Thus, he marries Bianca Trao, even though she has been seduced by her young cousin, Baron Nini Rubiera, because he realizes that it is necessary to marry a "name" in order to achieve a certain prestige in business circles; he sends his daughter Isabela to the Santa Maria [Boarding] School even before she is five years old, hoping that by so doing she will receive an education that will enable them to cancel his humble origin—only to discover that her school companions, well aware of her situation, ridicule her, tease her, and jeer her. It is understandable that, in view of such a situation, all human rapports should be conducted with the ultimate scope of exploiting and using people as means, not as end in themselves. Indeed, Verga's characters live in a world where *la roba* is the only meaningful, lasting symbol of reality, the only available expression of power, prestige, and importance, the sole instrument capable of shaping the character and destiny of the individual, the only means through which the very course of history can be changed. In the novel, property becomes the focal point of reference, the element that propels people into prominence, hence giving them dignity and purpose. In Mastro-don Gesualdo's case, and in the Baroness Ribiera's, *la roba* attains the kind of meaning the old house had for the Malavoglia family. "Listen," warns Baron Zacco shortly before the wedding of Gesualdo and Bianca is to take place, "today the world belongs to those who have money."

Not everyone is possessed by the greed for riches, even when the purpose of wealth is not necessarily to acquire more power but to be used as an instrument to receive affection. Gesualdo's faithful servant, Diodata, for example, is hopelessly in love with her master; yet hers is a love that Verga aptly compares to that of an obedient, faithful dog. She has witnessed the slow, difficult rise of Don Gesualdo; she has been with him in spirit and in person every inch of his climb up the social ladder, up to the peak of what he can aspire—affluence and meaning—and finds herself brushed aside through his insensitivity and calculations. Although hurt and slighted, she returns to him in his dying days to assist him in his illnesses (among them, cholera contracted after his wife's death) in the tormenting and painful last hours of his life. Mastro Nunzio, Don Gesualdo's father, is another character who silently and regretfully is forced to watch over the inevitable march toward the final total rejection of those values he had treasured so highly. He scorns his son's futile attempts to be what he clearly is not, and can never be, and reminds him of his humble origin: "Your mother's name was Rosaria," he says, looking at his grandchild Isabella. Likewise, he is ready to frustrate the attempts his friends and relatives make to turn him into something he cannot be. "I was not born to live among rich people," Mastro Nunzio reminds his son. "My name is Mastro Nunzio," he proudly but modestly tells Baron Zucco, and "I don't put on my son's airs."

With all his hunger for material possession, Don Gesualdo is neither incapable of yearning for affection and love, nor does he forget the meaning and implications of his condition. As Verga presents him to us, he is able to understand the agony and toil his riches have cost him, and is equally sensitive both to the power made possible by money and to the "poetry of working" to accumulate the wealth he so obstinately wants. Precisely because of the way in which the author presents his hero to us, when the decay and disintegration of his empire begins one feels more sympathetic toward his defeat. Don Gesualdo, victim of a cancer-like disease that wastes him away, ever so slowly, is turned into a poignant creature, himself an impotent witness to the despicable manner in which his son-in-law devours his substance. Ultimately even money, yes the money he had so preciously treasured, becomes meaningless and absurd when its limitations are forcibly understood: "Money! You can none of you take your eyes off the money I've earned! What good is it to me if I can't buy even my health? A lot of bitterness it's brought me—always!" Indeed, as Gaetano Mariani lucidly put it, "*la roba* has induced him to betray his origins, *la roba* will alienate his father's love, and all his relatives who will end by dragging him to court, *la roba* will draw Don Gesualdo away from his daughter, who through foolish ambition he has educated like a noble girl, tying her to a noble husband who marries her for her dowry: all his life, built on *la roba,* is destroyed by *la roba.*"

Because his true allegiance is to property, Don Gesualdo must endure the loneliness of a man who lives only to work, and works only to accumulate money, despised by the aristocrats, scorned by his rich relatives, hated by his competitors, and envied by the people: "Everyone was against him because he was rich. . . . Everyone conjured against him. . . . Now everyone deserted him." As the prototype of the materialistic man, Don Gesualdo must learn the meaning of the importance of people only when he loses them: his wife dies in the cholera epidemic, his father dies of old age, his daughter marries a nobleman who has nothing but contempt for his father-in-law and everything he is and stands for. After his wife passes away, Don Gesualdo's fortune declines rapidly, and, while he is not one to surrender easily, still the going is tough. His illness administers the *coup de grâce:* confined to his bed and incapable of personally supervising his affairs, he slowly understands that there is no longer any hope for him. He dies knowing that no one has really understood him, or indeed has understood what his property, his beloved *roba* for which he had sacrificed the best years of his life, really means to him.

2 ITALO SVEVO:
ZENO'S LAST CIGARETTE

John Freccero

Que si maintenant quelque romancier hardi, dé-
chirant la toile habilement tissée de notre moi conventionnel,
nous montre sous cette logique apparente une absurdité fonda-
mentale, sous cette juxtaposition d'états simples une pénétra-
tion infinie de mille impressions diverses qui ont déjà cessé
d'être au moment où on les nomme, nous le louons de nous
avoir mieux connus que nous ne nous connaissons nous-mêmes.

> Henri Bergson, *Essai sur les
> données immédiates de la
> conscience*, p. 99.

"A written confession," Zeno remarks, "is always a lie." For
this reason literature is most false precisely when it aspires to
being most true: when it attempts to tell the story of the
author's life. Inevitably, the attempt to abstract self from self
and to make the past in each of its successive moments some-

Reprinted by permission of the author and the Editorial Board from
Modern Language Notes, Vol. 77, No. 1 (1962), where it originally
appeared.

how consistent with the present, distorts the image which was the object of the search. Any "portrait of the artist," if it is to be an image at all, must be set off at a distance from the dynamic present—as a young man, Joyce insisted—as though there were an unbridgeable gap between then and now, and as though time were not a continuum connecting the present with both birth and death. Analysis presupposes the detachment of the writer from his subject, a perspective impossible to achieve when the subject is the self. Thus, for a writer to speak of his childhood or of his senility, the successive images of which his life seems to be composed, is to speak of empty abstractions which cannot be observed from the flow of his consciousness.

The titles of Italo Svevo's novels hint at this, his central preoccupation: *Una vita* (*A Life*), *Senilità* (*As a Man Grows Older*), *La coscienza di Zeno* (*The Confessions of Zeno*), all seem to be meditations upon the attempt to capture the essence of his life in retrospect—meditations ending with the realization that to recapture the past is to falsify it, to invent it as though it had belonged to someone else. In Svevo's last novel, his whimsical *persona*, Zeno, begins his written attempt to recapture his childhood at the insistence of a somewhat obtuse psychiatrist, Dr. S., who does not believe that the problem has its roots in metaphysics rather than in psychology. Zeno's first words state his problem succinctly:

> See my childhood? Now that I am separated from it by over fifty years, my presbyopic eyes might perhaps reach to it if the light were not obscured by so many obstacles. The years like impassable mountains rise between me and it, my past years and a few brief hours in my life. . . . The present surges up and dominates me, the past is blotted out.

In Zeno's purely spatial imagination, the present moment is conditioned by the one that went before, that one in turn conditioned by its predecessor, and so on, back into the past, toward the origin of the individual and of the species. In a sense, then, the past exists in the present, and moves with it into the future. This continuous chain is life itself, and consciousness is the present moment, the spearhead of the past thrust into the future. Because one cannot stop the trajectory, and because the present carries with it all that went before, one cannot speak of one's past without a vantage point from which retrospective abstractions can be made. Zeno attempts to construct for himself a place to stand in his effort to find the cause of his disease, chain-smoking, and his attempt results in the creation of a lie—literature:

> And by dint of pursuing these memory-pictures, I at last really overtook them. I know now that I invented them. But invention is a creative act, not merely a lie. . . . I thought my dream-pictures really were an actual reproduction of the past. . . . I remembered them as one remembers an event one has been told by somebody who was not present at it.

Zeno's consciousness converts memory-pictures into dream-pictures, perception into creation, and thereby constructs of barren truth a rational lie. He chooses elements from his experience in order to construct an essence, to "characterize" himself in a plot of his own choosing, omitting the myriad irreducible details that add nothing to the portrait, or indeed seek to obfuscate its general outlines. Like the novel it so closely resembles, Zeno's lie is a work of art.

In a sense, a novelist is at once a creature and a creator, for the story he tells is necessarily his own invention, yet it must be drawn from his own experience. He must be within it, in order for it to be "alive," yet in another sense he must be outside of it in order to understand. It is the use of a fictional plot that enables him to know the story's end before its beginning, and to stand to his own experience like the medieval God Who was *auctor naturae*, able to take in past and future with His synoptic view. This transcendent foreknowledge gives his characters a rationale and an inner consistency which makes

them intelligible. At the same time, however, that foreknowledge foreordains the characters and deprives them of the liberty that real persons seem to possess. They are oppressed by
their destiny, or by what Pirandello would call their "form,"
unable to assert themselves against the crushing exigencies of
plot. The dialectic of the novel is then the struggle between the
freedom of a God-like novelist to write the plot as he chooses,
and the resistance of his experience, seeking to establish its
own true, although chaotic, liberty. So it is with Zeno's confession: the truth of his story varies inversely with its degree
of intelligibility. By the act of making his own experience
(which he cannot understand) into a *story* (which he understands for having invented it), Zeno rationalizes away the
history of his own freedom and with the miracle of the lie
becomes his own God, seeking to justify, at least in the world
of fiction, the flesh and blood reality from which he has abstracted himself.

The traditional novelist of the self turns from life to literature and in his fiction takes the place of the God *manqué* in his
life. But just as the God of tradition has been reproached for
the tyranny of predestination, so in recent times the existentialists, recapitulating the history of theology in their phenomenology of the novel, reproach the novelist for knowing what
his characters are about. They revive the medieval analogy
between the author of a book and the Author of the Cosmos,
and attempt to banish the former as the Enlightenment banished the latter. So anxious are they to preserve human freedom
even in the world of fiction that they suggest the abdication of
the author from his own experience in favor of the liberty of
his creatures. If it were possible for the novelist to be *manqué*
in the same way that God is missing from the world, then the
new novel would indeed hold up a mirror to life: a mass of
senseless detail, signifying nothing. Its characterless characters
would be doomed, just as Pirandello's six characters are
doomed, to wait for an author, possessed of the absolute

liberty of indeterminacy. Unlike the world, however, an authorless novel cannot come into existence: the *anti-roman* of Robbe-Grillet remains the written record of some other author's refusal to write a novel, as the play of Pirandello remains the successful dramatization of some other author's refusal to write a play.

Curiously enough, however, while the theorists of the novel have been seeking to make it resemble their image of life, ordinary men like Zeno have turned away from that life and behave as though they were searching in their lives for the logic and plot of the hack novel. The liberty of indeterminacy given by the author-manqué to his novelistic creatures is a tour-de-force; in everyday life, however, the same gift is a source of anguish. The underground man in our day attempts to withdraw from himself in order to superimpose a logical pattern upon the unrelated fragments culled from his imagination and with an act of *mauvaise foi* which the psychologists call "rationalization," paints a reasonable portrait of himself with the gray pigments of his life. The objective is always the same: In Zeno's words, "an excuse for doing what I wanted or which would prevent my doing it." The unfortunate (and inescapable) secondary effect of the novelist's art, the negation of his characters' freedom, is for Zeno the primary objective. His intention is precisely the reverse of Svevo's.

Justification is the object of Zeno's literary rationalization, just as it is always the object of the stereotyped romantic "confession." It is achieved by retrospectively denying one's freedom and therefore one's responsibility. From the perspective which he invents for himself, Zeno sees all that has happened as something that had to happen, given his image of himself and his self-imposed novelistic destiny. The historic Zeno was a mere puppet, "understandable" and therefore blameless. Or so we might be led to believe were this a simple trial of the accused before the gullible jury of a literary audience—were this a nineteenth-century novel of confession. We are able to see through Zeno's literary subterfuge, however, for we have a place to stand, outside of his life and his lie, from which the ironic gap between the two can be measured. Dr. S., the psychiatrist who is Svevo's naive surrogate, introduces Zeno's story with a few remarks that succeed in casting into doubt all of that which is to follow: "He little knows what surprises lie in wait for him, if someone were to set about analyzing the mass of truths and falsehoods which he has collected here." The ironic introduction makes of the confession a novel-within-a-novel, precisely in order to reveal the mechanism of rationalization for what it is: the creative lie of defense. Svevo's technique is much like Dostoyevsky's biting satire: both *The Confessions of Zeno* and *Notes from the Underground* are directed against the vanity of those who, like Rousseau, would seek to prove their innocence by a process traditionally reserved for the admission of guilt. Specifically, it accuses the man who would paint the truth after his own image of himself.

Before he embarks upon his writing adventure, Dostoyevsky's man from the underground meditates upon his sincerity along the same lines (and with the same degree of sincerity) as Zeno:

> In any case, I have not long since decided to recall to mind some of my former adventures; up until now, I had avoided them, not without a certain uneasiness. At this moment, however, while I am evoking them and even writing them down, I am trying an experiment: Is it possible to be frank and sincere, at least with oneself, and can one tell oneself the whole truth? I note in this regard that Heine assures us that there can be no such thing as an accurate autobiography and that a man always lies when he is talking about himself. Rousseau, according to him, surely deceived us, even deliberately, in his *Confessions,* out of sheer vanity. I am sure Heine is right . . . but [he] had in mind public confessions; I am writing only for myself, and I wish to make clear once and for all that if I seem to be addressing a reader it is merely for convenience.

His greatest lie is that his confession is not public. Since the whole point of confession, whether theological or novelistic, is justification, it becomes difficult to imagine how it can succeed without a judge from whose perspective the penitent can be absolved, or, more correctly, acquitted. In the ordinary literature of confession of the nineteenth century, by the process of publication, we the readers are judges before whom the author attempts to exculpate himself. It is the genius of Dostoyevsky, however, and of Svevo after him, to put us at one remove from the trial scene, so that we may have some other testimony besides that of the accused, and may see each of his lies for what it is. In a profound sense it may be said that the novel-within-the-novel is the novelist's indictment of all public confession, particularly (and this explains the savagery of the attack) of his own. The novelist who *is*, confessing his guilt, accuses the novelist who *was*, seeking to proclaim his innocence. We must pause to discuss the gap that separates them.

The novel of justification, the false confession enclosed within the novels of both Dostoyevsky and Svevo, can never succeed because it can never end. Zeno abandons his attempt at writing his confessions when the war breaks out and the man from the underground, we are told, would go on interminably were he not interrupted by Dostoyevsky. The audience may be taken in by the lie within the temporal and spatial confines of the novel; in real life, however, the neurotic must go on and on in order to convince himself. The moment he ceases to abstract he must once more take up the tedious task of living; he then realizes that he has attempted to judge and to justify a life which he is still in the process of creating. Paradoxically, he knows that he can never fully be all that he is until he ceases to be; he can never know his own essence until he dies, when he will have ceased to know anything at all. Only death will provide the necessary gap between the man and an accurate self-portrait.

Death has many faces, however, one of which, we have

come to learn from the existentialists, is purely epistemological. The act of reflecting upon one's own consciousness is a type of death of the self which involves no physical decomposition: *je pense, donc je ne suis pas*. The great novelists extend the process of Sartre's *pour-soi* throughout a whole novelistic duration, and become all-knowing impersonal observers. However, this death of the self, in order to be more than simply a striking metaphor, must be complete, and if complete, can permit of no return to "the old man." The gap that exists in the novel-within-a-novel between the lying *persona* and the novelist (Dr. S[vevo]., Dostoyevsky) who accuses him is a kind of absolute separation between the experience of the novelist who was and the novelist who is. If this were a merely temporary and purely epistemological separation, then the novel-within-a-novel would also be a lie, capable of being in turn inserted into another novel (and another and another) in an infinite regression of false journals in the manner of Gide, the sum total of which might approach but never reach the truth as a limit, and the purpose of which would always be to justify, because of the essential vital continuity of subject and object. On the contrary, however, the sincerity of a Dostoyevsky points to the seriousness of his undertaking, and proclaims the truth of his perspective. Thus the death of his former self is total and complete, and his work can be described as a kind of resurrection. Such a process of spiritual death and resurrection has a traditional name—"conversion"—and the early history of the written record of such conversions is intimately linked to the history of the novel.

From the perspective of St. Augustine, the inventor of the genre, it was possible to believe that an autobiography could be the truth, that one could discover a principle of intelligibility in one's life and need not invent it. This is not to say that Augustine was unaware of the fundamental problem; he knew as well as any modern novelist how futile is the attempt to make a verbal abstraction from the flow of time, and his meditation was a lesson to all who would discover themselves in the present moment. "The present," he wrote "occupies no space." The moment one attempts to transfix time, to set off the past and eternalize the self in the present moment, that moment has slipped by from proximate future to proximate past. The present progressive is an abstraction, a mere grammatical convention when applied to the self, for the self is perpetually changing. In order to capture its essence in retrospect, one must establish a gap between then and now; in order to take stock, all transactions must first be concluded; in order to have the static word correspond to the dynamic flesh it seeks to express, one must die and be born again. In effect, the Augustinian solution of the epistemological problem of confession was identical with the Pauline solution of the moral problem facing all Christians. All confession, literary or sacramental, is either a lie or the record of a conversion, a death and resurrection. Self-knowledge is necessarily death of the self, a descent into Hell, while self-expression in its profoundest sense is necessarily re-birth.

For the Middle Ages, in order to make one's confession (or to write one's "confessions"), one needed a point of Being in the stream of becoming. Such a point could only be provided by grace, a sacramental place to stand outside of time from which the *ek-static* penitent might examine his conscience, from which the "novelist" might analyze his consciousness (the two processes are one for Augustine, as they are in the "*Coscienza* of Zeno" [sic]). The miracle could be brought about only by the God who had Himself died and been reborn, the Word made flesh, and its effect was so profound that it was said to mark the beginning of what St. Paul termed a "New Life." Similarly, the novelist of today seeks to reconcile a stable principle of intelligibility, his ontological "word," to the liberty and flow of life. This too can only be brought about with a kind of conversion, and in the greatest of novelists, with a kind of "incarnation romanesque," to use the expression of

René Girard. But Zeno's hilarious attempt to stop smoking, which is presumably his search for a conversion to a "new life," is an act of bad faith, for his self-accusation, like Rousseau's and like that of the man from the underground, is in reality self-justification. Zeno's frustration is the ironic proof of the fact that in Svevo's eyes, such a conversion is impossible in human terms. St. Augustine, presented with a similar situation, might have quoted the Psalms: "In the sight of God shall no man living be justified." Zeno looks everywhere for his moment of truth, except within himself.

It must not be imagined that this is merely a fanciful application of moral theology to esthetic phenomenology; the fashionable literary theology of the existentialists is at least as old as Dante. The *Vita Nuova (New Life)*, a spiritual biography which owes much to Augustine, records the poet's transition from old to new life, from inferior poet to great artist, through the grace of his lady, in the language of conversion that Zeno parodies in his first chapter. The scholarly arguments about the "reality" of Beatrice and the more recent refusals to see her as an analogue of Christ betray at once a modern misunderstanding of the Middle Ages and an old-fashioned misunderstanding of the profundities of literary creation. She is Dante's Word and flesh, his death and resurrection, his perspective on himself, necessary for the Christian and the artist.

So closely does Zeno's search for salvation parody the language of conversion in the *Vita Nuova* that we must pause to recall a few essential features of the latter story. Dante's book begins in a moment of calm recollection:

> In that part of the book of my memory, before which there would be little to read, I find a rubric which says: *"Incipit Vita Nova"*—here begins the New Life. Beneath that rubric I find written the words which I intend to copy into this little book, and if not all of them, at least their substance.

The substance of a book of memory, it would seem, is the essence of a life, distilled in memory out of many seemingly unrelated fragments, and expressed with the serenity of artistic and psychological detachment. The poet believed that his new life had begun in a moment of Grace made sacred by the powers of the number three, when he first met Beatrice: "Nine times already since my birth had the heaven of light returned to the same point with respect to its own revolution, when the glorious lady of my mind first appeared to my eyes. . . ." The stars themselves seemed to mark the moment, as if heaven and earth, God Himself, had pre-ordained this meeting of two nine-year old children which began the poet's authentic life and one of the world's great love stories. Dante's tiresome insistence upon the numerically exact moment is explained by the conviction, formulated by the poet as he looks backward over his life, that his love for Beatrice made time stand still, and gave the new life its meaning.

But precisely because of that story's neatness, it would strike Zeno as a poetic lie. Dante glosses a book of memory which seems already a creation of the imagination; the real book of memory, to Zeno, is his dictionary, whose order is the arbitrary alphabet, a pure convention applied to an amorphous mass of detail heaped up by the passing of time.

> I find the following entry on the front page of a dictionary, beautifully written and adorned with a good many flourishes: *2 February, 1886. Today I finish my law studies and take up chemistry. Last cigarette!!*

With confidence in himself, a sense of victory, with "hope for strength and health in the future," he smoked his interminable last cigarettes, one very much like another, at each moment renewing his vow to begin a new life. Somehow he seemed out of touch with whatever cosmic force makes moments propitious and presents each of us with his salvation in the form of a last cigarette, last puerility or weakness:

> I had a partiality for certain dates because their figures went well together. I remember one of the last century which seemed as if it must be the final monument to my vice: "Ninth day of the

ninth month in the year 1899." Surely a most significant date!
The new century furnished me with dates equally harmonious,
though in a different way. "First day of the first month in the
year 1901." Even today I feel that if only that date could repeat
itself I should be able to begin a new life.

But he waits for a new life, a conversion in a propitious
moment, which is no more likely to come than is the next year
1901. He passes from cigarette to resolution and back to cigarette again, searching for the key to his destiny from the mass
of possible permutations: "Third day of the sixth month, in
the year 1912, at 24 o'clock," or even a date which is striking
because of its very inconsequence: "third day of the second
month of the year 1905 at six o'clock!" But one date is very
much like another, as one cigarette or one bead of time is much
like another, and in a world where any number may serve as
the mystic key, no number will do. Zeno the *persona* will not
achieve the detachment of Svevo the author until death over-
takes him.

But if there is no number, there is at least the dictionary—
the alphabet—and for a man so desperate for order it suffices.
Zeno finds his wife, not as Dante found his Beatrice, through
an apparently chance encounter that had in reality been
planned by God Himself, nor again by the merest accident, as
one suspects that healthy men do, regardless of the rationalizations they construct in retrospect, but rather through a syste-
matic, rational and therefore ludicrous search, in alphabetical
order. Or so he would have us believe:

> Their names, which I immediately committed to memory, were
> Ada, Augusta, Alberta and Anna. I was also told that they were
> all good-looking. That initial seemed to me more significant than
> it really was. I dreamt about those four girls linked together so
> closely by their names. I almost felt they were a bunch of flowers.
> But that initial meant something else too. My name is Zeno, and
> I felt as if I were about to choose a wife from a far country.

He proposes to the sisters in alphabetical order, skipping only
the infant Anna: Ada, Alberta and then Augusta, who finally

accepts: "I don't mind confessing that at that moment a feeling
of immense satisfaction pervaded me. I had no longer any
decision to make. Everything was decided for me. At last I had
obtained certainty." Later, when the adulterous Zeno must face
the decision to leave his mistress, again his emblematic dictionary serves as a book of memory: "During those hours of
torment I wrote the date of the day in my dictionary against
the Letter C (Carla) with the comment: 'Last Betrayal.' "

The dictionary is the intellect's parody of the book of memory, the result of the mind's attempt to transcend itself and
to give order to chaos with its own static "word" in an imitation
of the divine process. Ideally, it represents the sum total of all
of reality bound up in a single volume, with a sequential order
(and therefore an apparent continuity) and an apparent rationale. Only a mad-man would mistake it for the meaningful
account of a life and thus be taken in by the obvious counter-
feit; yet the lie that the dictionary represents is little worse
than the lie of the completely contrived plot. It is dead because
it is a spatial, discontinuous order, lacking the temporal flow
of life just as the intellect is dead for analyzing atoms and for
not being able to account for change. In the process of retro
spective reconstruction the intellect attempts to capture life,
but intellect and life, the fragmentary dictionary and the flow,
are inalterably opposed because they pull in opposite directions, the first seeking the scientific certainty of dead determin-
ism, the other seeking the future flow of liberty. This incompatibility is at the source of Zeno's paradoxical nature, for even
the healthiest organism would appear pure mechanism under
the scrutiny of the intellect's retrospective gaze.

Zeno's book of memory has no essence; the dictionary has
many characters but no plot, for the course of life has had no
rationale and no privileged moments which he can observe in
retrospect: one cigarette is exactly like another. Together all
those cigarettes go to make up his life, measured out in discontinuous parcels which disappear as they are lived, leaving
behind an ash which mingles with all the ashes of history. We

live in this world with our ashes, which each of us carries with him. In order to recall, Zeno must "invoke the aid of all those many cigarettes I have smoked, identical with the one I have in my hand now." But even this one is gradually disappearing and in a moment will belong to the past. Zeno cannot stand still in the course of life, and yet it is precisely this which he must do in order to remember. One cannot recall the past while one is creating it; one cannot begin a new life while continuing to smoke. Zeno's homely, sensible wife unknowingly stumbles upon the truth when she remarks that "smoking is one way of living, and not such a bad one, either." One day Zeno will quit smoking: when the chain comes to an end and he finally succumbs (and thus is cured) of the disease that afflicts him—life itself—the only disease, he tells us, which is always fatal.

Authentic life, true health, is no more aware of itself than is perfect vision, perfect movement, or perfect breathing. Life is a rhythm into which one must enter; it is recapitulated "in the most rudimentary of sounds, that of a sea-wave, which from the moment it is born until it expires is in a state of continual change." Like music, its whole substance is rhythm—*tempo*—time itself, and not the string of beads that Zeno imagines. Guido, Zeno's rival in love, improvises upon Bach and produces beautiful music—"the rhythm of a healthy organism." "When I can play like that," Zeno remarks, "I shall be cured." In spite of his theoretical knowledge of music, however, or perhaps because of it, his violin will produce only cacophony. His intelligence is acute but mechanical, and like his eyes, it can never focus on the present—that which is at hand. A friend tells Zeno about the mechanics of walking:

> He told me with amusement that when one is walking rapidly each step takes no more than half a second, and that in that half second no fewer than fifty-four muscles are set in motion. I listened in bewilderment. I at once directed my attention to my legs and tried to discover the infernal machine. I thought I had

succeeded in finding it. I could not of course distinguish all its fifty-four parts, but I discovered something terrifically complicated which seemed to get out of order directly I began thinking about it.

I limped as I left the café. . . .

If Zeno is ridiculous, it is because in telling his story he would apply his cinematographic intelligence to the flow and change of life, hoping desperately to reproduce movement from separate and isolated states, like a machine imitating life. Unfortunately, the moving-picture camera of the mind cannot work quite fast enough, and even if it could, we would not be taken in by our own illusion: in this Bergsonian world, the myopic man of science and the far-sighted philosopher alike fall flat on their faces.

Zeno's wife, with her crossed eyes and her animal health, lives in the present without a thought of birth or death, attached to those stationary objects—jewelry or furniture—which prevent men "from becoming sea-sick in a world perpetually turning." For the far-sighted, chain-smoking Zeno, on the other hand, the present lies just beyond his last cigarette, a present into which his intelligence, or at least his imagination, plunges, leaving behind the will-less creature rooted to life by his past and by the weed that is burning in his hand.

> I understood at last the meaning of perfect health in a human being, when I realized that for her (Augusta) the present was a tangible reality in which we could take shelter and be near together. I tried to be admitted to this sanctuary and to stay there, resolved not to laugh either at myself or her; for my skepticism would only be a symptom of disease, and I must at least beware of infecting someone who had given her life into my keeping. It was my desire to protect her that made me act for a while like a normal human being.

It is Zeno's intelligence which converts the rhythm of life into disease, by analyzing and dissecting, by searching for stability in the present and substituting self-consciousness for action, chain-smoking for life. It is his delusion that he can find himself, capture his ego, undergo a conversion, and thus elude the pressure of his past forcing him along a pre-destined track. His intelligence dupes him into believing that he can stand still, outside of himself, and begin anew from a clean slate, in the present moment. His cigarettes represent his discontinuous duration, his connection with the past and his direction in the future. To make one of them the last, while such a resolution might satisfy the mind's desire to fix reality in static images and thus render it intelligible, would nevertheless result in breaking the continuity, in fixing life only by ending it. To renew the resolution each moment, however, and *then* to break it, would be to satisfy the life instinct while throwing the intellect its necessary bone. But this double operation leaves time for nothing else, and brings with it only paralysis. Zeno's dilemma is that he would walk and know that *he* is walking, would live and know that *he* is living, endure and know that *he* is enduring. He would be the man defining his own ego, giving direction and purpose to his life, ignoring the dictionary dragging behind him that is his past (and the past of his father and of his species), in order to begin a new life a moment from now, to be determined only by himself. It cannot be done, for to think is to kill reality by freezing it, to live is unconsciously to flow. The last cigarette is a desperate, compulsive attempt at a compromise between action and thought:

> I was irritated by canon law, which seemed to me so remote from life, and I fled to science in the hope of finding life itself, though imprisoned in a retort. That last cigarette was emblem of my desire for activity (even manual) *and* for calm, clear, sober thought.

He is then two men: an intellect perceiving separate, disjointed states, powerless to control an organism whose liberty is gained only by following its trajectory. A "last" cigarette satisfies both the hope of the intellect, and the demand of the organism:

In order to make it seem a little less foolish I tried to give a philosophic content to the malady of the "last cigarette." You strike a noble attitude, and say: "Never again!" But what becomes of the attitude if you keep your word? You can only preserve it if you keep on renewing your resolution. And then Time, for me, is not that imaginable thing that never stops. For me, but only for me, it comes again.

The attitude, a pose struck for the moment, is a pause in the stream of life. In the next moment, a new pause, a new resolution. But because time, like nature, abhors a vacuum, something must fill the gap between these instants. Imagining a third moment will not do, for this only succeeds in halving the instant, as a fourth and fifth will only succeed in quartering it. No quantity of renewed resolutions will succeed in working the qualitative change from spatially fixed points, the time that "comes again," to the stream of authentic time. Zeno tells his formerly-fat friend why dieting is so much easier than curing the smoking habit:

I explained to him that giving up three meals a day seemed to me nothing compared with the task of making a fresh resolution every moment not to smoke another cigarette. If you use up all your time making resolutions you have no time for anything else, for it takes a Julius Caesar to be able to do two things at once.

The intellectual desire to know liberty leads to the paralysis of discontinuous time—disease, Zeno calls it—whereas the flow and rhythm of animal health preclude the exercise of what is distinctively human—thought. The closest thing to freedom that he can reach is a compromise between the two—Zeno can play the violin only on condition that he beat out the rhythm with his foot. Perfect liberty would entail the reconciliation of separate points with a continuous line, making of discrete perceptions of the self the smooth trajectory life.

The first chapter of Zeno's novel presents us with an old paradox in unique form: how can one reconcile the movement of life, animal health, with the transversal static cuts made by the intellect? How can one be and know that he is being? The paradox is a form of the ancient paradox of Zeno of Elea, transposed from the mysteries of space and motion to those of Augustinian duration and time. Svevo has called his character Zeno precisely because he is an embodiment of the spirit of the Eleatic, seeking to reconcile reality to reason. The effect of transposing the puzzle from space to human time, however, is to make the conundrum the anguish of a soul.

The puzzle of Zeno of Elea may be stated in one of its forms in the following manner: If we imagine the trajectory of an arrow flying through space, it must be said that at any given moment it occupies a given space and is therefore momentarily motionless, requiring another moment before it can occupy the next successive position. Hence the trajectory is made up of an infinity of successive moments for the gradual transition from place to place. But these infinite moments cannot be said ever to reach the continuity that we perceive. Motion itself cannot be deduced. At each separate moment the arrow is motionless, all the time it is moving. Just as one can never place enough mathematical points side by side in order to make up a straight line, it is impossible to deduce the trajectory of the arrow from the logical stages, the transversal cuts, that go to make it up. It will never reach its target.

If we substitute for the arrow the present moment, the spearhead of consciousness moving from past to future, we have the paradox in Svevo's terms. Bergson himself transposed it to a temporal dimension. In *Creative Evolution* the philosopher wrote:

> Nothing would be easier, now, than to extend Zeno's argument to qualitative becoming and to evolutionary becoming. We should find the same contradictions in these. That the child can become a youth, ripen to maturity and decline to old age, we understand when we consider that vital evolution is here the reality itself. Infancy, adolescence, maturity, old age, are mere

views of the mind, possible stops imagined by us, from without, along the continuity of a progress. On the contrary, let childhood, adolescence, maturity and old age be given as integral parts of the evolution, they become real stops, and we can no longer conceive how evolution is possible, for rests placed beside rests will never be equivalent to a movement. How, with what is made, can we reconstitute what is being made?

Svevo suggested the paradox in several different ways. Music provides one of the analogues:

> I could play well if I were not ill, but I am always pursuing health even when I am practicing balance of the four strings of a violin. There are certain slight inhibitions in my organism which are more obvious when I play the violin, and therefore easier to deal with. Even the most undeveloped being, if he knows the difference between groups of three, four, and six notes, can pass rhythmically and accurately from one to the other just as his eye can pass from one color to another. But in my case, after I have been playing one of those rhythmic figures it clings to me and I can't escape from it, but get it mixed up with the following figure so that I play it out of time. If I am to play the notes right I am compelled to beat time with my feet and head; but good-by to ease, serenity and music!

Again, Zeno has an hallucination when he attempts to recall the past:

> I dimly see certain strange images that seem to have no connection with my past; an engine puffing up a steep incline dragging endless coaches after it. Where is it going? How did it get there at all?

Its significance becomes clear at his father's deathbed:

> I realize that the image that obsessed me at the first attempt to look into my past—the image of an engine drawing a string of coaches up a hill—came to me for the first time while I lay on the sofa listening to my father's breathing. That's just what engines do when drawing an enormous weight: they emit regular puffs,

which then become faster and finally stop altogether; and that
pause seems dangerous too, because as you listen you cannot
help fearing that the engine and the train must go tumbling head
over heels down into the valley.

Zeno's attempt to go back to his childhood is to retrace his
steps, coach by coach from the present moment, "invoking the
aid of all those cigarettes." With the mistake characteristic of
the Eleatic intellect he asks, "Who can stop those memory
pictures once they have taken flight through time, which never
before seemed so much like space." He is his past, just as the
engine is the train, and to stop puffing in order to look back
over the past, to refuse to follow the cigarette track, is indeed
to begin a new life:

> Copler, with the death-rattle in his throat, was measuring out his
> last hours of breath. His noisy breathing consisted of two sounds;
> one hesitating, as if produced by the air he breathed in; one hur-
> ried, when he expelled the air from his lungs. Was he in a hurry
> to die? A pause always followed these two sounds, and I thought
> that when the pause grew longer the new life would have begun.

The moralists tell us that a pause is necessary, that the
beginning of knowledge is to know one's self. But how can one
reconstitute the self if it does not as yet exist except as an end
term? How can one justify the belief in one's identity? Bergson
seems to have dismissed the problem: "all we have to do is to
give up the cinematographical habits of our intellect." But
these habits are all that the *persona* Zeno possesses, since he is
himself the product of an intellectual exercise. Hence, he must
struggle to survive:

> I limped along, trying in vain to contend with my bodily distress.
> I sometimes have attacks like these; I can breathe perfectly well,
> but I count each breath I draw, because each requires a special
> effort of the will. I have the feeling if I were not careful I should
> die of suffocation.

Zeno is a rational construct, the justification of the historical Zeno, with being but without life. Small wonder if he must be on his guard against the spontaneity of the vital force. If he were to apply the mathematician's solution of Zeno's paradox to his own life, $S_\infty = A / (1 - r)$, he might conclude that he need only place himself at the end of the series to see that the transition from point to point has indeed been a continuous trajectory aimed at the "sum to infinity." If he were to use the maxim of Hegel and of Sartre after him, he would see that *Wesen ist was gewesen ist:* being is that which has been. Essence is then simply the *raison de la série*, the mean or average of all of the successive appearances. These solutions will do for the mathematicians and for the philosophers, who have merely to dismiss Zeno's paradox, close up shop and go home to their wives and children at the end of their day. Not so with Zeno, or, we may guess, with any man seeking to know himself. When we apply the scientific solutions to the existential problem, we see the enormity for what it is—for how can one take the sum to infinity, the *raison de la série*, unless the trajectory is finished and the series closed? When the sum means being and the series life, we are left with the inescapable conclusion that one cannot know one's self until one is dead. The process of finding one's identity, essential to the process of justification, is necessarily spiritual suicide. And in the world of the neurotic Zeno, there can be no Augustinian resurrection.

To be delivered of his anguish, Zeno has one of three choices: he can stop living, stop thinking, or lie. If the reason and reality, thought and action, self-consciousness and health are contradictory, one must abandon either one camp or the other, the word or the flesh. Or one can create for one's self an essence, an autobiography, and present it to the reading public or the psychiatrist to make of it what they will. One can leave the rhythmic brooding of the armchair to approach the writing-table, as does Zeno when he first begins to write his memoirs, in order to create literature, itself a rationalization as closely related to the truth as are Zeno's interminable vows to quit smoking. Zeno's retrospective gaze will never capture his evolution, but rather invents a story written in Tuscan from a life lived in the dialect of Trieste, and presents us with a single character who can never change and never evolve, because he does not move.

In the successive chapters of the novel, to which we can only allude here, Zeno constructs mad rationalizations about his father, his marriage, his mistress and his business. Because of the perfect logic of all of his motivations, as he recounts them, we understand them for what they are: ludicrous attempts to justify himself. We learn to suspect all of his emotions and passions, precisely because he is a shadow of a man, without the flesh and blood of which real, illogical life is composed. He seems not to exist but to know, while those around him exist and are unaware of it. Similarly, he understands freedom, but for that very reason does not possess it, whereas those around him seem unconsciously free. Thus, all normal human relationships are impossible for him, for, lacking the principle of life, he cannot communicate with those around him more than he can communicate with the stones or the stars. He cannot give himself to the vital forces of destiny, as do the rest of society in the seance, for instance, but instead remains outside seeking to manipulate those forces with a God-like omniscience. The result is that he becomes the unwitting victim of the very destiny he tries to elude, while those around him achieve their liberty because they are unconscious of their own limitations.

Zeno is nevertheless in society and so must enter into relationships of various kinds with the people around him. This would be an insurmountable difficulty, were it not for a variation of the technique of the lie, his *modus operandi* throughout the novel. Since he is a shadow of a man, he can only resemble other men by imitating them, by counterfeiting their movements and their gestures. Forever an outsider to the bourgeois society around him, he can at least struggle to look like them and his mechanical efforts to fit in, to conform to the patterns about him, are the principal source of much of the humor in the book. It is the humor of the intellect imitating life's dynamism with the mechanical movement of the Chaplinesque filmstrip, composed of successive frames which move a shade too slow to look like life. When he reads newspapers, Zeno is "metamorphosed into public opinion." With a friend in a restaurant, he absently orders the same soft drink, "even though I hate lemons." He goes so far that he even chooses a wife, not logically, as he would like to have us suppose, but simply out of fascination for her father, whose "quiet strength" he envies: "When I admire anyone I at once try to be like him. So I began to imitate Malfenti. I soon began to feel myself as astute as he was." At the same time, the people whom he imitates are also his judges before whom he must justify himself, as a perpetual performer imitating his audience, who receives howls of laughter for his clumsy efforts.

As his models, those around him stimulate his admiration and envy; as his judges, they inspire his hatred. So it was with his father, so it was with Malfenti, so too with Guido, his rival in love. Zeno's reaction to his father and all his successive father-surrogates is necessarily ambiguous, composed of love and hate, for his reaction to life itself is ambiguous. He turns to the women in his life for deliverance, just as the man from the underground in Dostoyevsky's novel turns to the prostitute for deliverance from his love-hate fascination for the officer. But the same ambiguity prevails here, for his perpetual analysis precludes love, and casts the shadow of disease over every relationship. Zeno's wife offers him shelter in the present moment, which for her really exists, and he can repay his cross-eyed Beatrice only with indifference, precisely because she is willing to accept him.

But Zeno's mad rationalizations and his love-hate relationships will end when life, or rather life's ultimate paradox, breaks in upon his "Oedipal" microcosm with the thunderclap of the macrocosm: war. Just as his father launched him into the world with an act of violence which was at the same time his condemnation, the death-bed slap, nature's vengeance against the poison of reason, so his world (and ours) will end with the final slap that will shatter the cosmos and return us to our primal, if somewhat antiseptic, purity. The World War is at once the product of reason's conflict with life, and nature's vengeance for the schism.

The sudden shift in the novel from what has been the private world of Zeno to a universal dimension should not surprise us, for we are after all dealing with confession, and confession ends in apocalypse. For Zeno, "death was really the great organizing force of life," and when one approaches the great moment in one's own life, one approaches the "conversion" that will bring about an integration in society. It is then that one realizes that history too, if organized, if at all intelligible, is also directed toward death and suffers from the same malady that afflicts the individual. "For a long time now," Zeno says in his old age, "I have been smoking cigarettes and have given up calling them the last." One can no longer believe in facile constructions of the mind when one is confronted with personal death and universal holocaust:

> The war has reached me at last! . . . I found myself right in the middle of it, and was surprised then to think I had not realized that I must sooner or later become involved. I had lived quite peacefully in a building of which the ground-floor had caught fire, and it had never occurred to me that sooner or later the whole building, with me in it, would go up in flames.

Descending from the tower of the solipsist, he realizes that self-justification is withdrawal from one's fellowman in an act of vanity, while the admission of guilt is acceptance of one's (equally guilty) fellow-men in an act of love. At last Zeno can be successful in business, the commerce between men, when he forgets his schemes and trades the resin of medicine for the incense of secular adoration. In the reason there is little hope, when the reason is merely a tool for setting one's self off from the rest of mankind.

"Our life," says Zeno, using that pronoun for the first time, "is poisoned to the roots." The fact is that the world's reality is not the reality of the mind:

> Today we have reached the middle of the month, and I am struck by the obstacles that our calendar places in the way of carrying out a straight-forward, well-ordered resolution. All the months are a different length . . . except for July and August, December and January, there are no two successive months that have an equal number of days. Time is really very ill-ordered.

It is by manufacturing their own order, by playing God to nature, that all of men have sinned against her. By applying to nature reason in the form of the machine, man first offended her. He abstracted himself, or attempted to, from the natural evolutionary progress which alone could guarantee health. Now man gets more and more cunning and more and more weak. His mind increases daily in its power over the elements, but his eyes begin to require thicker and thicker spectacles. The bespectacled eyes are directed in envy toward his neighbor and his cunning directed toward theft and violence. The process in the macrocosm can end only as it does in the microcosm: universal war and death, the inevitable end of reason's struggle, of Zeno's story, and of the world itself:

> Perhaps some incredible disaster produced by machines will lead us back to health. When all the poison gases are exhausted, a man, made like all other men of flesh and blood, will in the quiet of his room invent an exposive of such potency that all the explosives in existence will seem like harmless toys beside it. And another man, made in his image and in the image of all the rest, but a little weaker than they, will steal that explosive and crawl to

the center of the earth with it, and place it just where he calcu-
lates it will have the maximum effect. There will be a tremendous
explosion, but not one will hear it and the earth will return to its
nebulous state and go wandering through the sky, free at last
from parasites and disease.

The word of man, yoked with violence to the world it seeks to
redeem, justifies itself with annihilation under the shadow of an
Author who is no longer there.

3

LUIGI PIRANDELLO:
MAJOR WRITER, MINOR NOVELIST

E. Allen McCormick

Far better known in Italy as playwright and *novelliere,* and celebrated internationally for a handful of plays that seem to offer us the quintessence of *pirandellismo,* the novelist Pirandello still remains largely on the periphery, important enough perhaps in the history of a genre unquestionably weak in Italian literature but central neither to the man's total literary achievement nor to the European novel as a whole.

This is no unusual fate. Secondary efforts in another genre have a way of being all too frequently subjected to analysis as illustration of something else. One thinks of Shaw's novels or those of the German expressionist Georg Kaiser, recalling thereby that criticism likes to extract from a less satisfactory form the ideas and often even the techniques that seem so much more comfortable elsewhere. Each of Pirandello's seven novels has come in for this kind of treatment; once the ideas and their place in *pirandellismo* have been discussed, the novels themselves qua novels come off rather poorly. *L'Esclusa,* 1893 (*The Outcast*), we are told, has too much analysis (Starkie); *Il turno,* 1902 (*His Turn*), is interesting for its local color and will be appreciated by readers of Verga (!), yet it too ends by wearying us (Starkie); *Uno, nessuno e centomila,* 1925–1926

(*One, None and a Hundred Thousand*), is a monologue of notes (Ulrich Leo), a series of disconnected observations on the motif of plurality of personality (Büdel). One may easily extend the list, or one may find criticism occasionally saying nice things about one or the other novel—generally *Il fu Mattia Pascal,* 1904 (*The Late Mattia Pascal*), but more recently and surprisingly *Quaderni di Serafino Gubbio operatore,* 1914–1915 (*Notebooks of Serafino Gubbio, Cameraman*)—or, finally, one may point to those who really prefer to de-emphasize distinctions between playwright, novelist, and short-story writer and speak of Pirandello's writing as "one interpenetrating whole" (F. May).*

In criticism pluralism begets extremes of one sort or another, and we need therefore offer no apology for centering these remarks squarely on the question of Pirandello's novels as novels—for asking what their achievement is apart from Pirandello's philosophy, which is to say, their vehicular value to *pirandellismo,* and apart from their particular niche in Italian fiction. Our attempt to answer this question involves a brief discussion of the novels in their order of publication, with special emphasis on an early, a middle, and a late novel. (*L'Esclusa, Il fu Mattia Pascal,* and *Uno, nessuno e centomila*).

In his first novel, *L'Esclusa,* a young wife is accused of infidelity and cast aside by her husband, then by her father, and finally by society. Her return, after a scene of anguished forgiveness, is predictable and conventional to the point of triteness. But there is a peculiar twist to the story, one we have come to recognize as typically Pirandellian: reality and appearance are at odds. Marta, the heroine, begins her exile as an innocent victim of her husband's insane jealousy and her father's outsized concept of honor, yet her bitterness toward them and the society that joins in condemnation gradually nourishes in her a desire to be guilty in fact. And so she does

* For more complete reference, see the paragraph on criticism in the section on Pirandello in the Bibliographical Notes.

commit adultery, with the admirer whose letters (uninvited though not unanswered) caused the scandal many months before. But her lover eventually encourages her to accept the reconciliation which the story finally provides: his analysis is uncomfortably precise:

> When you were innocent, they punished you, they drove you out, they insulted and defamed you. And now, when pursued by neither your passion nor your will, but driven by everybody, you have committed the sin—you view it as such!—which others accused you of when you were innocent of it—now they want you back, they insist on taking you back! Go back then, go back! You will be punishing them as they deserve, simply!

The speaker has been interpreted by Starkie as a Don Juan who "only looks on Marta as prey for the moment," but it is really more a matter of the author using Marta's lover throughout a considerable part of the novel as disputant and even as mouthpiece. This, more than any convincingly villainous quality, renders him cold and lifeless, and what promised to be a description of human suffering in a Sicilian bourgeois setting ends up as rather tedious psychology. Marta is reconciled with her husband at the end (at his dying mother's bedside), but their avowed vigil is lamentably strong in melodrama:

> She is looking . . . my mother is looking. I forgive . . . Stay here . . . stay! . . . We'll keep watch together. . . .

Pirandello seems to have forgotten the punishment Marta was somehow to have inflicted on a rigid, ununderstanding society, and the heroine's despair strikes one as altogether out of keeping with the outcome. It appears that the subject of their *roman a these*—the contradiction of appearance and reality—is far more important than the lives created to give it solidity.

Pirandello's second novel, *Il turno*, translated as *His Turn* and, more felicitously, as *The Merry-Go-Round of Love*, remains in the Sicilian landscape and contains much of what we

associate with regionalism. It is in several ways a more satisfactory work than *L'Esclusa* but, ironically, what seems to be
a decided advance in Pirandello's art and technique—his character portrayal and the gallery of characters he provides—is
the very thing that leads him away from the novel, or at least
toward greater formlessness. The theme of *Il turno* is indicated
in the title. A Sicilian girl is married off to an old man who is
four times a widower, her revulsion having been overcome by
repeated gifts of jewelry (left over from the other wives) and
by her father's insistence that union would be a stroke of business genius.

When the unconsummated marriage is finally annulled
through the conniving of a clever lawyer, it becomes "his
turn." He marries the beautiful, headstrong Stellina, who had
flirted outrageously with several young men during her first
marriage, and immediately retreats to the country to isolate and
enjoy his prize. His sudden death from apoplexy (one of Pirandello's favored means for disposing of the male; Marta's father
in *L'Esclusa* meets the same fate) is brought about by insane
jealousy and leaves the way open for Pepè, Stellina's first
suitor—a melancholy, weak-willed young man who at the end
of the novel is sitting expectantly beside the deceased husband:

> With his eyes fixed sorrowfully on Stellina, he waited, waited for
> her to raise her eyes from her handkerchief, look at him in this
> condition and understand.

First senility, then obsessive jealousy and possessiveness in
a true Sicilian primitive, now the pathetic and expectant *spasi-
mante*; the movement is circular within an incomplete rounde-
lay. And the somber "what next?" of *L'Esclusa* becomes here
the wryly humorous "next, please."

In these early novels Pirandello is ironic and at least partly
indulgent rather than openly compassionate. There is more
indignation in *L'Esclusa*—its theme demands it—and much more
comedy in *Il turno*, but their similarity is more fundamental

than this obvious difference. In both, the author refuses to sentimentalize or idealize; life as he makes us see it (in his Sicilian period, at least) is unpredictable, often harsh, and always mined with obstacles to torment or to evoke laughter—or sometimes both at once. The characters in these novels are foolish but not fools, for the guiding sentiment is irony rather than satire. The attacks on social conventions are blunted by the characters themselves, who are not at all outright victims of society but frail individuals—*macchiette*, oddballs—whose difficulties are as likely to be self-created or fated (i.e., artificial) as they are to be social.

It is worth noting that the presentation of *L'Esclusa* and *Il turno* is in the main traditional. Perhaps for this reason Pirandello's next novel, *Il fu Mattia Pascal*, has seemed to some a boldly experimental work and a more or less abstract study in typical Pirandellian problems. This is overstated, as is Starkie's claim that *Il fu Mattia Pascal* is central to Pirandello's works, "the centre from which radiate all his other characteristic works." One can agree with the latter only in the sense that this novel stands thematically at a point midway between the early stress on man as a "type" within a (disapproved of) society and the later emphasis on man's inner world, on the man behind the mask; and structurally between the novels which have regional settings, use local color, and concentrate on story in the sense of the world of surface and those which leave external reality and turn inward to seek out and explore the characters' selves.

In this sense it is best to see *Il fu Mattia Pascal* perched somewhat unsurely on the line separating situation and story on the one side and issue on the other. The story is simply told: Mattia Pascal is eminently unsuited for life. Cheated out of his inheritance after his father's death and married to a woman with a detestable mother, Pascal seems doomed to spend the rest of his days as a henpecked husband and father and as a useless librarian in an equally useless library. When his brother unexpectedly sends him some money for his mother's funeral, Pascal escapes, goes to Monte Carlo and wins a modest fortune. On his way home, after thirteen days, he reads in a newspaper that he has committed suicide and that his body has been recovered from the millrace. Finding himself without debts, wife, and mother-in-law, he goes to Rome to enjoy the freedom of a new life. Under the name of Adriano Meis, Pascal lives for a time on the outside looking in. As a "walking invention" he must forever remain apart.

> witnessing the lives of others, observing them minutely . . . and at the same time I saw all my own snapped threads. Could I take these threads and knot them to reality again?

He finds that he cannot. Doling out his money to himself like a pensioner on fixed means, he gradually discovers that he has in fact pensioned himself from life: he cannot buy a dog because, having no legal identity, he cannot pay the dog tax; he cannot marry his landlord's daughter Adriana; he cannot denounce the thief who steals several thousand lire from him; he cannot even fight a duel for lack of proper identification.

> After two years of roaming like a shadow in that illusion of life beyond death, I saw myself being forced to carry out the sentence they had passed.

In despair Pascal (as Adriano) kills the "shadow of a life" by simulating suicide. Reverting to his original self after this double death, he returns home only to find that his wife has married again and given her new husband a child. In one of the most delightful scenes in all of Pirandello Mattia Pascal confronts his wife and her new "husband," who is holding a baby.

> "My . . . my daughter . . ." Pomino stammered.
> "Ah, you criminal!" the widow [Romilda's mother] shouted.
> I still couldn't answer, I was so dazed by this news. "Your daughter?" I murmured. "A daughter, too? . . . And now. . ."

"Mamma, please, go to Romilda," Pomino begged her. But it was too late. Her blouse unbuttoned, the infant at her breast, Romilda came forward, all disheveled as if she had got up in a hurry. She glimpsed me.

"Mattia!" And she sank into the arms of Pomino and her mother, who dragged her away. In their confusion, they left the baby in my arms.

Pascal renounces his rights and refuses to have himself declared legally alive; he desires only that the townspeople see him and know that he *is* alive. But even this modest wish is not fulfilled in any satisfying way.

Nobody recognized me, because nobody thought of me any more. . . . Profoundly disillusioned, I was annoyed, depressed, embittered more than I can say.

Finally Don Eligio, the old librarian with whom Pascal had worked, presents him to the town. When the excitement subsides Pascal returns to his old job, aided by the wisdom of Don Eligio:

outside of the law, and without those individual characteristics which, happy or sad as they may be, make us ourselves, we cannot live, dear Signor Pascal.

But because Pascal is still legally dead and has not regained his individual characteristics, he must conclude "I don't know who I am." When a townsman does occasionally ask, the answer is inevitably "I am the late Mattia Pascal."

If Pirandello is right in defining humor as an awareness of contrasts between man as he is and man as he thinks he is or wants to be (*L'Umorismo*, 1906), *Il fu Mattia Pascal* may be said to rank among the successful comic novels. But clearly the comedy here is precariously close to tears, to the bitterness that comes with the realization that man must wear a mask. Having once removed it, he can no longer live but must restore the mask (*L'Esclusa*) or go "mad" (*Uno, nessuno e centomila;*

Henry IV; and many others) or die a Pascalian death. It is this last which, beyond all comedy and certainly beyond all critical reflections on the derivative ideas Pirandello uses, makes *Il fu Mattia Pascal* an important work. We shall return to the mask and other aspects of the story after a brief comment on the other novels.

I vecchi e i giovani (The Young and the Old), written some five years after *Mattia Pascal* and not published as a book until 1913, marks a regression in Pirandello's novelistic art in that its structure and cohesiveness is no better than (or even as good as) its predecessors; nor does it represent any vital advance in the domain of relativism based on man as appearance or fiction. Neither Pirandellian concern is satisfied here, and to see it (correctly but somewhat irrelevantly) as the crown of Pirandello's *verismo* (as Arminio Janner has done) is to ignore the obvious: this long and meandering account of the Sicilians, from Garibaldi's campaigns to the present, is hardly a novel at all. To call it panoramic or to admire as Starkie has the "dramatic method by which . . . [Pirandello] describes the crumbling of the heroic generation of the Risorgimento" is to return to what was referred to earlier as reading a novel qua illustration of something else. Many of the most recognizable Pirandellian elements are present: the colorful eccentrics; the large number of little scenes, episodes, and vignettes; the carefully realistic descriptions of Sicilian peasants, middle class, and aristocracy; even—in modest degree—the dualism of life and form (Tilgher's original formulation of Pirandello's opposites). But the focus is lacking; not even the conflict or contrast suggested in the title emerges in the course of the novel's more than 400 pages. Despite occasional assertions that *I vecchi e i giovani* is of central importance, a more sober view must deny it any real prominence.

Suo marito (Her Husband), written in 1911 and in its second edition given the title *Giustino Roncella nato Boggiòlo,* likewise does not need much discussion. After the original edition went out of print, Pirandello refused to publish it again without extensive rewriting, which was never completed. (It was, however, included in the 1957 edition of his novels in the form he left it: the first four chapters reworked; the remaining ones in the text of the original edition.) Although Janner calls this novel a *romanzo mancato* and sees it as an important and highly personal source of *pirandellismo,* it is commonly agreed to be inferior writing.

The two remaining novels—*I quaderni di Serafino Gubbio operatore* (until 1925 it was called *Si gira*) and *Uno, nessuno e centomila*—represent a new departure in Pirandello's fiction and at the same time a continuation of much that is significant in *Il fu Mattia Pascal.* Both are more obviously subjective than the earlier novels, and their style and techniques have moved perceptibly closer to Pirandello's theatre and philosophy. Critical opinion of the two works shows the same lack of unanimity observed in assessments of the other novels. Janner, for example, considers *Serafino Gubbio* slight, another *romanzo mancato,* whereas de Castris laments a general neglect of the work, finding it Pirandello's "most interesting and technically original experiment." *Uno, nessuno e centomila* pleases no one as a novel. To some it has other qualities that are singular and significant; to others it is a failure in most respects. Whitfield and Starkie believe that the author is most himself in this work, and Büdel applauds the novel for its adherence to Pirandello's doctrine of decomposition, of disconnectedness instead of coherence, adding that a "work which follows such criteria is therefore not less of an artistic creation." Such evaluations are of course somewhat off center so far as novel criticism is concerned. But if, as Angioletti reminds us, we ought never to forget that Pirandello was above all artist and poet, it should be worthwhile to ask more directly than has been done *how* his late novels represent that art. *Uno, nessuno e centomila* may serve as our example.

Plot is at once clear and yet almost irrelevant in this work.

Gengè Moscarda's story, told by himself, is a clever psychological study in growing insanity. When his wife innocently remarks one day that the right side of his nose hangs a bit lower than the left, Moscarda's entire life changes:

> I was immersed all of a sudden in the reflection that it meant—could it be possible?—that I did not so much as know my own body . . . it was from there that my sickness started. . . .

Throughout the first half of the novel Moscarda weighs the implications of his discovery that as a man he is unknown both to himself and to all those around him. Jolted out of the illusion that he is someone, *uno,* he concludes that he must be no one, *nessuno,* "a poor, mortified body, waiting for someone to take it," or else a hundred thousand, since each person must necessarily see him differently.

Trapped in this dialectic and thus aware for the first time of his (and man's) agonizing solitude, Moscarda resolves to live as though he "weren't." As Sartre might put it, the others have stolen his identity or world; they now gradually convince themselves that he is mad. Moscarda's revenge is to prove that they have misjudged him, that he is not what they think they see:

> Each one snug in his illusion of another, so that he might be assured that all the others were wrong, should they tell him no, that each one was not as another saw him. I felt like shouting to all the world: "Come! Come! Let's play the game! Let's play the game!"

This is what Moscarda does, principally through the second half of the novel. He mistreats his wife, causing her to leave him; he begins to give away his property and money; he courts Anna Rosa, his wife's friend, who is overcome by the horror of an act to which she feels herself drawn and who resolves the matter by shooting and seriously wounding Moscarda. He survives and is able to bring about Anna Rosa's acquittal by convincing the court of his own madness. Having earlier allied himself with the church, Moscarda succumbs to priestly persuasion that he seek salvation by donating everything to the church for works of charity and by living henceforth (legally sane, thanks to church influence) as a pauper and penitent. In his asylum outside the town Moscarda reflects happily that a name is but an epitaph, something befitting the dead. But "I am alive, and I reach no conclusion. Life knows no conclusion." Moscarda's "success" rests finally on the conviction that he is "dying every instant, and being born anew and without memories: alive and whole, no longer in myself, but in everything outside."

This brief summary of the story line is of course deceptive to the degree that it suggests a simple structure to the novel. Fully one-half of *Uno, nessuno e centomila* is so concerned with Moscarda's speculations that it remains peripheral, that is to say it simply refuses to become absorbed in the story's few events. Viewed optimistically, the novel betrays a return to Sterne's method of writing (Starkie); however, the usually delightful parentheses, meanderings, and interruptions in *Tristram Shandy* are more clearly a case of successful experimentation with form than can be claimed for *Uno, nessuno e centomila*. Or, in more recent times, Max Frisch's *Stiller* can claim greater success in experimentation while remaining within the confines of the novel.

One observes this penchant for straying beyond form in virtually all of Pirandello's longer fiction, from the early veristic novels (especially *I vecchi e i giovani*) to this work of some thirty years later. In the late works Pirandello *is* experimental, certainly, but far more so in result than in intent, if one is willing to look beyond the ideas and themes. Man is frozen into a form; life itself cannot be. Replace the word *life* with *novel*, and you see how well *Uno, nessuno e centomila* illustrates this Pirandellian axiom without perhaps really meaning to.

If we turn more directly to technique and to the problems that arise in expressing *pirandellismo* in the novel form, it becomes apparent that these works are essentially variations on a single theme: man breaks out of a pattern of existence—quite unexpectedly, and in this respect the breaking out is similar to the unguarded moment which exposes Kafka's heroes—and attempts to reweave a life that has been aimless and a failure. Much like the figures in Gide's novels, Pirandello's characters experiment with other ways of life, commenting on themselves as they do so. Their running commentary, grounded in a realization of the fissure between life and man's awareness of self as a part of it, means simply that the characters are narrators as well as actors: they watch themselves live (Tilgher), often self-consciously, and in consequence fail in the attempt to turn mind into action, intellect into passion. Moscarda virtually discusses himself to death. Marta in *L'Esclusa* is more emotional, but if her actions are less reasoned, they are not therefore less firmly based on self-awareness in collision with an unreasonable society (the careful reader discovers that despite Marta's copious tears the world outside her is truly the emotional and emotionally volatile aspect of the story). Pascal, another outsider, likewise suffers from the inability to react with the same intensity as those about him (Adriana, Signorina Caporale, even Pomino).

To see oneself live is to reduce by that much genuine participation in life. To theorize on one's own life, which is perhaps the outstanding feature of Pirandello's rebels, intentional and unintentional, is to carry a set idea—the point of departure for all the novels—too fully into the life and action of the novels themselves. If there is still value to Henry James' dictum that the novelist should depict and not render, Pirandello failed to appreciate it. And there is evidence that the medium took its revenge upon him.

This first major feature of the novels—man as theorizing, commenting rebel—invites a consideration of their second major feature—the social world with which the characters contend. For while it is true that Pirandello prefers to explore the narrower world of the mind, it is precisely what the mind confronts—as participant or spectator or both—that shapes both fiction and philosophy. Having gained his freedom and left society as much by accident as by design, Mattia Pascal sets out to construct a new man, to rectify the injustice that is his life. But to effect a metamorphosis this side of the fairytale world and with no other materials than those dragged along with him (an eye operation to remove the telltale cross-eyes and the Monte Carlo winnings are externals and cannot really shift the balance) would suggest that Pascal is ultimately his own master. Pirandello does not believe this; his pessimism demands that all such experiments stop short of success. Mattia Pascal may claim to be happy, but the end of the novel represents the euphoria of limbo.

Similar to Adalbert Chamisso but with an opposite end in mind, Pirandello employs the shadow to express Pascal's dilemma. Chamisso's famous hero, Peter Schlemihl, sells his shadow and thereby loses his social identity, the expression of solidity that makes Schlemihl and the world compatible. Without a shadow he is condemned to isolation. Pascal, too, relates his shadow to the problem of man's social identity; in calling himself, as Adriano Meis, "un'ombra d'uomo" and "l'ombra d'una vita" ("a shadow of a man" and "the shadow of a life"), he betrays his insight that as shade or ghost he can have no reality outside of society. Thus life in the shape of the unhappy Pascal turns out to be more tangible and hence more valuable than Adriano, the shadow that he becomes.

It is a significant reversal: whereas Schlemihl's loss of his shadow leads to irrevocable isolation, it is Pascal's acquisition of a shadow and the consequent substitution of shadow for man—Adriano Meis for Mattia Pascal—that isolates him and proves his undoing. However, in contrast to Chamisso's hero, who barters away what is essential to his legitimacy and can never regain it, Pirandello's Pascal-Adriano is given a choice: he may remain forever a shadow, that is a nonlegitimized fiction who lurks on the fringes of society with a fortune as worthless as Schlemihl's, or he may return (he believes) to his role as Mattia Pascal.

I have indicated earlier, however, that such an alternative is really no alternative at all but a defeat. In *Il fu Mattia Pascal* the shadow may be seen as a version of Pirandello's mask. As another form of clothing or as an invented form, it cannot but conceal the truth that lies stifled beneath. To cast it aside, however, is to return to the earlier mask of Mattia Pascal, the husband and father who was in Pirandello's view as much a living death as the fictitious Adriano Meis. The injustice of Pascal's life is in sum its inauthenticity, the mask which society has created for him.

In a similar sense, the act of adultery of which the protagonist of *L'Esclusa* is accused is a version of the mask. In attempting to cast it off and live outside society (as an honest, dignified woman who supports her family by teaching in another town), Marta ends by making the mask a reality and returning to her husband. To acquiesce in the wearing is to accept the image others make of us. The narrator of *Uno, nessuno e centomila* likewise reverts to an image and shows most clearly of all that the personal defeat—which is at once a social defeat—is not actively tragic but imbued with the tragic sense of life. In these representative novels Pirandello has his characters abdicate rather than die. The presentation may be dramatic; the results never are.

The society of Pirandello's novels is best defined by observing those who withdraw from it. It is unnecessary to review the gallery of eccentrics to remind ourselves that the world of Sicilian town life (or the bourgeois Roman setting of *Mattia Pascal*) comes alive only when the misfits and all the outlandish personalities intrude upon the narrative: Professor Falcone in *L'Esclusa*, Mauro Mortara in *I vecchi e i giovani*, Ciro Coppa in *Il turno*, Signorina Caporale in *Il fu Mattia Pascal*. The line grows noticeably thinner, however, in the later works; there are inevitably a few *machiette* around, and for the most part they still convey enough of society's foibles to suggest a richer world behind the increasingly austere settings, but the greater abstraction and intellectuality of the novels written after 1909 crowds out one of Pirandello's greatest gifts as a writer of fiction. It remained for his *novelle* to continue the tradition of original and unforgettable characters.

A third outstanding feature of the novels is directly related to Pirandello's portrayal of society through types, primarily its most colorful and eccentric ones. We have referred to the fact that Pirandello proceeds from a set idea or an abstraction which needs to be fleshed out fictionally. When brought into focus, its various formulations (best summarized by Adriano Tilgher in a study which influenced Pirandello himself) illuminate the overwhelmingly central assumption that life and society are a chaos of provisional forms. Whether intentional or not, the refusal to organize the array of minor characters and peripheral episodes in such a way as to produce a more or less traditionally constructed novel is fully consistent with (and a reflection of) a human society that is mystifying and, despite its frozen conventions, amorphous. Pirandello's longest novel is an example of this failure to enunciate the kind of discernible structure the novel as genre aims at: *I vecchi e i giovani* is in no sense experimental; its rambling form clearly results from the lack of a sufficiently strong central theme, one that would immediately give associative meaning to the numerous episodes that make up so much of the work. What, for instance, is the import of Dianella Salvo's visit to the *camerone,* that decaying reminder to old Mauro of his hero, General Laurentano? Little more than that, a reminder: Mauro is and remains a secondary character, and his fate, not unlike that of the old generation altogether, is to lose himself in the vastness of a work whose epic potentiality is lost among the details.

But it is neither original nor especially profitable to lament Pirandello's epic incapacity. More to the point is to say that the underlying technique, that is to say Pirandello's most natural narrative form, is something other than that which customarily holds a novel together. We are reminded that this "revolutionist of world theatre" (Cambon) has almost always been guided by the dramatic impulse—which, however, ought not to lead us too quickly to the conclusion that Pirandello the dramatist is paramount. The best and purest expression of his art is the *bozzetto*, not the drama and certainly not the novel. To indicate briefly what is involved in this form as Pirandello uses it should enable us to see more clearly the main compositional features of the novels as well. The *bozzetto* is usually based on an anecdote or anecdotal situation. Two or three characters (only rarely more) are introduced to perform or act out, sometimes as narrators, the situation. As types they are generally a mixture of the comic-grotesque and the pathetic —which is to say that the sympathy and sense of participation we associate with irony (despite the aesthetic distance in which it is grounded) are combined with the less personal stance of satire and caricature.

L'Esclusa offers an interesting example of this basic narrative unit. Marta has been transferred to a school in Palermo. Among the tenants in her building are Don Fifo and his wife, who call one day to pay their respects. In a bare two pages of text (in the Mondadori edition) their story is told: married for only three months now, Donna Maria Rosa had previously been the wife of Don Fifo's older brother, who had died a year before. During their visit Donna Maria Rosa speaks tearfully of nothing but her deceased husband.

> Don Fifo meanwhile, sat motionless, listening with lowered eyes and arms crossed on his chest to an interminable funeral eulogy of his dead brother. He represented the sarcophagus of the deceased, one might have said, and his wife the cenotaph.

Husband, wife, and brother-in-law had always lived together, "one soul in three bodies." On his deathbed the brother had blessed the two unhappy creatures he was leaving, offering them to each other as mutual consolation. After asking everyone's advice, and waiting out of respect for appearances, they married as soon as the nine months required by law had passed. At the end of his wife's tale Don Fifo burst out with: "A melancholy fate, signora, a melancholy fate, God knows!"

The episode is complete in itself; nothing of possible further interest can happen, nor does the reader expect it. The tale, one knows, will be repeated countless times (though of course not in the novel itself), and Don Fifo will presumably follow with the same exclamation, which closely resembles the *pointe* of any anecdote. As types, Donna Maria Rosa is fat and blonde and sighs lugubriously; and Don Fifo, long and lank, his trousers tight, and his general appearance that of someone precariously fastened together. With their physical appearance as with their situation, no further embellishment is necessary or possible.

Such insertions are numerous in the novels and serve to remind us once more that Pirandello is most original and convincing when sketching out with light irony a few colorful types engaged in the antics or the pathos of a moment. What they betray of themselves, often with overt help from the author by way of inserted commentary, is invariably enough, and past and future are irrelevant. Some of Pirandello's best known stories, "La Giara," for example, or "Il Tabernacolo," are not essentially different from the Don Fifo anecdote and would hardly seem out of place in any of the novels.

In discussing Pirandello's essential narrative form—predominantly the scene which is set in motion by a few striking individuals; we relate it to the *bozzetto* and the anecdote—little mention has been made of the relationship between the novels and the better known novella. Their meeting ground is in the area of the drama. Criticism, notably that of de Castris, has made us aware of some of the transitions that occur in moving from fiction (in general) to drama, and one often encounters the statement that Pirandello was essentially dramatic. At one level this is difficult to contest: there is the fact of several major plays; there is the knowledge that his attraction to the theatre, dating from the years just before World War I, continued unabated to the end; and there is finally the interesting transformation of his novella—no less than twenty-eight of them—into plays.

Beyond these biographical commonplaces, however, we encounter difficulties. Pirandello's drama is itself primarily thesis drama, rich in ideas and abstractions—in short, the drama of words or thought rather than action. Seeing it as "dramatic," which in certain obvious ways it is, leads one to look back into the novella, especially the ones later converted to plays, to discover in them the short, concise dialogues, the striking moments that are resolved by the kind of conflict associated with drama, the characters with traits more given than developable—in sum, many of the things that led one of Germany's best *Novellendichter* to assert that the novella is sister of the drama (Storm).

But one is equally justified in pointing out that in Pirandello's hands the novel is no less a sister to both, the novella and the drama, inasmuch as all three forms derive their peculiar Pirandellian shape through the interplay of plot and commentary on plot. What is dramatic in the one is dramatic in the others, and the term 'dramatic' takes on new and unusual meanings. Action and exposition of action, when presented together, traditionally tend to cancel each other out, which is to say that epic and dramatic are by nature opposed. But where they are not, i.e., where we experience the one adding to the other by enriching and intensifying conflict, truly dramatic works may result. Auréliu Weiss, in an excellent essay on Pirandello's "Technique of the Unseizable," speaks of the fusion of scenic and ideological levels of conflict, a process in which the two opposites mutually dramatize each other. This, it would appear, is the underlying principle in novel, novella, and play alike. When the fusion is unsuccessful, a certain monotony results; *L'Esclusa, I vecchi e i giovani,* and most of all *Uno, nessuno e centomila* suffer from this. But where the intellectual reaction to life is portrayed as emotional reaction as well and where the commentary which reveals it is an integral part of the character's adventure in exploring possibilities of being, the result is a convincing work of art. *Il fu Mattia Pascal* is surely for this reason Pirandello's most successful novel. The tendency toward decomposition, toward fragmentation, is apparent here too, but Pirandello succeeds (almost) in convincing the reader that discrete and often irrelevant chunks of life represent the damning logic of that life the protagonist is seeking to stabilize in his quest for the truth of his identity.

We may add a final word on the relationship between life's fluidity (an essential part of Pirandello's relativism) and the structure of the novels. On a visit to his notary Moscarda ruminates on the pleasures of history:

> Nothing is more restful than history. Everything in life is continually changing under our very eyes; there is nothing certain; and that restless desire to know how accidents shape themselves, to see how facts take on stability, facts that keep you so breathlessly agitated! Everything, on the other hand, is shaped and stabilized in history; however sad the accidents may be, however dolorous the vicissitudes, you there behold them put in order, or at least fixed, in from thirty to forty pages of a book. . . .

Moscarda ends his day "living wholly without." Appropriately, he is in a shelter, an *ospizio.* Pascal concludes by withdrawing from life to put those vicissitudes in order and fix them in a book. The Henry IV of the play retreats into history again; and even the heroine of *L'Esclusa* is returning to a stability, a frozen situation that will never again change. One might easily apply the thought, in reversed form, to *Il turno,* which suggests a treadmill or a continuing circle much like that of Schnitzler's *La Ronde.*

Such fixing within the safe, restful circle of history finds its symbolic equivalent in the enclosing structure of the anecdote, the episode, the *bozzetto*, the little scene. It is the ultimate stability, the immobilization that art can give to life. The thirty or forty pages Moscarda visualizes are of course extended in the novels. That is on the one hand their weakness; but on the other it is a profound expression of Pirandello's insistence that life is, as Serafino Gubbio saw it, a spectacle of chaos, "this ceaseless parade of phantoms" out of which man fabricates his existence.

4 ALDO PALAZZESCHI: A SURVEY

G. Singh

One cannot fail to be impressed by the array of first-rate novelists and storywriters in the twentieth century Italian literature, such as Svevo, Bacchelli, Gadda, Tomasi di Lampedusa, Moravia, Pavese, Vittorini, and Calvino. It is to this group that Palazzeschi, even though in virtue of only two or three novels, undoubtedly belongs.

Palazzeschi, like Bacchelli, is one of the most prolific Italian writers, and his writing career stretches over the span of half a century or more. His first published work—a collection of poems, *I cavalli bianchi* (White Horses)—appeared in 1905; and his most recent work (to the time of this writing) is the novel *Il Doge* (The Duke), which was published in 1967. As is almost inevitable in a prolific writer, there is a remarkable degree of unevenness in his *oeuvre* more or less comparable to the unevenness of D'Annunzio, who, incidently, exercised a considerable influence on Palazzeschi's earlier work. Moreover the fact that Palazzeschi made his debut in the literary world as a poet and not as a novelist is not without significance. In Palazzeschi the poetic element is to be found not only in the style and language of the novels—a sort of lyricism that was the result of Palazzeschi's own experimentation and innovation in verse—but also in the very nature of themes and dialogues, reflections and ideas, that form part of the novelist's material. That is to say, most writers would have chosen to deal with them through the medium of verse, if they had had sufficient mastery over that medium. In a way this may be true of many other novelists—novelists like Hardy or D'Annunzio—but it is true in a particularly significant way of Palazzeschi.

Aldo Palazzeschi was born at Florence on February 2, 1885, into a middle-class family. His father was a well-known businessman. A materially prosperous but convention-ridden social and family background strengthened in him the instinct for self-assertion and independence, which at times took the form of intellectual anarchy and was reflected in his writings. This instinct expresses itself through the independent and experimental character of his writings from first to last. It is also due to this that, like Saba, Palazzeschi is the least 'literary' among the major writers of this century, and he possesses what Solmi calls "an accent of intact, almost disconcerting virginity."[1]

His individuality is also responsible for his lifelong love of solitude, which characterizes some of the personages in his novels. A confirmed bachelor, Palazzeschi believes in the organic link between his inclination to solitude and his artistic and psychological development:

> I love solitude as others love speed, height, power, agility, risk. I find solitude gives me all these things, and even if I owe to friendship some of the most unforgettable hours of my life and maintain a very close link with my friends in spite of my having to live away from them for practical reasons, the hours of happiness which I owe to solitude constitute a different kind of joy; something something sharper and profounder, something destructive and painful, something I would even say too sad for a writer; something beyond words. I must overcome a certain vague and natural feeling of reserve in even admitting to it; almost as if it were something I was enjoying too deeply, something that was too deeply mine for me to be able to tell others that it even existed.[2]

Here one would easily recognize the creator of Valentine Core in the novel *Allegoria di novembre* (November Allegory).

There is—and it could not have been otherwise—something of the nature of aristocratic reserve and even delicacy about the writings of one endowed with such a disposition and sensibility, and this reserve and delicacy leads to the feeling of detachment from the political turmoils of his time. What Montale said some years ago apropos of the unique quality of Palazzeschi as a poet and novelist applies more today than ever before.[3]

Palazzeschi started his literary career as a poet in 1904 and most of his poetry—to be found in the volumes entitled *I cavalli bianchi*, 1905, *Lanterna*, 1909 (Lantern), *L'incendiario*, 1910 (The Incendiary), second and enlarged edition, 1913—was written and published in the next ten years. As a poet Palazzeschi will rank, at best, as a good minor poet; and yet his poetry is both historically and autobiographically important. It tells us much not only about the spirit and impulses behind the Futurist movement in Italian poetry in particular and of the spirit of the times in general, but also about Palazzeschi's own involvement in it and the impact it made on his novels and other prose writings. The uniqueness and authenticity of a very personal note and style which we find in his language and in his narrative invention owes a good deal to Palazzeschi's connections with Futurist poetry and with its main exponents like Papini and Soffici, who were Palazzeschi's friends.

One of his most famous and characteristic poems is "E lasciatemi divertire!" ("Let Me Have Fun!"), embodying, as it does, that *joie de vivre*, that zest for life, that spontaneous intensity of living and the indomitable sense of humor and irony which go into the making of Palazzeschi the novelist.

> *Infine,*
> *io ho pienamente ragione,*
> *i tempi sono molto cambiati,*
> *gli uomini non domandono più nulla*

> *dai poeti:*
> *e lasciatemi divertire!*
>
> *Finally,*
> *I am perfectly right,*
> *times have changed a lot,*
> *people ask nothing more*
> *from the poets:*
> *hence, let me enjoy!*

It was only during the postwar years, when Palazzeschi had definitely turned away from poetry, that he concentrated on the novel and the short story and came to assert his status as a major writer. In 1914 he published what would be his last volume of verse.

But even during the period between 1907 and 1914 when Palazzeschi was writing poetry, he had published three novels: *Allegoria di novembre*, 1908, *Il Codice di Perelà* 1911 (*Perelà's Code*), and *La piramide*, 1912–14 (The Pyramid). In one form or another these novels reveal a certain psychological tension and conflict in him—a conflict between the old world of the nineteenth century and the new world of the twentieth. This conflict revolves around the awareness, to quote Matthew Arnold, though in a slightly different sense, of "wandering between two worlds"—on the one hand the world of the memories of early life tied up with the nineteenth century and on the other the new visionary world conceived in terms of futurism. Together with this conflict, which presented itself in the form of a moral and psychological need for liberation and autonomy, there was in Palazzeschi the passionate idealism of one who wanted to change and reform everything around himself.

> Bliss was it in that dawn to be alive,
> But to be young was very heaven

wrote Wordsworth of the early phases of the French Revolution. But for Palazzeschi, writing and subscribing to the manifesto of the Futurist movement and, following that, the experience of war itself must have given a hard blow to his ideals and amounted to a very mixed sort of bliss indeed.

The first novel describes the experiences and vicissitudes of the Roman prince, Valentino Core. He falls in love with an English youth named John Mare and retires into a solitary family villa in order to keep his ideal of beauty and love for this man as pure and intact as possible. He does not want to contemplate the change that the passage of time and the wear and tear of everyday life would produce on his young friend and, at the same time, he wants to escape the physical temptation which, in case he yielded to it, might compromise his own idea of the purity of love and beauty. He keeps writing letters to this friend and thus maintaining a sort of spiritual contact with him. This is his method of living his passion of love for this youth at a higher and more refined level of consciousness than a bodily contact would have enabled him to attain and at the same time of achieving a kind of peace with himself in this self-imposed banishment and retirement. But the sort of peace he desires, the peace that comes from self-possession and self-contentment, cannot be realized in this villa, even though the disturbing presence of the English youth is not there. And it cannot be realized because the memories of Valentino's early life and childhood keep haunting him—especially the memory of his mother, who committed suicide. The epistolary contact with his friend and all the intensity of passion and craving that underlies it give him the illusion of having accomplished some kind of sublimation. But Valentino is at once too intelligent and too restless to find much satsfaction in that state of things for long. The hero of the novel has been called a D'Annunzian hero because of his obsessive quest for the rare and exotic sensations and instincts. There is certainly something romantically metaphysical and metaphysically romantic about Valentino. In his attitude and passion toward the English youth there is a characteristically curious admixture of refined sensuality and decadent sentimentality, an almost carnal version of Platonism or pseudo-Platonism.

But this kind of bond, and the psychological character it presupposes, is a seriously limiting factor in a novel because it does away with the need for any plot, dialogue, or dramatic incidents. Some traces of this weakness, so evidently present in this novel, are to be found also in the other two novels written during this poetic period and as a matter of fact in practically everything Palazzeschi wrote, except *Sorelle Materassi* (*The Sisters Materassi*, 1953). The only thing that happens in Valentino's everyday external life is the walk he takes every evening, lugubriously brooding over the thoughts and passion and delights that link him with his far-off friends. His search for the past, for the meaning of his early childhood, does not help him much. The villa is there and he can listen to all the anecdotes concerning his past from the old housekeeper and her daughter, but the past and what he is looking for somehow elude him. The real attachment—even though it has something even more morbidly insubstantial about it than his love for this boy—consists in his feeling for the dead mother, who remains for him the embodiment of ideal love. What withholds him from loving John with all the passion that he instinctively and naturally feels for him is the fear of having his ideal, so perfectly and so safely embodied in the intangible and invisible figure of his dead mother, realized in a less perfect form. Moreover, real form entails real experience—and he is afraid of precisely that. For him, real love is inseparable from the fear of losing it, from a sense of betrayal, and from the consideration of such exigencies as chance and change may force upon him. The only way out of this emotional and existential impasse, as it were, is death. Valentino dies—or, rather, mysteriously kills himself. His body mysteriously disappears. And this ends the first and epistolary part of the novel.

In the second part we have the comments of others concerning the strange life, love, and death of Valentino. And

here the nature and style of the prose have an ironical edge
and a narrative flow that characterize Palazzeschi's later and
more mature novels.

The next novel, *Il codice di Perelà* [1911; subsequently revised editions 1920, 1943, and 1954; in the last edition the title
is changed to *Perelà uomo di fumo* (*Perelà, the Man of
Smoke*)], sheds all traces of poetic vagueness and lyricism. It is
the story of a man of smoke who has lived for thirty-two years
in the chimney. One day he comes out of the chimney and
gets to know the world of men in its various aspects—political,
cultural, and social. At first he is well received by the world,
and is held in such high esteem that he is entrusted with the
job of formulating a new code. But all of a sudden, for some
unaccountable whim, people turn against him and condemn
him to life imprisonment. An airy and insubstantial creature,
he easily escapes and dissolves into thin air. The novel has an
allegorical purpose—to state convincingly the author's opinions
and reflections on the problems and various aspects of contemporary life. Perelà, a thinly disguised alter ego of Palazzeschi,
represents the ideals of absolute freedom of thought, action,
and imagination that Palazzeschi writes about and celebrates in
his poetry. In this novel, more than in any other, we can see
the influence of futurism and its ideological tenets. They actually form part of the subject matter of the novel.

According to some critics, *Perelà* is Palazzeschi's most accomplished novel. It is certainly a witty and brilliant allegorical
satire of fascism (not yet in power) and of the sort of leader
that Italy was to know in Mussolini, whose moral and spiritual
physiognomy one finds so vividly and convincingly delineated
in this novel. Prince Zarlino is playing the role of *un pazzo
volontario* (a voluntary madman). "The madman," he says,
"never announces what he is going to do; on the other hand, I
always announce everything. I say, for example: now I shall
let out eighty-eight shouts. . . ."

In the third novel, *La piramide*, the relation between the

personality of the author and the story and characters of the
novel is even more complete. Here too the story serves mainly
as a vehicle for an idea—the idea of individual liberty carried
almost to an anarchic extreme. The idea itself reflects the state
of Palazzeschi's own mind and personality under the combined
forces and influence of D'Annunzio and of the Crepuscular
and Futurist movements. The characters in this novel serve as
the author's mouthpiece and no more. Hence they do not ring
true, a besetting sin of practically all Palazzeschi's early novels.
This novel also illustrates another fundamental weakness of
Palazzeschi's early novels—their almost morbidly subjective
character as a result of which there is very little room for
action or incidents and plot. It was the First World War that
drove all idealism from Palazzeschi's mind and brought him
face to face with the reality of war and living from day to day.
And the experience of war paved the way for the maturity in
Palazzeschi's subsequent work.

The novel *Due imperi . . . mancati,* 1920 (Two Empires . . .
That Came to Nought) covers the period from 1914 to 1919
and relates the author's reflections on his attitude to war. Here
again the story, the plot, and the action (whatever there is of
them) merely serve as a vehicle for a sincere and impassioned
diatribe against the futility and immorality of war (and this at
a time when military triumph and national glory and patriotic
love were exalted and eulogized all around). Palazzeschi's anti-
war spirit leads him to turn against D'Annunzio, in whom
Palazzeschi saw the embodiment of the spirit of war. To the
spirit of nationalism, Palazzeschi opposes the spirit of Marxism, conceived not in terms of an economic doctrine but as
an ethical imperative related to the essence of Christian ethics.
This novel—which may be considered the antithesis of the
aesthetic and decadent surrealism of the previous novels—contains the core of Palazzeschi's social and political idealism,
which is based on a blend of the teachings of Christ and the
philosophy of Marx. Palazzeschi's expression of the concept of

universal brotherhood is characteristically opposed to Alfieri's celebrated dictum, "nessun paese mi è patria" ("No country is my motherland"):

> There is not the tiniest part of this earth which is not my country. I belong to all the countries and all the countries belong to me; if I have told you that I am the Emperor of the whole world how can I feel myself to be a subject of a small part of it? I am not even a man and I don't care to be one; I am a sensual creature, something throbbing freely in the air.

Similarly, the D'Annunzian or Nietzschean concept of the superman is replaced by Palazzeschi with the concept of the poet or the artist as champion of the fundamental values of man and civilization. His aversion to war is all the more convincing when, while in military barracks during the war, he lets his imagination be transported by the thought of a sudden cessation of war and the return to normality and peace:

> Oh! if only the sound of a trumpet could wake us all and if someone could shout: "The gates are open, you can go away; all go home" . . . , we shall see all run away naked, as if they had gone mad; not a single person would stay in.

The experience of war and his moral and spiritual revulsion from it lead Palazzeschi to conceive of a Utopia without war and, further, without social taboos, conventions, and sterotyped patterns of morality. This Utopian world is not so much described as suggested in his overall criticism of various social and institutional evils, including marriage.

In this novel, too, both the ethos and the criticism of life seem to be superimposed upon the story rather than emerging from it. Palazzeschi has not yet been able to achieve that complete fusion between form and material which would make what the poet states directly and what he lets the plot and the story suggest indirectly look like two complimentary aspects of the same reality. This is not merely a matter of technique, but essentially a question of artistic depth, moral depth, and maturity. Nevertheless this novel does register an advance in Palazzeschi's treatment of human experience as something more solid and substantial than the abstractions, ideals, and ideologies, which are, in one form or another, the dominating theme of the earlier novels. This is in itself a sign of growing awareness and depth.

Due imperi . . . mancati, in fact, opens the way to the novels and short stories of Palazzeschi's artistic and psychological maturity—that is to say, the novels *Sorelle Materassi*, 1934, *I fratelli Cuccoli*, 1948 (The Cuccoli Brothers) and *Roma*, 1953 and the collections of short stories like *Il Re bello*, 1921 (The Handsome King), *Stampe dell'800*, 1932 (Nineteenth Century Prints), *Il palio dei buffi*, 1937, and *Bestie del 900*, 1951 (Beasts of the Twentieth Century). In these works there is both a poise and a tension between contrasting dramatic and psychological pressures, as, for instance, between the nostalgia and the desire to revolutionize the present, between irony and humor, between philosophical meditation and a realistic grasp of the facts and circumstances of everyday life.

In many respects *The Sisters Materassi* is what has been generally claimed for it—Palazzeschi's masterpiece. It is above all a masterpiece in the sense that it offers a closer and a richer synthesis of all—or most—of the characteristic qualities of Palazzeschi both as a novelist and as a prose writer.

It is the story of two elderly unmarried sisters, who are tailoresses and embroideresses by profession, and of the profound cataclysm—moral, sentimental and even passioned—brought about in their dull, drab, and bourgeois lives by their young and attractive nephew, who enters their lives when he is fourteen years old (but looks somewhat older). This youth exploits the aunts even before he comes to realize their infatuation for him—more so, after he has become aware of it. In the end, having both sentimentally prostrated and economically ruined these two aunts, who are obliged to foot all his extravagant bills, he marries and goes to the United States with a foreign woman who is a millionaire and whom he met in Venice.

There are other minor characters who, nevertheless, play quite a significant role. There is, for instance, the youngest sister Giselda, who has had a disastrous marriage in her past and has come back to live with her elder and richer sisters. It is interesting (and Palazzeschi makes much of this contrast) to note how utterly different her attitude to this nephew is— different in that she is already armed and prejudiced against him and any other male, whereas the elder sisters just dote on him and adore him.

Then there is the maidservant Niobe, who has a shady past. But she has no prejudice against men and shares, though not openly, the sisters' infatuation with Remo. The two sisters assume an air of moral superiority to Niobe because they know she has had sexual experiences which they have not; beneath their superior airs, however, they obtain vicarious pleasure from what they think her experiences have been. Niobe does not make any secret of her admiration, and the nature of that admiration, for Remo, at whose service she has secretly put herself and her money. As usual, it is money more than anything else that Remo wants, and he has no difficulty or moral qualms or compassion about using Niobe's savings of a lifetime.

Remo's friend Palle, from a modest family background, is in some ways a male counterpart of Niobe. Although he doesn't have a handsome physique or any particular grace or elegance in his comportment, he does have a manifestly virile personality which expresses itself vulgarly in all he says or does. He is not the type to appeal to the middle-class sisters, who are concerned with appearances and find in Remo the happy union between external charm and polish and exuberant and uninhibited sensuality. The only feeling they have toward or against Palle is jealousy—jealousy that he has been able to win Remo's friendship and confidence, which to them amounts to practically stealing a part of what they want to possess completely.

One of Palazzeschi's qualities, as we have noted, is his power of inventive realism and evocativeness. The very first passage in the book and the whole chapter describing Santa Maria a Coverciano illustrates it as well as anything else:

> To those who don't know Florence or know it only superficially, having had a hasty glimpse of it while passing through it, I shall say that it is a very beautiful and charming city closely surrounded by extremely harmonious hills. By "closely" I don't mean that the poor inhabitant should raise his nose in order to look at the sky as if from the bottom of a well. Quite on the contrary. Moreover, I shall add the word "sweetly" which seems so appropriate to me, since the hills around descend gradually and smoothly, from the highest of them which are even called mountains and which come as far down as a thousand metres in height, to those gay odd hills only a hundred and fifty metres high. I shall go even as far as to suggest that only on one side and over a brief stretch, the hill, while bordering on the city, dominates it almost perpendicularly, forming thereby a sort of balcony over which we can lean out with the utmost pleasure. One gets over there through stairs:

> > per le scalee (che si fero ad etade ch'era sicure il quaderno e la doga)

> > [through the stairs (which were made in the times when the records and the measure were safe)]
> > >   Purgatorio, XII, 104–105

In case one has not understood this allusion, it is necessary to explain that this original way of regarding one's contemporaries as thieves and forgers is also a Florentine custom; and we, who would never be so audacious as to contradict the divine poet, acknowledge that they did it, and go ahead. Hence the stairs, or extremely steep roads whose very names reveal their particular nature: Costa Scarpuccia, Erta Canina, Rampe di San Nicolo.*

* The words costa, erta and rampe mean respectively steep slope, ascent, and ramp.

The dominating hill is that part of the "Viale dei Colli" which stretches as far as Piazzale Michelangelo, and which many people, even though they may not have seen it, would have heard about or would have imagined with the help of the photographs, prints and picture post-cards.

That is why between the city and the hills surrounding it there are more or less vast plains separating it from them, sometimes by two or three kilometres, sometimes more and sometimes less.[4]

Another quality is the element of satire, which, together with other elements of humor and compassion, runs through this novel with results which are both artistically fruitful and psychologically revealing. All Palazzeschi's inventive power as a novelist and as a poet comes into brilliant play, for instance, in that superb scene of one of the aunts' reaction to Remo's suggestion that the best way of paying all the debts was to sign the promissory note:

[Teresa] felt offended and upset by that terrible word which during the last forty years had never been uttered under her roof, which had so sadly filled the period of her early youth, and which she thought had been banished for ever; the promissory note. The note that was to be paid: the squalor of the house under its threat, the mother's eyes red with tears. How often when she was a child, this word had weighed over this house. The father ill and the note to be paid. The mother dressed herself up, would wipe her eyes and would go to Florence after having been from door to door in her own village, to visit her friends and acquaintances in order to avoid the protest, the visit of the bailiffs and the attachment. And sometimes, being unable to collect money in time, the note had been protested in the anguish and in the impotence of all the members of the family, the mother and the poor daughters; while from his invalid's arm-chair, the father would shout curses and oaths. The ghosts of her childhood appeared again: the mortgages, the bills, the protest, the attachment, the creditors, the bailiffs . . . appeared again through doors and windows, re-entered the house, and took the form and body of an inexorable fatality.[5]

In the finale, clinching the moral of the story, there is a characteristic touch of the sarcasm-cum-sympathy which is the keynote of Palazzeschi's novels and short stories in general and of *The Sisters Materassi* in particular. It is the prose counterpart of what Papini noted and admired in Palazzeschi's poetry—a certain "counterpoint of white and black sensitivity." Palazzeschi knows the art of using humor, irony, and sarcasm in his novels without altogether harnessing his creative and inventive powers and experience to them. In other words, he extracts humor and irony from the situation, plot, or characterization that he has chosen to create rather than fashion the plot and characterization in conformity with any humorous or ironical plan. The sense of humor is pervasive even in the description of a landscape, as in the following passage:

> If then in this land the hill occupies the position of the lady, and almost always a true lady, a princess, the plain holds the position of the maid-servant the waitress or the maid; and even the most benevolent and courteous of the passers-by has for this plain that cordiality of condescension which one has for the woman who opens the door when one goes to visit her mistress.[6]

His sense of humor as well as his power of characterization and psychological insight are most happily and fruitfully exercised in depicting the Materassi sisters, as, for instance, when he distinguishes them from other elderly spinsters.

> Elderly ladies, rather old in fact, old not only on account of years but also by choice; ugly and wrinkled with impunity, who do nothing whatever in order to attenuate or hide the cruel work of nature, and the relentless effect of time on their faces and forms but who rather anticipated old age by running happily to meet all its catastrophic consequences; and dressed in such a shabby and old-fashioned way, and going beyond the limit indifference towards the current fashions to such an extent as to seem offensive.[7]

And it is not merely what he says about their person or character but also how they act and behave. One of the most

humorous scenes in the novel is the description of these sisters'
visit to the Pope:

> When the prelate said that they were the two embroideresses
> of Florence, who had offered the stole to His Holiness, he ten-
> derly took their hands in his own hands in order to look at them
> as he said to both "Very good, very good." The poor women,
> who were on their knees, could not help crying, and at last
> managed to speak, their speech broken by sobs. Teresa, while
> the Holy Father, with His caress on her front, gave her the
> papal blessing, cried in a burst of enthusiasm: "For our father's
> soul! For our mother's soul!" And the Pope, broadening his
> smile, nodded with his head, since she, having once broken the
> ice, gave no sign of stopping: "For our sister at Ancona! For the
> one at Florence! For all the inhabitants of our village!" And the
> more the Pope nodded with his head to make her understand
> that the blessing was also for them, Carolina, who had not been
> hitherto able to open her mouth, but who had listened, with great
> wonder, to everything her sister had managed to ask, opened her
> mouth and burst out with "Niobe": whereat the Pope, smiling
> even more broadly, up to the point of showing his red mouth
> without some of the teeth, and having clasped Carolina's face
> with his hands, as one does with a child, said to her before pass-
> ing on to the others: "For everyone, for everyone!"[8]

Elements of caricature and grotesqueness are also introduced,
but they too are a means of psychological exploration into the
character of the Materassi sisters. This analysis sometimes proceeds on the lines of Freudian psychology, but it never loses
touch with the creative side of the narrative that consists of
interdependent humor, pathos, and caricature. One of the focal
points of interest in the novel is the complementary as well as
counterbalancing role that Remo (so splendidly self-centered
and unscrupulous) plays in relation to the aunts who are path-
ologically infatuated by him. There is a kind of reason in their
infatuation insofar as their own responsibility in this affair is
concerned. And this reason is the masochistic fulfillment they
gain from their dealings with Remo. Both at the conscious and
unconscious level of their minds, they refuse to take Remo for

what he *is* to them—neither more nor less than a young nephew; they persistently project their own suppressed and unfulfilled sentiments and aspirations on him. He serves as a personification of the drama's objective, the pathos and the rancor of a sexually and emotionally frustrated life.

There is in *The Sisters Materassi*, as in other novels by Palazzeschi, no straightforward narrative proceeding stage by stage; instead, what we have is a series of scenes and situations which do not necessarily emerge one from the other and are not always organically linked. Palazzeschi provides these links by introducing numerous descriptions, anecdotes, and digressions, which, besides holding our interest, enrich our comprehension and enjoyment of the characters' psychological, cultural, or social milieu. And the way these episodic, descriptive, and illustrative elements are fused to form a convincing substitute for the narrative thread and unity makes for that architectonical unity, that rich and complex pattern of subtly orchestrated notes and intensities, that is undoubtedly Palazzeschi's forte as a creative novelist. It is also the most impressive and unmistakable proof of his artistic and creative maturity—the same maturity that one can see operatively present in the prose style that has practically done away with the lyrical flamboyancy and subjective overtones and undertones of the earlier novels. And the characters of Palazzeschi's more mature novels seldom fail to move us or convince us, no matter in what light they are presented—whether humorous, ironical, or farcical. In *The Sisters Materassi* there is also a more marked detachment and sharper perspective dividing the novelist from the characters than in the earlier novels. The characters act and behave with the utmost naturalness in conformity with the role and the nature assigned to them, and such artistic and psychological naturalism and autonomy are the hallmarks of living and individual characters.

Palazzeschi has a dual approach to his characters in that he manages to remain objectively aloof from what he is creating or describing, and at the same time to participate in it. There is both involvement and detachment, a basic sympathy and consideration for what he has created and a subtle ironic laugh or grin at the follies or self-deception of those characters. For instance, even when he laughs at the expense of the two sisters, there is, underneath his laughter, a positive element of human comprehension and even sympathy or compassion. It is, moreover, significant that even when Palazzeschi is criticizing something or making fun of what his characters say or do or think, there is no trace of cynicism whatsoever in his attitude toward them. However grotesquely and comically these two sisters or their actions or thoughts may be represented, we are never allowed to lose sight of their basic humanity and individuality or, above all, of their creative vitality and psychological veracity. These sisters appeal to us both as types and as individuals, a proof of Palazzeschi's ability to deal at the same time with what is general and what is particular and to embody these traits or qualities in one and the same character. It is a measure of the depth of insight he has in the psychological, moral, and, above all, human possibilities and potentialities of the creatures of his own imagination and inventive power.

Of course, Palazzeschi, too, as a man and as a novelist, has preferences and grades of affinity to and aloofness toward his characters. Whereas his attitude toward the two old sisters is that of amused tolerance and curiosity, his attitude toward Remo is that of an instinctive and impassioned admiration. He seldom exposes Remo to the same cruel light of searching irony, sarcasm, wit, or caricature as he does the two sisters. Remo is a key figure in the story, not only because he exercises such a powerful and possessive influence over his aunts—an influence that frequently amounts to a calculated and preplanned attempt to exploit their infatuation for him—but also because he serves to bring out what is essential in their character much more so than they serve to bring out Remo's character. It is possible to contemplate Remo existing independently of his two aunts, so long as he has some other persons whom he could use to fulfill his egotism. But we can't imagine the aunts existing the way they do for us without him and without the special relationship the three of them have. The physical attraction and something much more complex than a merely physical and sexual attraction that he exercises upon them is in fact a curiously psychological amalgam of what the aunts instinctively feel Remo is really like and what they just as instinctively wish him to be. They both want to possess him and to be possessed by him—and all this under the fairly innocent pretext of being nice to one who was left without parents and needs someone to care for him. It is difficult to say exactly at what stage Remo comes to understand the real nature of the fascination he has for them and the power he involuntarily exercises on them or the extent to which it is altogether involuntary. For instance, when he kisses the younger aunt, Carolina, he does it with such a prolonged intensity that even Teresa, the elder sister, protests, partly out of jealousy and partly out of false prudery. But there is no doubt that soon he adopts an attitude toward them—and not only when he is kissing them passionately or with a cold and calculated design—that is meant to fan the fires of a morbid kind of sensuality in them. For instance, when he subtly differentiates his behavior toward the female clients of the laboratory and the ecclesiastical clients, being more provocatively personal toward the former and more formally reverent toward the latter, the jealous sisters can't help noticing—and are not intended by Remo (or by Palazzeschi) not to notice. Remo both dupes and satisfies the aunts not only because of his irresistible physical charm and diabolic cleverness but also because of the sisters' masochism. Every lie or deceit, however petty, that he so casually administers in his dealings with them, is charged with a sense of betrayal, which they cannot but perceive and suffer from—and this all the more so since their professed desire is to help him in life. The more they pamper him by spending more and more money on him, the more blatantly and unscrupulously he displays and indulges in his egoism. And yet in his physical beauty and unscrupulous exploitation, there is something paradoxically innocent—something that refuses to come to terms with the moral issues or problems involved. His sincerity is, of course, synonymous with an astuteness of which he himself pretends to be both aware and unaware, according as it suits him, so long as he can thereby exploit others. In all his dealing with others—his aunts and his friends included—he goes as far as he can, with an infallible shrewdness that tells him where to stop and how to wriggle out of situations safe and unscathed.

The more Palazzeschi analyzes Remo's character or reveals it through his own actions and utterances, the more mysterious and unanalyzable some essential part of it seems to be. It saves him from being, and from appearing to be, one who is diabolically astute and calculating but at bottom an awfully simple character. This mysterious element in his personality is also, perhaps, the most subtle and psychologically interesting source of his ultimate charm. In his portrayal, Palazzeschi shows more or less the same insight and understanding of the dark and labyrinthine layers of Remo's egoism as Meredith does in *The Egoist*.

But underlying these varied and brilliantly humorous, farcical, tragic, or pathetic manifestations of egoism, one seldom or never in *The Sisters Materassi* meets with a moral comment or commitment—with something amounting to the criticism of life. And this is true of almost all novels by Palazzeschi. He is engrossed mainly in the representation—sometimes direct and sometimes allegorical, sometimes ironical or farcical, and sometimes poignantly pathetic—of the multifarious aspects of human experience and human nature and of the interplay between the conscious and the unconscious, the rational and the irrational. He observes, analyzes, and describes in a brilliantly witty and creative way but avoids moral evaluation; and this accounts for the amorality of his novels.

No wonder traces of the aestheticism of D'Annunzio and Wilde have been noted in Palazzeschi's novels and verses. But what is conspicuously absent in them is the rigor and vitality of thought that one finds in a novelist like Svevo or Lawrence. The extraordinary success and originality of individual scenes in the novel—for instance, the visit of the sisters to the Pope, the fair of Fiesole, the signing of the check—are isolated phenomena of intense creativity. The wealth of witty, detailed, and colorful descriptions and anecdotes in Palazzeschi's novels do not give it the organic unity it needs.

Luigi Russo, one of the earliest critics of Palazzeschi, makes a drastic criticism of his fundamental unconcern with any of the moral complexities of human experience that must be treated on a level other than the witty humorous, or pathetic. "His humour," says Russo, "has a fable-like character, and his paradisaic tendency is an attitude rather devoid of history and life experiences."[9] And to this,[10] we must add only that in spite of his limitations, Palazzeschi is to be considered one of the major Italian writers of the twentieth century, because he belongs to that amphibious group of poet-novelists, who are increasingly rare.

NOTES

1. Sergio Solmi, *Scrittori negli anni* (Milan, 1963), p. 153.
2. Aldo Palazzeschi, *Piacere della memoria* (Milan, 1964), p. 437.
3. Eugenio Montale, "Palazzeschi, ieri e oggi" in *L'Immagine*, II, no. 8, March-July 1948, p. 438.

As one who cannot be reduced to any system today any more than he could have been so many years ago, a Tuscan without professing the Tuscan mannerisms, a poet who is not in touch with the lyric poetry of the day, a short story writer and a novelist who does not write novels and short stories, but *tableaux vivants* worthy of the *Anime morte*, a man of his times, without being a prisoner of his times, Aldo has brought into our literary world an altogether individual type of independence and a lesson that is valid for everyone. He teaches us that poetry needs a profession; that a writer cannot last long unless he is rooted in that *amor vitae* which very few people know, since very few people have a liberal spirit. He shows us that art is not a gift that everyone can have, but the result of a heroic predestination, of a grace, if one will, that one must know how to deserve and that does not choose its elect by chance."

4. *Sorelle Materassi,* 23d ed. (Vallecchi, Florence, 1963), pp. 7–8.

5. Ibid. p. 265.

6. Ibid. pp. 10–11.

7. Ibid. p. 22.

8. Ibid. p. 39.

9. Luigi Russo, *I narratori* (Milan, Principato, 1958), p. 218.

10. And this criticism more or less applies to the subsequent novels —*I fratelli Cuccoli* (1948), *Roma* (1953) and *Il Doge* (1967)—and to the bulk of his short stories.

5 FEDERIGO TOZZI: A PSYCHOLOGICAL INTERPRETATION

Giacomo Debenedetti

The short stories of Tozzi—those we knew, those we never thought to find again, and a large number hitherto unpublished, all gathered together in a collection which seems, for the present, to be definitive[1]—raise once again the whole problem of his fiction. Indeed, Tozzi's narrative work is now shown to be so much more prolific than he had previously appeared, revealing an originality which we had never suspected, even after we have read so many other books, listened to other music, and looked at other paintings.

The point of departure for our evaluation might be a review Pirandello wrote in 1919, immediately after the appearance of the pregnant, labyrinthine, inexorable masterpiece of the novel *Con gli occhi chiusi* (With Closed Eyes). With its involution and intuition, we might say that it was written in invisible ink, which only the passage of time could bring to light, especially when we see it run up against the criticism that such a narrative method "might be called naturalistic but actually is not." Pirandello, too, from the very beginning, had taken up naturalism as an optical device in order to lend credibility and acceptability to characters and events which had lost all civic rights

Reprinted by permission of Renata Debenedetti. Translated for this volume by Frances Frenaye.

in the world in which they continued to trespass; his was a naturalism, in short, that laid charges of dynamite in its own path. In his review, whether he knew it or not, Pirandello offered Tozzi a testimonial to the congeniality between them. Actually, both contributed to the portrayal of the "new man" of modern art, a man animated by reasons of his own, who continues to be ignored by accredited and traditional reason that still claims a monopoly of the rational. They did this by quite different means, but their breaks with the past eventually converge. Pirandello is more demiurgic, more aggressive and autocratic in the manipulation of his material; to use an expression familiar to those who look at contemporary art, his narrative might be called "squared." Tozzi is more unaware; his subject leads him to results whose existence he ignored, and perhaps would not choose to follow; but on the other hand, he is more of a poet, more of an artist, in the classical and still persuasive and moving sense of the word.

"Il faut être absolument moderne," Rimbaud once said. But for readers and critics like ourselves can modernity be the criterion of excellence? Perhaps not, we agree. Nor should I like to give the impression that an attack upon naturalism is today the essential, even if not the complete ground for being taken seriously as a writer. We continue, to be sure, to admire the achievements of the great naturalists—of Zola, for instance. If we couldn't do so, we should feel like orphans. But when we tell of ourselves, of people of our own time, then the natural-istic point of view no longer satisfies us. What was this point of view, anyway?

A well-known epigram of Svevo, only superficially cynical, says: "It's not so much that I enjoy eating a steak as the fact that I'm eating it and others aren't." Naturalism took for granted a public of steak-eaters. The pleasure, edification, and participating, the satisfying compassion, the life-giving intellectual gain, registered by its reading public were to be found precisely in the feeling of superiority on the part of conventional, successful men who, by following the rules of the game, had won their steak while the heroes of the novels were starving or else eating the bread of affliction. Indeed, the greatest novels of the period presented stories that were implacably bound to end in catastrophes. And even those with happy endings pointed up the difficulties which the hero had to overcome in order to win his steak, beyond which he no longer appeared worthy of interest.

We can extricate ourselves from these metaphors by clarifying our parallels. A beefsteak stands for worldly goods, or, more abstractly, possession. It is not by chance that Giovanni Verga has been demoted to a mere leader of *verismo*. His masterpieces have been interpreted as being about things, and their psychological correlative, possession. The identification of personality with worldly goods or things is particular to the man of the middle class, the capitalist. Even in the realm of feeling the bourgeois is a capitalist and owner; he is the one who defines as possession his most ardent and purposeful relationship with a woman. And naturalist novels that deal with love are novels of possession. The pathos of the hero betrayed by his wife or mistress is that of the dispossessed man or, more precisely, of the man who has been robbed of his belongings. Marcel Proust, who, with a blunted ax and melancholy mildness, dealt the hardest blows to the naturalist novel, did not realize that he was epitomizing his objections to this genre when, in one of the love episodes of *A la recherche du temps perdu*, he declared that the word "possession" is absurd, that it mythologizes the impossible. Actually the loves which he narrates are for the most part explicitly or implicitly homosexual in character, which means that they reduce the idea of possession to absurdity, since such possessions are of a kind considered illicit and out of order.

Indeed, the society which was coming to birth with our century, through a travail whose upheavals we are still experiencing, was moving toward the elimination of Svevo's steak-eaters, at the cost of bringing everyone—as long as it was really everyone—down to the level of eating from a can. Now it happens that Tozzi won a name with *Tre Croci* (*Three Crosses*) and *Il podere* (*The Farm*), that is, with two novels that seem concerned with *things* but actually deny the capitalistic *fetishism* of worldly goods, or possession. By using traditional, apparently conservative plots, he upset the mechanisms and the motivations and broke the springs of the positivistic, deterministic, middle-class novel. Of course, in spite of his youthful anarchistic socialism and his enduring Christian anarchism, he did not write, or even attempt to write, a novel of social protest. But his development as an artist can be deciphered here and now—far better than yesterday, far better than when he was alive, and a great deal better than he ever suspected it would be—under the discernable content of his short stories and novels.

We know that the first boost to Tozzi's fame—which thereafter marked time—was given by Giuseppe Antonio Borgese, a critic generally considered more of a special pleader than a man distinguished for his sensitivity and intuition. In the case of the campaign he waged for Tozzi the opposite turned out to be true. Intuition told him that he had come upon a writer who upset customary perspectives, while his gift for special pleading counseled him to base his advocacy on backward-looking reasoning. It was sufficient for him to recognize that, with Tozzi, there was an end to the rule of impressionistic fragmentation in the tradition of *La Voce* and *Lacerba*, that it was once more "a time for building," that narrative form was freed from its enslavement to frivolity and raised to an artistic genre of the highest artistic importance. And he pointed out as a model the well-built, concise, splendid and tragic perfection of *Tre Croci*, in which he saw a brilliant "return to the past," understandable only in terms of naturalism. He did not use this word, but he proclaimed that, after the toilsome and admirable apprenticeship of the "autobiographical trilogy"—*Ricordi di un impiegato*

(*Diary of a Clerk*), *Con gli occhi chiusi,* and *Il podere*—Tozzi
had finally attained, in *Tre Croci,* such an impersonal material
that it opened up to him the "broader road" that was unfortunately cut short by his death. We need not add that impersonality was the criterion of excellence of the naturalistic novel.

The proof of this misunderstanding, which was, at that time,
perhaps, providential in winning Tozzi his rightful place in the
history of the Italian novel, was made evident when Borgese,
as literary executor of his friend's unpublished work, mutilated
the first and posthumous edition of *Ricordi di un impiegato.*
Only in 1960, when Tozzi's son brought out the complete text
of this very early (1910) work, was it clear that the figure of
the supposedly naturalistic Leopoldo grew out of a ganglion of
obscure and untamable motives, of amorphous and unassimi-
lated matter, of existential bewilderment strangely evasive in
relation to the role which he plays under the spotlight of the
stage. It would take a long time of citing passages which may
seem, as they did to Borgese, parenthetical and digressive, with
no bearing upon the plot, to analyze the perturbatory function
exercised upon the outward development and coherence of the
story and upon the plausibility of the *tranche de vie.* I am
reluctant to speak in terms of music when our discourse is of
literature, but I might briefly say that here is a case where the
insertion, here and there, of a few bars of atonal notes makes
us realize that the whole composition is written without the
harmonical and accoustical conventions to which our ears are
soothingly accustomed. These create in us a state of alarm and
tension which cannot be calmed by the satisfyingly familiar
cadences, the succession of notes and chords with a reassuring
pattern of cause and effect that follow.

We need only look at the episodes of the apparitions, mentioned here not merely as an example but, rather, as the indispensable evidence for the point I am making. Up to this point
the hero, Leopoldo, may have seemed the product—however

unhappy—of a legitimate union with so-called natural reality and average experience. Now, all of a sudden, he appears as the son of an as yet nameless chaos, in which ordinary classifications do not hold sway. We have a stage crowded with flesh-and-blood presences of reincarnated memories, which push their way, confusedly, to the foreground, without any rationale of time, space, or causality, bound together only by their power of vexation and evil. Their impellent was fear, as we may see from the declaration that precedes their entrance: "Every time that I am approached by someone I don't know I am afraid; and sometimes even a friend affects me the same way. I'm not afraid, actually, of him, but of the consequences which I may suffer when he starts talking." What consequences? What harm can Leonardo suffer from the unknown farmer whom he evokes as one of the many maleficent figures?

I remember how, outside of Florence, just beyond the suburbs, I had to pass by the green wooden gate of a farmer. Every time, as I drew near and saw the farmer standing at the open gate, I either turned back or crossed over to the other side of the road, in order not to meet him face to face.

It is understandable that, in the same place, Tozzi says in the words of his mouthpiece, Leopoldo: "I never wanted to be brought close to certain people." *Brought close,* he writes, rather than *bring myself close,* as if he were at the mercy of unknown impersonal and deplorable forces that control him. His way of avoiding the farmer has on the one hand, something of a superstitious ritual, and on the other hand something of a fear of the watchdog, of fierce and noxious beasts, of the dragon at the gate. Both fears have the same root, since superstition is always linked to a taboo, to a feeling of guilt and the fear of punishment by something that cannot be concretely foreseen but only guessed at by virtue of certain flashing and impenetrable signs. Animal fear is born of the presence of a living creature, similar to us inasmuch as he is alive, but giving out an alien and incomprehensible message, foretold yet not concretely stated.

If we are to come out with the whole point, let us say that Tozzi's characters are born in the same way as the apparitions to which Leopoldo is enslaved. We know this from a passage written several years later, when Tozzi was even more strongly driven by his storyteller's vocation. This is in that chapter of *Bestie* where he recalls how, as a boy, he watched a craftsman put red lead paint on the wheelspokes of peasant wagons, set them out to dry in the sun and then remove, with the handle of his brush, any fly that got stuck in the paint. The boy enjoys the sight of this simple, unproblematical work, deriving from it a feeling of physical well-being which makes him first hungry and then sleepy. In this euphoric condition, he is led to mull over his dreams and ambitions as an aspiring artist. "I thought how, when I was grown, I would write a book different from any I knew: an ingenous and tragic story like one of the vine-leaves that the wind blew down between my knees; yes, my book would be just like one of these vine-leaves." Then, suddenly the space around him is filled with characters invisible to the kindly craftsman: "The whole road was filled with people, with a light, transparent nightmare which stirred, like my soul, at the least breath of wind. Eventually I had to ask them to let me off; I felt them cluster around my youth like insects around a newly-lit lamp." Surely a crystal-clear allegory, with many facets, with responding echoes and understanding nods exchanged between inspiration and professionalism, between the sure hand of the craftsman and the anxious bewilderment of the artist. At the center there is the peremptory image of people seen as insects or animals, *Bestie,* as they are called in the title of the book, which is the most seminal work of Tozzi's entire literary production.

So preoccupied a vision of his characters has something obsessive about it, and indeed Tozzi speaks of a nightmare. It is as if he had to defend himself against them before putting them down on paper. We are brought into the realm of the unhealthy, the threatening, the evil which is to be averted. Yet it would be a mistake and an oversimplification to attribute this artistic dilemma to a pathological condition. Alfredo Gargiulo tried something of the sort, on the basis of shaky clues in both style and content and of literary associations. The result was an off-key hatchet job, which does not add to his critical glory even if, among those who put him on the wrong track, we must include Tozzi himself, with his fear of illness, particularly mental illness, which he makes quite explicit in his *Diary of a Clerk* and elsewhere. With quite different intentions, and in spite of the affectionate tone of his portrayal, even Borgese seems to make us suspect that there was something morbid about him, when he says: "He used to walk close to the walls, like a man who thinks he is being followed." If we are to bring pathology into it at all, then we must remove it from a clinical angle and consider it in relation to certain spiritual ills to which we are condemned in our century, thanking Tozzi for having sublimated them in his art and, where his personal life is concerned, thinking of them insofar as he is concerned as painful tricks played upon him by Providence.

Let us look again for a moment at Leopoldo, in *Diary of a Clerk*. If he makes his job as a railway employee so tormenting and unbearable, it is because he sees in it the external, concrete, perhaps still curable evidence of a *mal de vivre* so deeply ingrained that it is inseparable from his personality. In reality Leopoldo is a perpetual employee, an employee of life, which to him is an incessant rain of orders, unspoken but inescapable, of orders and threats on the part of a boss who is no one in particular, but everyone and everything and everywhere. There is another such figure in literature: Gregory Samsa, the petty employee who is the protagonist of Kafka's *Metamorphosis*. We see how this fellow wakes up one morning to find himself transformed into a centipede. This disgusting insect is the sym-

bolical incarnation of his true identity as a humiliated under-
ling, condemned to blind obedience by a world which domi-
nates and despises him and continually makes him feel that
it can get along without him. Gregory, too, was an employee
of life. Tozzi's very personal anxiety caused him to discover, in
the everyday figure of Leopoldo, a character of the most revealing and symptomatic family of man that has appeared in contemporary fiction.

For Kafka, the insect was the final metamorphosis, on its
way to a tragic and liberating end. For Tozzi it would have
been, rather, the symbol of a point of departure, which he must
make into a man, while preserving the alarming stigmata of his
previous animal existence. If we go beyond the borders of the
literary and artistic Italy of Tozzi's day, we shall find even
more striking parallels and analogies. In the early years of the
century the German painter Franz Marc, a friend of Klee and
one of the most convincing practitioners of expressionism and
abstraction, wrote an essay entitled *Constructive Ideas of
Modern Painting,* in which he systematically demolished naturalism, from the end of the Renaissance to, and including, the
impressionists. The seed of his argument was the need "to
return by another path to the images of spiritual life, which
does not follow the laws of a world conceived on a scientific
basis." (We may say, parenthetically, that Tozzi too was to
speak of "new intimate and spiritual perceptions.") For Marc
it was a question of releasing the latent forces behind matter,
that worn object of copying and photography, of "tearing off
the mask," as one of his critics puts it, "from the superficial
image of nature, in order to reveal the powerful laws that hold
sway behind its bland appearance." But these theoretical prem-
ises are less important than the remedy which Marc sought to
pit against "naturalizing," and which he called "animalizing."

Thus Tozzi's most keen-minded contemporaries consciously
and theoretically formulated his earlier, spontaneous, and inevitable vision. For him, other men and the other self were

"animalized" from the start, as we have seen in the halluci-
natory and prophetic passage—a passage which dispenses us
from quoting numerous other examples drawn not only from
the metaphorical *Bestie* but also from *Con gli occhi chiusi*,
where even the physical aspects of inanimate nature are animalized. How, then, does Tozzi react to what he calls this
"insidious animation"?

Fiction seemed to him the only way to assimilate, by portraying them, the live beings and things so tightly closed and
so reluctant to communicate to him the reasons for their
existence. His isolation turned into a potential springboard for
storytelling on the day when he said to himself that "any
mysterious [his italics] human action," however apparently
insignificant, (for instance, that of a man "who at a certain
point on the road stoops down to pick up a stone and then goes
on his way"), is of deeper interest than the most remarkable
fictional invention. The words just quoted are from Tozzi's
volume of collected essays *Realtà di ieri e di oggi* (Realities of
Yesterday and Today). Here we may see another amazing parallel, this time with Joyce's theory of the "epiphany." But we
shall more profitably read into such essays the fact that for
Tozzi to write meant to capture these mysterious actions and
their inexpressible mystery. His was to be a narration not of
cause and effect but of inexplicable patterns and ways of
appearance and being. Hence Tozzi's innate antinaturalism.
Naturalism narrates by virtue of explaining, whereas Tozzi
narrates inasmuch as he cannot explain.

An animalizing vision, with the superstitious uneasiness
and terror that it entails, illuminates the essence of Tozzi's
novel of behavior from within. The way of looking at things
that imposed itself upon him goes back to remote antiquity,
indeed to the prehistoric cave-drawing. Our primitive ancestors, fearful of animals and dependent upon them, sought from
them fertility and the capture and death of their enemies by
painting these acts on the walls of their caves for purposes of

imitative magic. Diggers have discovered the preparatory sketches for some of the wall paintings, from which it is clear how meticulously the artist studied his model in order to ensure the accuracy of its reproduction, and hence its efficacy, as an instrument of magic possession and deliverance from fear. Tozzi, too (I hope the reader will forgive the ingenuousness of the phrase), tormented himself in order to make things come out as he saw them. This, of course, is true of any artist; but in him there was a strong element of craftsmanship, which drove him to make the best possible rendition of the mysterious actions which he portrayed. Besides the practical results which primitive man set before him there was the reward, the compensation, the triumphal transfer of the actions and powers of the portrayed subject to the portrayer, who with his own hands reproduced them. Thus he redeemed his condition of succubus, becoming master of the man of whom he had formerly been the slave and establishing a *modus vivendi* between himself and his fears.

The reader may ask what connection there is between this archaic and pagan process and the art of a Tozzi who, under his hard-won status as a self-taught man, preserved the heritage of Tuscan and Christian culture. The fears, nightmares, and feelings of dependency and persecution to which he was prey dwelled deeply within him and worked upon elementary levels of his psychic makeup, levels which are primitive and react in a primitive manner. By a coincidence which gives further proof of Tozzi's accord with the time in which he lived, these were the years when the great art centers of the world went in for discovering the artefacts of primitive man; there was a special enthusiasm for African art, stemming largely from Paris and the studio of Pablo Picasso. This art (and here lies the reason for our mentioning it) permitted the reintegration with the cultivated ego of Western man of a baggage of long-lost, censored, in short, "savage" notions which for some time had indicated that they would no longer tolerate the psychological colonialism by which they had been checked. Picasso and his friends worked from ethnological documents and artefacts; they adopted and stylized the original signs and language that they found therein. Tozzi, on the other hand, ingeniously repeated the basic processes of what was described by an ethnology being imported in Europe—an ethnology he himself ignored. Once more, by virtue of a wonderful coincidence of fate and vocation, which became, in him, a dramatic daimon, he instinctively followed the path of modern art, while fundamentally expressing his own personal makeup and attempting—with a boldness which he often deemed insufficient and unsuccessful—to absorb the signs and language of a national illustrious and homely native tradition. He was an isolated, suffering, unconscious, yet eloquent guinea pig, involved in a crisis which was far more widespread than he imagined and was being experienced, at the same time, by artists more sophisticated than he, who handled it with greater awareness and managed to give names to phenomena which he confusedly and anxiously adumbrated truly "with closed eyes."

In order to understand how all this came about and reconstruct the human model from which Tozzi's poetry sprang with an impulse even more overwhelming than that of the creative will, we must turn to psychology. And this, to purist critics, is the most corrupt, sinful, and, in short, inadvisable of tools. But whether or not it is acceptable, there are times when nothing but psychology will do, and in this case we have ready proof that we are not calling upon it in vain, or without an enrichment of understanding. We have already seen that something, undefined, persecuted Tozzi to the point of obsession, producing images, resentments, and a whole chain of coercive reactions. Psychology would call these manifestations of the unconscious. But we have already noticed—indeed, Tozzi has told us so himself—that they were accompanied by another symptom, that of fear. With such a complete picture we might expect a classical picture: a youthful trauma which caused a chronic inhibition of his freedom to choose his own repressions or to cope with those to which he gives way. All this could well amount only to a psychological conjecture, called upon in order to reinforce a dangerous critical scaffolding. And if by any chance the trauma cannot be found, then the whole theory falls apart. Without wishing to sound overdramatic, I must confess that it was with considerable trepidation that I searched for the unknown factor that would confirm my theory.

A superfluous search, the reader may say, since a father complex is shouted out by Tozzi's life story and his major works, in every one of which there is an inhibited son. Yes, but all this is too generic, it is a plight shared by millions of other men and perhaps by dozens of great artists. Besides, Tozzi would be wasted as a mere case history in one of the lesser manuals of psychoanalysis. There must be something more personal, capable of explaining why his protagonist is condemned to live "with closed eyes," without the power to open them to everyday reality which, indeed, appears to him through a veil of apprehension, in both the physical and the spiritual sense of the word, as an agglomeration of monsters. Closed eyes, blindness to life, here is Tozzi's central myth, the open or secret connecting theme that runs through all of his most important fiction.

And it is in the novel *With Closed Eyes* that the trauma which we postulated is revealed in the course of a scene that seems to reproduce, in a terrifyingly realistic and at the same time symbolic condensation, the event that started the whole thing. This scene is not necessary to the plot; to a highly aesthetic critic it may seem merely picturesque, reminiscent of the rustic and bloodthirsty D'Annunzio, of whom the young Tozzi was a fanatically enthusiastic reader. Indeed, it breaks into the fabric of the book like an extraneous body, propelled by a sudden necessity that knows no law. In other words, it has the character of an involuntary confession. Briefly, the young hero Pietro looks on, stunned, at the general, almost indiscriminate castration of all the animals of the farm, in the presence of his father who has ordered it. It is hardly necessary to add, by way of explanation, that the idea of having to submit to a mutilation of this kind, willed by a father, is one of the basic features of the Oedipus complex. Pietro has visual evidence that his father is capable of such a gesture. What relation, we may ask, is there between this episode and the loss of sight, of the ability to look at things as they are, that is, the specific and quite different lesion from which Tozzi himself suffered? We ask this rhetorical and naive question in order to recall that Oedipus, the youth who bears the name of the complex, when he wants to atone for the murder of his father, that act of unconscious revenge and reconquest of his own destiny, blinds himself. He perpetrates upon himself, with his own hands, the mutilation which his father, anxious to preserve his life, his wife, and his kingdom, had inflicted upon him when he was a babe in swaddling clothes, hanging him up by his feet and leaving him to be found and brought up by shepherds, ignorant of his identity and his right to the throne. Here, from the very beginning of the myth, we have the connection between the loss of sight and the terrifying castration operation.

The letters collected in the volume entitled *Novale* show that Tozzi's demandingly affectionate father insisted that he make his way in the world, in compliance with a model which his father had set up but did not follow, preferring to indulge in all the pleasures to be had from life without ever paying for them. The mutilation has altered the son's initiative; it blocked the confrontation with reality which could have opened his eyes. He begins to vegetate like a blind man, both in real life and in the novel *With Closed Eyes*. To begin with, he was lazy and did badly both in and out of school, as if he were making a sort of negative affirmation in order to reproach his father for having forbidden him a positive posture. We have already said that the Leopoldo of the *Diary of a Clerk* was an "employee of life." When his father forces him to submit to the frustrating ordeal of a competitive examination for a petty government job, his bitter revenge is to wear his sleeves rolled up, as emblems of what his father has done to him, of the incurable incapacity to which he has been reduced. Once his father is dead, he leaves his job and takes over the administration of the family property. Now that his father is not there to make demands on him, there is no longer any reason for him to protest by refusing the task.

But the lesion still hurts, and calls for destructive compensations. *With Closed Eyes* is essentially the story of a willful failure in love, with which Pietro tries to punish the person who has made him psychologically impotent. *The Farm* and *Three Crosses* retell the drama of mutilation in an apparently more detached and objective guise.

In *The Farm* the protagonist, Remigio Selmi, quits his job in a small-town railway station (as did Tozzi) in order to go look after the farm left to him by his father. With a sort of passive rage and guile he lets himself fall into the hands of cheats and vultures; he is caught up in devious lawsuits and evasions that bring him close to outright violation of the law; he turns to dishonest or inept lawyers and signs promissory notes, perhaps for the very purpose of losing his newly acquired property. This property is, of course, the symbol of his father's power, and he must destroy it in order to obtain a morbid enjoyment out of the impotence to which his father had condemned him. As we read his story we want to tug at his sleeve, to save him, and yet every time we are disarmed by his stubborn and shapeless ingenuousness, by the innocence of his distraught face and wide-open, unseeing eyes. After the court has sentenced him for the shady dealings into which he had entered on the fundamentally hypocritical basis of saving his financial situation, the book closes in a poetical key: "A few hours later there was a hailstorm. Grape-leaves and green grapes were scattered over the ground together with pelted vine shoots and branches." Natural destruction is added to financial and moral ruin, and yet the impression left with us is one of brightness and shining. The havoc wrought by the storm, following upon the loss of Remigio's case in court, seems to release a feeling of peace and catharsis. Under the tarpaulin which the peasants hold over his head Remigio appears finally relieved. He has put down his father with an act of vengeance as irreparable as the lesion which his father had inflicted upon him.

Three Crosses repeats the same tale, against a different background—this time an antique shop which, if things were to go well, could produce material wealth. The wounded, antiheroic protagonist of Tozzi is this time split into the three Gambi brothers, owners in partnership of the bookshop. In the book there is not even a mention of their father. But his mute presence is immanent in the brothers' relationship. He left them the small estate which enabled them to make a living and go into business, and his presence endures in a thousand underlying ways. The novel tells how, by means of a false promissory note, the brothers go bankrupt. A lawsuit, financial ruin, and moral disgrace, and at the end three crosses which rise one beside the other in the cemetery of Siena.

In Tozzi's time, and in the social class to which he belonged, the promissory note was, to the older generation, a symbol of dishonor. By borrowing money against a promissory note, the Gambi brothers were, indirectly, fighting the memory of their father. But this was not enough. They had to destroy his power, and even his survival, by completely wasting his substance. These three characters, whom Tozzi, by anecdotes and description, makes into separate entities, are actually fragments of a single mirror, all of them reflecting the same view of life, each projecting a ray of light on the same psychological situation, that of a man who has been deprived of his power of getting his teeth into reality. And for this they substitute something as obvious and miserable as the joys of the table, striving to compensate their impoverished existences by orgies of greed and, through them, attaining a perverse euphoria and a physical enhancement like that of lovers' orgasm. They bleed themselves financially in order to buy the best fish, meat, chickens, and fruit on the market. With ribald arrogance they display their gastronomic satisfaction in the same way that a Don Juan brags of his sexual prowess; the table overflowing with delicacies is an assertion of virility, expressed by the literal devouring of their possessions. Their daily banquets are grim and tedious affairs, intended to damage the good name and reputation of their father, eliminating his enduring presence, incarnate in material things.

It has been said that the heroes of Tozzi's novels are inept and incapable of living. But the inept man is doomed from the start and cannot develop in a novel. The assertion holds true only if Tozzi is branded as a naturalist. But his novels are irresistibly dramatic; they are concerned not with an inept hero caught up in some kind of action, but with the origin and development of that mortal illness, the inability to live or, rather, to adapt to life. Naturalism examined what has been called psychology without a psyche, seen in the broad light of day. The contemporary novel, such as Tozzi wrote before its time, has a nocturnal point of view; it operates in a zone where there are no worldly explanations, no cut-and-dried solutions, in the true realm of the psyche, where chance cannot be abolished by a throw of the dice.

Tozzi thought, and stated quite clearly, that art should turn "toward the summits of more modern psychological components." He told stories that smacked of those of the preceding generation, hoping that the cases he described were exceptional and that other men would not have the same fate as that of his lonely heroes. Yet, unwittingly, he created a character who, with his "more modern psychological components," could not live in the way that had been taught him. The conflict between his inner being and his outward appearance takes place below the surface of the novel, and here is the unconscious and far-reaching secret of Federigo Tozzi.

Moved by impulses which caused him to be at war with himself and with his immediate artistic demands, his human desire for recognition, Tozzi portrayed a lost, suffering hero, a frail runner in life's race. A brother, this hero, to the passersby whose strained expressions and rude, alienated behavior mirror the travail of the man of today, trying to adapt himself to the incognita which he has discovered within, to find a meaning in the new structure of his future, which history still pushes away as if it were arbitrary and premature. Under a burden such as would have crushed many another artist, Tozzi found the courage, patience, and humility to go about his work with all the devotion of a scrupulous craftsman, like the wagoner of his youthful memory or dream who, with the handle of his brush, removed from the wheelspokes any fly that got stuck in the paint.

NOTE

1. Federigo Tozzi, *Opere: Le novelle,* vols. I & II, ed. Glauco Tozzi. (Florence, Vallecchi, 1963), 1083 pp.

6
IGNAZIO SILONE:
POLITICS AND THE NOVEL

Irving Howe

The central event of our century remains the Russian Revolution. For a moment, one of the most fervent in all history, it stirred the hope among millions of people that mankind had at last begun to lift itself, however painfully, from the realm of necessity to the realm of freedom. That hope, like the heroic phase of the revolution from which it sprang, did not long survive, and in the literature of our time there are few direct reflections of its original intensity. A "law" of history would seem to require that a considerable time elapse before a great event can be appropriated by the creative imagination—and in this case the event had been fatally disfigured before the novelist or poet could reach it. In two books, though hardly more than two, we can still see the revolution in its pristine enthusiasm: John Reed's *Ten Days That Shook the World* and Leon Trotsky's *History of the Russian Revolution*. The first is a work of journalism, a remarkably vivid rendering of the revolution as physical experience, while the second is history in the grand style and like all histories in the grand style, also a work of the literary imagination. Apart from its claim to being a faithful record and true interpretation, Trotsky's book is one of the few in our time that is able to sustain the kind of stylistic scrutiny now reserved for Shakespeare's plays, James' novels and minor poets. The book unfolds from a simple but commanding image: the meeting of Russian worker and Russian peasant, their first hesitant gropings toward each other, the pattern of retreat and reconciliation and finally, a clasp of unity. I quote a key passage:

> The workers at the Erikson, one of the foremost mills in the Vyborg district, after a morning meeting came out on the Sampsonievsky Prospect, a whole mass, 2,500 of them, and in a narrow place ran into the Cossacks. Cutting their way with the breasts of their horses, the officers first charged through the crowd. Behind them, filling the whole width of the Prospect, galloped the Cossacks. Decisive moment! But the horsemen, cautiously, in a long ribbon, rode through the corridor just made by the officers. "Some of them smiled," Kayurov recalls, "and one of them gave the workers a good wink." This wink was not without meaning. The workers were emboldened with a friendly, not hostile, assurance, and slightly infected the Cossacks with it. The one who winked found imitators. In spite of renewed efforts from the officers, the Cossacks, without openly breaking discipline, failed to force the crowd to disperse, but flowed through it in streams. This was repeated three or four times and brought the two sides even closer. Individual Cossacks began to reply to the workers' questions and even to enter into momentary conversations with them. Of discipline there remained but a thin transparent shell . . . The officers hastened to separate their patrol from the workers and, abandoning the idea of dispersing them, lined the Cossacks out across the street as a barrier to prevent the demonstrators from getting to the center. But even this did not help: standing stock-still in perfect discipline, the Cossacks did not hinder the workers from "diving" under their horses. The revolution does not choose its paths: it made its first steps toward victory under the belly of a Cossack's horse.

There is no novel of comparable stature which attempts to absorb the same experience. To be sure, the Russian Revolution had a lasting effect on the contemporary novel, as on every other phase of our life, but the effect was belated and indirect. The myth that one can see emerging from Trotsky's paragraph —I do not, of course, use myth as a polite synonym for lie— dominated the imagination of most political novelists until a very few years ago, but for the more serious writers it was largely "negative" domination, forcing them to think in terms of separation rather than unity, the split between worker and peasant rather than fraternity. The contrast between early political hope and later disillusion becomes the major theme of the twentieth century political novel: Malraux, Silone, Koestler —all are obsessed by the failure, or betrayal, of the revolution. Their books can be read as footnotes, half tragic half ironic, to Trotsky's paragraph.

Where Dostoevsky looked upon radicalism as a marginal conspiracy, a disease that had infected the intelligentsia and the *lumpenproletariat,* Malraux and Silone, in their major novels, recognize it as the occasion for the first independent entry of the masses into history. For Dostoevsky and Conrad the very possibility of revolution meant a catastrophic breakdown of order, a lapse into moral barbarism; for Malraux and Silone the breakdown of society is a long-accomplished and inevitable fact, and what matters now is the energy, the heroism, the pathos of the effort to achieve socialism. The view of "human nature" shared by Dostoevsky (at least the official Dostoevsky) and Conrad is one of radical pessimism: man must be strapped by ordained moral law so that the chaos within him will not break loose. Malraux's view is existentialist: man is whatever he makes himself, either in victory or defeat, and only through a chosen act can he fulfill the unmeasured possibilities of his being. For Malraux it is the appearance of millions of speechless men, climbing up from the silence of centuries, that is the overwhelming fact of our political life. From the feeble conspiracies of *The Princess Casamassima* and the feeble chatter of Peter Ivanovitch's circle in *Under Western Eyes* to the desperate revolt of the Shanghai workers in *Man's Fate*— that is the distance which the political novel, as indeed our world itself, has travelled.

The political novelist of our century feels the pressures of ideology far more intensely than his predecessors of the nineteenth century. He sees ideology not as a symptom of some alien disease but as both the burden and challenge of history: necessary in times of social crisis, frightening in its rigor, and precisely because it can be put to such terrible uses, a temptation most dangerous to those most in need of it. Yet he recognizes that ideology must be confronted, history allows no alternative; for like some discovery of atomic physics, ideology is in itself neither good nor bad, being a mode of thought that permits the widest spectrum of moral application.

From the nineteenth to the twentieth century there is a radical shift in perspective, in the distance the political novelist establishes between himself and his materials: Conrad and James probe beneath the surface of society to measure the plebeian threat while Malraux and Silone are themselves engaged in the struggles they portray. It is significant that both Malraux and Silone were active political figures shortly before they turned to literature, this very turn itself being a political act of the most desperate kind. In a sense, the true hero of their novels is the author himself: Kyo is not Malraux nor is Pietro Spina quite Silone but the problems of Kyo and Spina are the problems of Malraux and Silone. It is from their creators that Kyo and Spina draw their obsessive need to shift the direction of history, to put, as the hero of *The Royal Way* says, "a scar on the map." The result of this personal involvement is at once a gain in political authority and a loss of subtlety and range in the traditional skills of the novel. In the work of these writers there is far less penetration into individual motives and behavior than in the novels of, say, Conrad and James—and the difference is due not merely to the greater talent of the

nineteenth century authors, nor even to the advantages that
Conrad and James gained from working within a still vital
cultural tradition while Malraux and Silone venture into unex-
plored regions of mass consciousness and mass revolt; it is due,
rather, to the fact that Conrad and James wrote from positions
of isolated social comfort while Malraux and Silone expose
themselves, they are in their tragedies, their blood and hope are
ground into the defeated revolutions over which they mourn.

In Ignazio Silone's first novel, *Fontamara*, the image of
worker and peasant, which had achieved a symbolic elevation
in Trotsky's History, appears again, this time in a state of
decomposition, its two parts split into figures of hostility. One
of the few modern novels that has the genuine quality of a folk
tale, or perhaps better, a comic fable, *Fontamara* tells the story
of a peasant village in the Abruzzi resisting in its pathetic way
the onthrusts of the Mussolini regime. To the peasants, the
political problem first presents itself as one of city against
country, town against village—and they are not entirely wrong,
for they, the peasants, are at the very bottom, suffering the
whole weight of Italian society. Simple but not simple-minded,
unable to generalize very well from their suffering yet aware
that they must learn to, they show an acute insight, through
their complicated jokes and sly stories, into the nature of the
social hierarchy. When a minor government flunkey, the Hon.
Pelino, comes to gather their signatures for a petition that, as it
happens, has not yet been composed, one of the peasants tells
him a marvellous little fable:

> At the head of everything is God, Lord of Heaven. After him
> comes Prince Torlonia, lord of the earth. Then comes Prince
> Torlonia's armed guards. Then comes Prince Torlonia's armed
> guards' dogs. Then nothing at all. Then nothing at all. Then
> nothing at all. Then comes the peasants. And that's all.
>
> And the authorities, where do they come in? [asks the Hon.
> Pelino.]

Ponzio Pilato interrupted to explain that the authorities were divided between the third and fourth categories, according to the pay. The fourth category (that of the dogs) was a very large one.

From their bloody experience the peasants must learn that they need the help of the town, and one way of reading *Fontamara* is as a series of explorations into, or encounters with, the town where the peasants try to discover their true allies— not the priest, who is corrupt and bloated; not the old land-owners, who are being squeezed by Mussolini's agents yet remain as much as ever the enemies of the peasants, not the liberal lawyer, Don Circostanza, who betrays them with his windy rhetoric. Only when the most violent of the peasants, Berardo—it is significant that he owns no land and is therefore free from the conservative inclinations of even those peasants who have nothing more than a strip of rock or sand—only when he goes to Rome does he meet, after a series of tragic-comic blunders, the agent of the revolutionary underground. At the end of the novel, a union has been achieved—hesitant, not fully understood and quickly broken—between peasant and worker. The underground revolutionary brings to the peasants a miniature printing-press, a product of urban technology, and the peasants print one issue of a little paper called *What Is To Be Done?* As one of them explains with a truly masterful grasp of political method, the question must be asked again and again, after each statement of their plight:

They have taken away our water. What is to be done? The priests won't bury our dead. What is to be done? They rape our women in the name of the law. What is to be done? Don Circostanza is a bastard. What is to be done?

The question echoes, not accidentally, the title of Lenin's famous pamphlet, in which he first outlined his plan for a disciplined revolutionary party; nor is it an accident that both Lenin's pamphlet and the paper of Silone's peasants are written in times of extreme reaction. For *Fontamara* is the one important work of modern fiction that fully absorbs the Marxist outlook on the level of myth or legend; one of the few works of modern fiction in which the Marxist categories seem organic and "natural," not in the sense that they are part of the peasant heritage or arise spontaneously in the peasant imagination, but in the sense that the whole weight of the peasant experience, at least as it takes form in this book, requires an acceptance of these categories. What makes *Fontamara* so poignant as a political legend—despite the apparent failures, upon occasion, of Silone's language to equal in richness his gift for anecdote— is that he is a patient writer, one who has the most acute sense of the difference between what is and what he wishes. The peasants are shown in their nonpolitical actuality and the political actuality is shown as it moves in upon them, threatening to starve and destroy them; Silone does not assume the desired relationship between the two, though he shows the possibilities for a movement into that relationship, the book is both concrete—wonderfully concrete—in its steady view of peasant life and abstract—a brilliant paradigm—in its placing of peasant life in the larger social scheme. The political theories behind the book resemble the lines signifying longitude and latitude on a map; they are not the reality, not the mountains and plains and oceans; but they are indispensable for locating oneself among the mountains and plains and oceans; they are what give the geography of society meaning and perspective.

Fontamara ends in defeat yet it exudes revolutionary hope and *élan*. Silone's next novel, *Bread and Wine*, is entirely different in tone: defeat is now final, the period of underground struggle at an end, and all that remains is resignation, despair and obeisance before authority. The novel's hero, Pietro Spina, who partly reflects the opinions of his creator, is a revolutionary leader who from exile has returned to the peasant areas of his native Abruzzi in order to reestablish ties with his people and see whether his Marxist theories will hold up in experience. As he wanders about the countryside, the sick and hunted

Spina gradually abandons his Marxism, but not his social rebelliousness; the priest's frock that he has adopted as a disguise
begins to be more than a disguise; he must fulfill the responsibilities of his public role or what appears to be his public
role, and must adjust his private emotions to this necessity;
he becomes or aspires to become, a revolutionary Christian
saint. He asks—in the words of Albert Camus—"Is it possible
to become a saint without believing in God? That is the sole
concrete problem worth considering nowadays." But he sees
even further than Camus: he dimly envisages, and in *The Seed
Beneath the Snow* tries to realize, a fraternity beyond saint-
hood and then beyond good and evil.

Soon after arriving in the Abruzzi, Spina decides that the
usual kinds of political propaganda are irrelevant in a fascist
country. People have been misled by slogans too long and too
often; they instinctively distrust all phrases. To refute the
government propaganda is pointless since no one, least of all
its authors, believes it. Why argue against ideas that everyone
realizes to be absurd? People understand the truth well enough;
it is courage and energy that they lack, not understanding;
they are not ready to sacrifice themselves. Spina feels that what
is now needed is not programs, even the best Marxist programs, but examples, a pilgrimage of good deeds: men must be
healed, they must be stirred to heroism rather than exhorted
and converted. Something more drastic, more radical than any
kind of political action is needed to cope with the demoraliza-
tion and corruption Spina finds in Italy.

Before coming to these conclusions Spina had already been
uneasy about his political allegiance: "Has not truth, for me,
become party truth? . . . Have not party interests ended by
deadening all my discrimination between moral values?" The
political doubts prompting these questions, together with his
feeling that the Marxists in exile have lost touch with the
realities of Italian life, lead Spina to the ethical ideal, the love
concept, of primitive Christianity, which for him becomes "a

Christianity denuded of all religion and all church control."
Spina believes not in the resurrection of Jesus, only in his
agony; Jesus figures for him entirely in human terms; in fact,
the significance of Jesus is that he is the first, and perhaps the
last, fully human being. To live as a Christian without the
church means, for Spina, to shoulder the greatest possible inse-
curity before man and God. Spina rejects that duality between
means and ends which is common to all political movements;
unwilling to stake anything on the future, he insists that the
only way to realize the good life, no matter what the circumstances, is to live it. "No word and no gesture can be more
persuasive than the life, and, if necessary, the death of a man
who strives to be free, loyal, just, sincere, disinterested. A man
who shows what a man can be."

Abstracting this political view from its context in the novel,
as Silone virtually invites us to, we reach mixed conclusions
about its value. Much of what Silone says is undoubtedly true:
anyone trying to organize a political underground would have
to demonstrate his worthiness not only as a leader but as a man
and a friend. But here we reach a difficulty. Once Silone's
militant and saintly rebels acquired followers, they would have
to be organized into some sort of movement, even if it claimed
to be nonideological and were not called a party; and then that
movement would be open to bureaucratic perils similar to those
of the Marxist party which Spina has rejected—bureaucratic
perils that would be particularly great in an atmosphere of
saintly, even if not apocalyptic, Messianism. Has not something of the sort happened to Christianity itself, in its transition
from primitive rebelliousness to a number of accredited
institutions?

Silone has here come up against a central dilemma of all
political action: the only certain way of preventing bureaucracy
is to refrain from organization, but the refusal to organize with
one's fellow men can lead only to acquiescence in detested
power or to isolated and futile acts of marytrdom and terror-

ism. This is not, of course, to deny the validity of specific organizational rejections; it is merely to question Silone's belief,
as it appears in *Bread and Wine*, that political goals can be
reached wthout political organization.

It is, however, entirely to Silone's credit that he recognizes
this dilemma and embodies it in the action of his book; he
does not try to pry his way out of it with some rusty formula.
One of his finest strokes in *Bread and Wine* is the scene in
which Spina takes off his priestly frock—this occurs, significantly, as soon as some possibility for political action appears.
He takes off his priestly frock but we are not to suppose that
his experience as Paolo Spada the false priest has not left a profound mark upon him. The duality between Spina and Spada
—between the necessity for action and the necessity for con-
templation, between the urge to power and the urge to purity—
is reflected in Silone's own experience as novelist and political
leader. Even after he wrote *The Seed Beneath the Snow*, a novel
in which he exemplifies a kind of Christian passivity and mute
fraternity, he continued to participate in the quite worldly
Italian Socialist movement. In his own practice as an Italian
Socialist, he has been forced to recognize that the vexatious
problem of means and ends involves a constant tension between morality and expediency which can be resolved, if resolved at all, only in practice.

Yet it is precisely from these scrupulous examinations of
conscience and commitment that so much of the impact of
Bread and Wine derives; no other twentieth century novelist
has so fully conveyed the pathos behind the failure of socialism. *Bread and Wine* is a book of misery and doubt; it moves
slowly, painfully, in a weary spiral that traces the spiritual and
intellectual anguish of its hero. The characteristic turning of
the political novelist to some apolitical temptation, is, in Silone's case, a wistful search for the lost conditions of simple
life where one may find the moral resources which politics can
no longer yield. This pastoral theme, winding quietly through

the book and reaching full development only in its sequel, *The Seed Beneath the Snow*, is not an easy one for the modern reader to take at face value: we are quick, and rightly so, to suspect programs for simplicity. But in Silone's work it acquires a unique validity: he knows peasant life intimately and, perhaps because he does not himself pretend to be a peasant, seldom stoops to pseudo-folk romanticizing; he is aware that a return to simplicity by a man like Spina must have its painful and ironic aspects; his turn to pastoral does not imply social resignation but is on the contrary buttressed by a still active sense of social rebelliousness; and most important of all, he employs the pastoral theme not to make a literal recommendation but to suggest, as a tentative metaphor, the still available potentialities of man.

Bread and Wine is a work of humility, unmarred by the adventurism or the occasional obsession with violence and death which disfigures the political novels of Malraux and Koestler. Whatever the ideological hesitations of Silone's novels, they remain faithful to the essential experience of modern Europe; and to the harsh milieu of political struggle they bring a cleansing freshness, a warmth of fraternity.

Perhaps as a sign of the drift of our age, Silone has gradually become one of the most isolated among Italian writers. In the intellectual world of Italy he is seldom honored or admired. The memory of his refusal to accommodate himself to the fascist regime stirs feelings of bad conscience among literary men who were more flexible. His continued rejection of the traditional elegance of "literary" Italian confounds and disturbs the conventional critics. And his politics—for in some vague but indestructible way he remains a socialist, indifferent to party or dogma, yet utterly committed to the poor and the dispossessed—annoys those Italian writers who have tied themselves to one of the party machines or the far greater number who have remained in the shelters of aestheticism.

This last factor may also account for the decline of Silone's reputation in the United States. Those American intellectuals who have settled into social conformism or a featureless liberalism find in Silone's politics little more than sentimental nostalgia—or so they would persuade themselves; those who have turned to religion, whether it be the Catholic Church or the crisis theology of Protestantism, cannot help realizing, with a discomfort in proportion to their sensitiveness, that Silone's struggle for the ethic of primitive Christianity has little in common with the religious institutions and doctrines of the twentieth century.

Yet each man, if he is to remain one, must go his own way; and Silone, in his clumsy uncertainty, his humorous irritability, his effort to speak without rhetoric or cant, has become a kind of moral hero for those of us who have been forced by history to put aside many of the dogmas of social radicalism but who remain faithful to the rebellious and fraternal impulse behind the dogmas. Silone's most recent novel, *A Handful of Blackberries*, has been received with some conventional appreciation and more conventional depreciation; neither of these is an adequate response. So deeply opposed is this book to the moods, the assumptions, the values of our time, so thoroughly is it imbued with the forgotten emotions of humaneness, that one can only assert that in years to come it will be looked back upon, if anything is looked back upon, as a cultural and spiritual act helping to redeem a terrible age.

Simply as a novel, *A Handful of Blackberries* has large, obvious faults: it reads more like a scenario than a realized work, it is occasionally flabby in structure and scratchy in style, it betrays a tone of great weariness (but from that weariness also comes a kind of greatness). One soon suspects that Silone, like many other novelists for whom writing is not merely portrayal but also a form of implicit prophecy, has become a little impatient with the mechanics of literature, the game of creating illusions. He has reached almost, but not quite, the position of the serious artist whose very seriousness causes him to shed the forms in which he has scored his greatest successes.

Yet these matters, though they have an intrinsic interest, are as nothing besides the overwhelming fact to which the novel testifies: that in an age of faithlessness Silone has kept faith. He has remained with the *cafoni*, the landless peasants in whose name he first began to write, and in this novel he tells us that, through the noise and the muddle of shifts in regimes and parties, nothing has changed for the peasants except the names of those who exploit them and the catchwords by which their exploitation is rationalized.

The surface action of the novel traces the disillusion of a young engineer who begins as a local leader of the Communist Party and comes gradually to realize that he must choose between the peasants who trust him and the party machine, which is as inhuman and repressive as the machine of the fascists. The inner action of the novel is a fable enriched with Silone's marvellous anecdotes[1]—a fable about a trumpet by which the peasants, when their misery becomes unbearable, called one another together and which the Communist Party, in its false claim to be their spokesman, now wishes to appropriate. But while it may be true that the peasants are unable to act positively in their own behalf, they do have a long and rich experience in collective resistance. They do not surrender the trumpet.

Once again, as in *Fontamara* and *Bread and Wine*, the city is counterposed to the country: neither can understand the other, and given the inequity of social arrangements it can hardly be avoided that the one should exploit the other. The life of the peasants remains as miserable, as buried in darkness, as ever before. And so long as this remains true, Silone sees no reason to make his peace with the world as it is. Nor is he at all sentimental about the peasants, for the sardonic humor that twists through the book is often turned against their coarseness and gullibility. But they are his, by adoption of blood, and he remains hopeful, with a hopefulness that has nothing to do with optimism, that from the hidden inarticulate resources of the poor, which consist neither of intelligence nor nobility, but rather of a training in endurance and an education in ruse—that from all this something worthy of the human may yet emerge. When will the trumpet blow again? "How can I know?" answers the peasant Lazzaro. "It doesn't depend on me, you know. Maybe next year, or twenty or five hundred years from now." But the trumpet remains.

Silone's novels contain the most profound vision of what heroism can be in the modern world. Like Malraux, he appreciates the value of action, but he also realizes that in the age of totalitarianism it is possible for an heroic action to consist of nothing but stillness, that for Spina and many others there may never be the possibility of an outward or public gesture. If we compare his view of heroism with that of Hemingway, we see the difference between the feelings of a mature European and, if I may say so, an inexperienced American. For Hemingway heroism is always a visible trial, a test limited in time, symbolized in dramatic confrontations. For Silone heroism is a condition of readiness, a talent for waiting, a gift for stubbornness: his is the heroism of tiredness. Hemingway's heroic virtues are realized in situations increasingly distant from the social world, among bullfighters and hunters and fishermen; Silone's heroic virtues pertain to people who live, as Berthold Brecht has put it, in "the dark ages" of modern Europe, at the heart of our debacle.

NOTE

1. "Silone's characters exchange anecdotes like gifts; it is all they have, but it is everything. If genuine life is communion, according to Silone, its seed is the anecdote; so that his notion of life and his notion of fiction are not to be detached. The role of fiction, like the end of life is (for Silone) to be companionable; and its nature is the

account of individuals failing or succeeding in coming together, in being companionable, in putting themselves in touch with reality and with each other by the telling of stories."

This fine observation appears in an essay about Silone written by R. W. B. Lewis, in *Kenyon Review* (Winter 1955). The essay has other such insights, but is, to my mind, marred by an unwillingness to take Silone's politics with full seriousness, that is, as an activity needing no "translation" into moral or quasi-religious terms. Thus, Mr. Lewis speaks of Silone's politics as a "fortunate fall, a bruising experience invaluable for both the man and the artist." This seems to me a curious view of the relation between life and literature, as if experience were merely fodder for composition. But most important, it indicates, I think, a refusal to understand that for Silone the failure of socialism, far from being a "bruising" experience—let alone anything so providential as a "fortunate fall"—was the decisive and tragic event of his life.

7

ALBERTO MORAVIA:
EROS AND EXISTENCE

R. W. B. Lewis

So as to have a new life": was what she wanted to
answer; but she had not the courage. That remote reason of
hers, now that she saw nothing was changed except her surrendered body, appeared to her ridiculous and unworthy.

Moravia, *The Time of Indifference*

Alberto Moravia is the most precocious and among the
most gifted and prolific of the novelists now referred to by
younger Italians as the second generation. Italian intellectuals
in their twenties have taken to calling themselves the third
generation (a periodical bearing that name was even founded
to promote the notion[1]); and they are now lumping together,
as their elders if not betters, all those novelists whose art was
formed out of the experience of the Fascist era: Silone, Moravia, Elio Vittorini, Cesare Pavese, Vitaliano Brancati, Carlo
Levi, Mario Soldati, and a number of others. Moravia belongs
properly with this group and is probably its leading practitioner
of the craft of fiction. But beyond that, he is perhaps the most
emphatic annalist anywhere of one widely featured explanation
of life.

Reprinted by permission of J. B. Lippincott Company from *The Picaresque Saint*. Copyright, 1956, 1958, by R. W. B. Lewis.

The explanation seems to have come to him, all rounded and complete, at the moment he first became aware of his own literary talent, and this was a very early moment indeed. He has complained with apparent seriousness that he was able to write nothing from his ninth to his seventeenth years; but his first and perhaps best novel, *The Time of Indifference*, was written before he was eighteen (though not published until 1929, when he reached his majority), and his first story—"Tired Courtesan"—came out in the Italian journal *Novecento* in 1928, when he was twenty years old. "Tired Courtesan" was published in French, in line with the magazine's policy of supporting a pan-European culture by offering its wares in any of the major languages. A good deal of Moravia was announced in the subject and tone of the title itself, and in the sophisticated trickery of the French translation. The substance of the tale—a murky assignation during an illicit affair that both parties, for diverse financial reasons, are anxious to terminate—introduced much of what has ever since been Moravia's controlling image of experience.

It is an image of the world in its sexual aspect: or at least of that part of the world that, according to Moravia, is touched and accounted for by the sexual aspect. To say merely that Moravia's fiction is erotic is a truism that can stifle rather than enlarge our sense of his achievement: like saying, with a final simplicity, that Dante's poetry is religious. For Moravia's fiction provides a major treatment of a minor but honorable and suggestive view of things: the sexual view, the view of human relations and of everything that arises in or impinges upon human relations as beginning and ending in the sexual encounter. Everything other than sex is, in the stories of Moravia, an extension of sex; or perhaps better, everything other than sex is sooner or later converted into it. Moravia, in fact, is a minor master of the strategy of conversion in literature: that is, of *artistic* conversion, of the transformation of one set of values into another. The typical Moravian narrative shows us, not the precise and detailed moment of the sexual encounter (in this respect, there is less "sex" in Moravia than in a good many other modern writers; much of the time the "sex" remains hidden, like the divinity in certain religious poems), but the full amount of life that culminates in the sexual encounter or is an observable deflection from it. And the purpose behind Moravia's strategy is strikingly similar to that of the other novelists we are considering. If Moravia's encounters are sexual rather than political, as in Silone, or religious, as in Greene, the aim is identical—to recover a more faithful image of man at a time when that image has been singularly deformed and betrayed. Measured against that purpose, Moravia's achievement is impressive but partial.

"The use of man as a means and not as an end," Moravia has insisted, "is the root of all evil." An ancient and recently urgent European tradition echoes in the remark; and in the case of Moravia, the urgency arose from the Fascist habit of reversing the formula. It was chiefly because fascism was the enemy of man that it was also the enemy of art. Moravia had to discover, as Silone rapidly discovered, that human reality in art was heresy in the Fascist view. *The Time of Indifference* was a notable public success, but its combination of clinical honesty and lyrical sadness went so against the official vulgar heartiness sponsored by the Italian government that an order was issued forbidding the mention of the author's name in any newspaper or magazine. His next novel, *Mistaken Ambitions* (1935), consequently went unreviewed, and Moravia was forced, like Silone, to adopt a pen name, "Pseudo," for articles, and the mild evasion of "Alberto Moravia" for stories (the author's real name is Alberto Pincherle-Moravia). Moravia traveled a good deal during the thirties—to Mexico, China and the United States.[2] In the same period he abandoned realism for more indirect and furtive pictures of the contemporary scene. Several of his literary colleagues were driven by the political climate of the day into the same area of the fantastic

and the hermetic, and not always to their disadvantage;[3] but
Moravia's surrealistic and satirical writings in the thirties
(*L'Epidemia*, for example) do not, in my opinion, show him at
his best.

Moravia's sufferings under Mussolini were not abnormal,
nor was his early life unduly adventurous; what was abnormal
was Moravia's creative sensitivity. He was born in Rome in
1907, and much of his childhood was colored by a painful bone
disease that required a prolonged stay in a sanitarium and the
use first of crutches and later of a cane. He still walks with
discomfort; but his illness was to serve him by recompense and
in a manner not uncommon in the history of literature, both as
stimulus and as sheer material for his fiction: "Sick Boy's
Winter" (1930) was a brilliant early fruit of the days at the
Istituto Codavilla in Cortina. His worst experience during the
war came toward the end of it, when he tried to flee southward
from Rome to Allied-occupied Naples, in 1943, and got stuck
en route. He spent nine months of hideous boredom, hiding
out with his wife and some shepherds in a kind of covered
pigsty, silent, inactive, watching the endless rain descend (as
he has said) "like a liquid wall and always the same." This
episode, too, was to be fruitful. Out of the discomfort and the
boredom, Moravia, fourteen years later, fashioned one of his
solidest novels: *Two Women,* a meticulous account of the
winter he still vividly remembered.

He had written *The Fancy Dress Party,* a curious short
novel, in 1941, and the eloquent *Agostino* three years later;
but his uninterruptedly fertile period began with the arrival of
spring and the Allied armies in 1944. *The Woman of Rome*
following in 1947; *Luca* (another short novel, coupled with
Agostino as *Two Adolescents* in English) in 1948; *Conjugal
Love* in 1949, *The Conformist* in 1950, and *A Ghost at Noon*
in 1954. It is in these works (along with *Two Women*) that
Moravia's image of human nature and human experience—
though present, as I have said, from the beginning—assumed
its full and unmistakably Moravian shape.

The Strategy of Conversion

Perhaps the element most often vitalized by the sexual impulse, in Moravia's treatment of it, is money—the element closest indeed to sex in the center of Moravia's vision of human affairs. Moravia's characters are relentlessly grasping; but they or their observers intermittently realize that it is not the acquisitive but the sexual instinct that grasps after satisfaction. One of *Racconti Romani*,[4] for example, shows us a real-estate agent with designs upon a beautiful and aristocratic young widow, some of whose property he has been asked to sell. His hopes fade as he discovers that the woman derives her sexual gratification not from men but from money—from the very fantasy of making money, from demanding many times more money for the property than she can possibly expect to get. The lines cross skillfully: the widow's interviews with prospective buyers are forms of flirtation aimed at increasing the price in the pursuit of an essentially nonfinancial pleasure. The agent gives up. "I had been the agent in a business affair, but now she had made me become the agent in a sordid love affair. Before I knew what I was doing, I burst out, 'Princess, I am a broker, not a pimp'; and red in the face, I hurried away."

The child Agostino (in the novella bearing his name), reveals only his innocence when he wonders—gazing in a country villa turned into a brothel—"what the relation was between money, which usually served to acquire well-defined objects of measurable quantity, and caresses, nudity, female flesh." A connection is readily intuited by the initiated. Adriana, the woman of Rome, remembers her surprising willingness to accept money the first time it is offered her—and by a man she dislikes, at a moment she believes herself "engaged" (in the fine free Italian meaning of the word) to someone else:

> The feeling I experienced at the moment bewildered me . . . a feeling of complicity and sensual conspiracy such as none of his caresses in the restaurant bedroom had been able to arouse in me.

It was a feeling of inevitable subjection. . . . I knew, of course, that I ought to refuse the money; but at the same time I wanted to accept it. And not so much from greed, as from the new kind of pleasure which his offering had afforded me.

The young woman who narrated "The English Officer" (1946) recalls, like Adriana, the "spontaneity" and "attitude of surrender" with which she took the first money offered her for going to bed with an Allied soldier.

Moravia's repertoire is not a large one; in fact, he has insisted that it must not be. "I never trust a writer who can say too many things," he has told a *New Yorker* interviewer. "By that I mean a writer who has too many tunes to play. One good tune is enough. Good writers are monotonous, like good composers. Their truth is self-repeating. They keep rewriting the same book. That is to say, they keep trying to perfect their expression of the one problem they were born to understand."[5]

The political dimension of life yields not much less easily than does the economic. Fascism and underground anti-Fascist activities enter *The Woman of Rome* as a shadowy other world; they are made to seem an unreal intrusion—via the insubstantial character of Mino—into the reality of the heroine's sexual history. In an essay on communism and the West (1954), Moravia alluded resentfully to the recent "politicization" (his word) of life; and he has attempted, in his own writings, to reverse that tendency. "Moravia distrusts politics," his friend and colleague Paolo Milano has said about him; "and he has a qualified indifference towards history—individual men interest him, not crowded events."[6] Moravia's distrust leads, in his fiction, to the conversion, or attempted conversion, of the political into the sexual: an effort which compares interestingly to that of Silone, who as we shall see, has sought to transform the political into the charitable, out of an even more radical distrust of the former.

Moravia's attempt is projected with entertaining directness in "Bitter Honeymoon" (1951), in which a young couple,

starting on their honeymoon, run into one of the bride's political colleagues, a fellow worker in "the Party." The husband,
Giacomo, is (he says) not interested in politics, though he is
vitally interested in consummating the marriage after a failure
to do so the night before. The Communist intruder, Livio,
argues that everything has its political implications: "How
could it be otherwise? Politics is everything." Simona, the
wife, wobbles between the two men in a state of uncertain
potentiality; she had failed to report her marriage to the Party,
but she had also resisted her husband's advances. Listening
to the two comrades talking together, Giacomo suspects
gloomily that "comrade" may represent a more intimate relation than "lover." But love conquers all, or nearly so; at least,
the human element seems vindicated; and the story ends with
the first instant of consummation. In *The Conformist*, an
admirably ambitious but on the whole unsuccessful novel,
Moravia attempts nothing less than a philosophical demon-
stration in narrative of the sexual origins of political commitment—the Fascist temperament as rooted in a youthful homosexual trauma. And in his "Portrait of Machiavelli" (1950),
Moravia intimates that the peculiar quality of Machiavelli's
political passion was the consequence of sexual frustration, or
the consequence at least of an utter moral exhaustion that
Moravia perceives in Machiavelli's cold comedy of seduction,
Mandragola, and which he defines by means of a close comparison with the Marquis de Sade.

Friendship, to judge from Moravia's fiction, is determined
and measured by a man's sexual conduct toward his friend's
wife or mistress: several rather amiable items from the *Racconti
Romani* underline this criterion. Family relations are shaped
in the same manner. The theme of *Agostino* is examined in
the context of the predominantly, almost overtly sexual relation between a young mother and her child. An awareness of
that relation is the beginning of Agostino's transition to manhood, of the decline of his innocence and the toughening of his

heart: when, secretly watching his mother undress, he says to
himself—with an attitude that "seemed to him almost scientific
but which in fact owed its false objectivity to the cruelty of
sentiment which inspired it"—"She is a woman . . . nothing but
a woman." In *The Time of Indifference,* the relations between
mother and daughter, mother and son, and sister and brother
are elaborately defined by the sexual aspect as incarnate in the
businessman, Leo, who moves in the novel from an affair with
the mother to an affair with the daughter, while the brother
looks on, alternating between a dreary effort to feel morally
indignant over his family's behavior and the thought that he
might turn his sister's quasi-incestuous degradation to his own
account by borrowing money from her new lover. "L'Archi-
tetto" (1935) is a lighter and less contorted variation on this
same singular design. And when Moravia wrote his first original play (he had already dramatized his short novel *The
Fancy Dress Party*), he was drawn quite naturally to the tale
of Beatrice Cenci and her repulsive father—"since," as he has
remarked, "the relations between father and daughter . . . lend
themselves to a psychological interpretation very close to the
modern sensibility, and have indeed an almost existentialist
flavor."

These illustrations are typical. These are the inhabitants and
these the characteristic involvements in the somewhat lopsided
Moravian universe. It is to be noted that there is no historical
or religious or mythological dimension to this universe, either
pure or converted; this is one of the many ways in which
Moravia should be differentiated from D. H. Lawrence, who
may also be said to have described the world in its sexual
aspect, but with a sense of incipient force and with a rich and
tender carelessness altogether distinct from the meticulously
ordered proceedings of Alberto Moravia. Nothing, for example,
could be more alien to Moravia than Lawrence's own achievement of deep-flowing artistic conversion in *The Man Who
Died,* in which the crucified but not wholly dead Christ is re-

stored to life by the sexual devotion of a priestess of Isis. The religious impulse is thus converted into the erotic impulse in a manner that converts near death into a *vita nuova*. Moravia's view of the mythic as well as of life in general and of family relations was plainly indicated in the comment introducing his second novel, *Mistaken Ambitions*, in 1935. "In *The Time of Indifference*," he wrote, "the author tried to create tragedy based on traditional motives—those, so to say, which grow out of the tensions and disequilibria of a badly tangled family situation: those for example of Aeschylus in the *Oresteia*, or of Shakespeare in *Hamlet*."[7] It should be added, in fairness, that Moravia has recently satirized his earlier attitude by including, in *A Ghost at Noon*, a preposterous interpretation of the *Odyssey* as a bleak story of sexual incompatibility—a view of that spacious poem that Moravia's hero-narrator is permitted violently to reject.

But the literary allusions are none the less significant: for perhaps the major tactic within Moravia's broad strategy of conversion—of transforming a familiar moral note into an essentially sexual note—is to invoke the literary echo, in a partly joking and partly jaundiced manner. He is quoted as relating the scene in *The Time of Indifference* in which Leo and Carla embrace behind the curtains, their guilty pleasure heightened by peeking out at the betrayed but unsuspecting mother, to the famous "curtain scene" in *Hamlet;* and it may be, as Daniel Aaron has suggested,[8] that the seduction of Leda by the barber in *Conjugal Love* wryly re-enacts, and willfully debases, the more ancient seduction of Leda by the god as swan. In *The Time of Indifference* again, there is a manifest echo—within the context of an affair gone stale before it has started—of one of the best-known and most poignant soliloquies in Italian literature. It is the classic *addio monti* passage in chapter eight of Manzoni's *I Promessi Sposi*, the farewell of chaste Lucia to her homeland and her lover: "Farewell mountains springing from the water and rising to the sky . . . farewell house that was still not hers. . . ." This turns up in *The Time of Indifference*, echoed by Carla's soliloquy as she hastens through the inevitable rain toward her mother's lover: "Farewell streets, farewell deserted quarters," and so on. The transformation implicit in the echo depends crucially upon the purity, the firm moral character of the original.

The Tragicomedy of Existence

All of this brings us to a central quality, or combination of qualities, in Moravia's fiction, a recognition of which must modify our first impression of frankness and realism. I mean its literary and especially its theatrical quality, and its pervasive semicomic mood.

Moravia's work is to some extent impressively realistic, and it has an exceptional vividness of presentation. His words at their best provide instantaneous openings on to the actions they describe; persons and things are observed with a camera-eye exactness, tinged all the while with an elusive wistfulness; but the style to rise to—the here-and-now, sharply delineated and sadly contemplated, is everything. But his scenes stay fixed in our minds, and our recollection is that we have seen them, not read them; we recall people and places, not words and pages. This is to say, precisely, that his writing is theatrical— and theatrical, it should be insisted, rather than dramatic. Italians for twenty years have been speaking of "the Rome of Moravia"—a crowded, hurried, modernized, and mechanized Rome, full of brief-cases and cocktails and very different from the Rome of somewhat older Italian literature; for example, the poetic, heroic, archeological Rome of D'Annunzio.[9] It is true that Moravia has accomplished one of the great feats of the artist in narrative; he has created a world, and he calls it Rome. But Giuseppe Borgese was probably right when, reviewing *The Time of Indifference* in 1929, he contended against the claim for Moravia of sociological accuracy in his portrait of

Rome: "There is not much Rome here . . . the scene is made up of lights and draperies, as in certain contemporary *mises en scènes.*"

When Moravia won the Marzotto award for fiction in 1954, he was introduced, aptly enough, as "the last Goldonian in Italy." The reference was to the eighteenth century Venetian playwright, author of several scores of comedies of intrigue and manners. Moravia works assiduously in the whole tradition of Italian culture; Boccaccio, Machiavelli, Ariosto, Manzoni, and many others are very notably reflected in his writing, and he is, in fact, one of the most incorrigibly literary novelists of his generation; but he is perhaps closest to Goldoni, and reading Moravia's stories we come upon startling confrontations, the heated dinner conversations, the mistaken identities, the cross-purposes, the deceits, the peepings, the gifts or billets-doux received and mislaid and inopportunely discovered: these are what move the plot in a narrative by Moravia, and they are the devices of conventional farce.

Above all, the device of the accidental witness to the intimate or even the shameful act. The use of it is endless: Agostino, lurking outside the window of a country brothel, peering in at a prostitute and her customer; Marcello, in *The Conformist*, returned unexpectedly to his Paris apartment, hiding in the dark to watch a Lesbian make overtures to his wife; the protagonist of *Conjugal Love* happening, during an evening stroll, upon an adulterous interchange between his wife and the local barber—and a host of other such occasions. One sign of the interesting development represented by Moravia's novel, *A Ghost at Noon*, is—along with the implicit satire it contains of Moravia's own earlier attitude to myth, as mentioned above —the way the hidden-witness motif is turned back on itself. The husband in *A Ghost at Noon* finds himself on one occasion seated next to his wife, badly rattled by her obdurate attitude toward him and furtively watching the fall of her *négligé*. "Suddenly . . . I told myself that this was what I had come to at last: to look at my wife's nakedness in hiding, with the pleasure of forbidden things, like a boy who peeps through a crack in the cabin of a beach resort." That reflection, typical of *A Ghost at Noon*, suggests a deepened moral estimate of the erotic theatricality with which Moravia has for long busied himself. But for much of his earlier work, the device of the secret observer was a valid necessity. It is, to be sure, a classic motif of pornographic literature as well as of farce; but in Moravia, it is primarily a piece of theatrical mechanics, not lingered over for its own sake (if there is a truly pornographic element in any of our five novelists, it is within the paradoxes of Graham Greene) but essential to the progress of the action. It is the turning point or even the climax. For the very core of Moravia's fiction is theatrical. He begins not on a clearly felt literal level, nor even on the so-called symbolic level; he begins on a theatrical level, with the dramatis personae poised toward each other in postures of skilled artifice; and the moral content follows from there. His fiction, that is, moves under the compulsive effort of both author and character to squeeze genuine sentiment out of traditional stage business.

Now genuine sentiment, in these stories, is the first dependable mark of being alive. In fact, given the human condition reflected by Moravia, it is precisely a sentiment about being alive; the Moravian character suffers from the need attributed by Moravia to Machiavelli—the need "to feel himself alive."[10] What is gradually revealed to us as Moravia's pervasive theme, a theme even more pervasive than sex and in fact served by the erotic theme, is nothing else than the sensation of existence. This is the end to which Moravia's fiction may be seen to be pressing; and it is to this that the sexual encounter regularly and treacherously seems to promise the clue.[11] As a consequence of his theme, Moravia's stories are more ridden by anxiety than the Goldonian comedies they draw upon; the stake is so much more important. Goldoni's work, too, had its measure of realism, along with a certain hardness of tone;

Goldoni lacked the warm romantic humor, say, of Goldsmith or the rational gaiety of Beaumarchais. But his comedies were firm in outline and unstrained in manner; they centered on the complicated steps of the intrigue in question, and intrigue could provide Goldoni with a set pattern of action in which he might take a detached, if sometimes uncharitable, delight. But despite the morbid amusement they may contain, Moravia's tragicomedies of intrigue are (like *Mandragola*) darker and more desperate; for Moravia focuses not upon the intrigue but—through the intrigue—upon the encounter the intrigue was to bring about, and upon the reward the encounter was to assure; and comedy dissipates in panic as the outcome of the adventure seems ever more dubious.

Or perhaps we should say that only the laughter dissipates: the comic mood, however discolored, remains. Traditional comedy, from the Greek stage onward, has defined a particular rhythm of experience that concludes with the unmasking of impostors and the celebration of marriage. Impostors are for the most part unmasked in the fiction of Moravia, but anything like a marriage is just what dismally fails to take place. That is why his stories may more properly be called tragicomedies; and why, in this respect, they are like many of the narratives of Henry James (a writer with whom Moravia might not otherwise be easily associated)—in particular, like *The Ambassadors*, where the imposthume represented by the adultery of Chad Newsome and Mme. de Vionnet is exposed, but where the potential marriage between Strether and Miss Gostrey is fastidiously renounced. The tone of that novel is explicitly stated at the moment of renunciation: "She sighed it at last all tragically, all comically away." With a shift in pronoun, the sentence could conclude Moravia's *Conjugal Love*.

James was congenitally interested in the question of living. Moravia has been obsessed with a more radical mystery—the mystery of existence itself, the fundamental enigma that, I venture to say, has been the chief concern of Moravia's literary generation, both in Italy and elsewhere: as this book will, I trust, sufficiently testify. What the concern amounts to in Moravia's case may best be suggested by tracing through his stories the process by which he arrived at it; as the sexual intention gradually invades the whole of observable life only to pause before the threshold of the source of life itself. I have rehearsed the "sexualization" of money, politics, friendship, and family relations; to these may be added the moral virtues —courage, honor, good will, kindness, truthfulness, self-respect, all of them tested and given their meaning in sexual terms. And even beyond those, the trivial rituals of the daily round: dressing and undressing, shaving, bathing, eating and drinking, the trip to the seashore, the afternoon walk, the leisurely times in the neighborhood cafe. The same inclination energized them all, the same atmosphere surrounds them. But here and there we detect a deepening and penetration to the more elementary conditions of human survival. Health and sickness, for example: we can cite the rapidly sketched "Infermiera" (*Racconti Romani*), in which the gardener of a Roman villa fails in the courtship of his patron's nurse because the latter was more attracted by sickness than by health. Her taste was "to make love with sick people; but I, unhappily, was healthy, and so there was absolutely no hope for me." Better than that, and one of Moravia's finest novellas, is "Sick Boy's Winter," the whole of which takes place in a sanitarium, with the narrative prose faintly breathing the sterilized air of its corridors. Here, the progress of the young hero's convalescence is entirely implicated in the development and expression of his sexual pride; he seduces a wan little English girl, a fellow patient, and both he and his mute pitiful victim suffer nearly fatal relapses. In *Luca*, adolescent sexuality leads through a grave illness to the longing for death, and then onward to partial recovery and the meager promise of a new life.

Dealing as he does so persistently with the sexual element, Moravia could scarcely help sounding the note already familiar in modern literature: the ambiguous relation between sex and death; and he has not failed to offer his own erotic variation on the grand pattern of death and rebirth—for instance, the combination of murder, suicide, and impending childbirth that turgidly concludes *The Woman of Rome*. But life and death are stripped by Moravia to their innermost essence. They are very simply existence and non-existence. They are the plus and minus of radical vitality, as affected by sexual action. In the fiction of Moravia, we have a recurring picture of Eros moving between being and nonbeing. It is this that distinguishes the fiction once and for all from pornography; for the incessant peeping and pryings in Moravia's stories are, beyond pornography and even beyond farce, symptoms of an insatiable desire to catch a glimpse of the secret reality of human beings —their primary existence, what is hidden or misrepresented by public morality, conventions and clothing. They are symptoms, in short, of a hectic and self-conscious and yet ambiguous romanticism; they are symptomatic, too, of an author whose characters, as inveterate spies, are surrogates for their creator, whose work may be called the most thoroughgoing job of private espionage in modern fiction. But again, a distinction must be pressed; for as to Moravia's anatomical concern, his repeated and detailed descriptions of the naked body, what this suggests, as more than one critic has asserted, is not a salacious interest in nudity but an aptitude for still-life painting. The Italian phrase for still-life, more telling than ours, is *natura morta*; and it is exactly Moravia's ambition and that of his principal characters to transform *natura morta* into *natura viva*.

The ambition offers a peculiar challenge to Moravia's artistic talent, for existence, as it seems to be conceived in the Moravian ethic, is anything but a dramatic subject. The ethic itself contains few seeds of the dramatic; it is personal and non-philosophical in its nature; it is a feeling, rather than a theory; a mood and a tone, rather than a discourse. We could perhaps say that it is a fragment of existentialism that evaporates at the critical moments; for while Moravia's characters, like those in certain of the writings of Sartre and Camus, reach for wholeness and identity through action (through cautiously staged sexual action, in the case of Moravia), they almost always fail.[12] Carla, the heroine of *The Time of Indifference*, enters the affair with Leo out of muddled desire for a "new life": a phrase that, in typical Moravian fashion, sings ironically in Italian with its flattened reminder of Dante's *Vita Nuova*, an account of spiritual rebirth through ennobling love. And Carla fails so abysmally that she cannot answer her brother Michele when he asks her why she had behaved so. Life, as she had anticipated it, was too scanty a thing to have striven for. " 'So as to have a new life': was what she wanted to answer; but she had not the courage. That remote reason of hers, now that she saw nothing was changed except her surrendered body, appeared to her ridiculous and unworthy." Michele and his sister are the first in Moravia's long catalogue of failures: mostly masculine failures, be it noted in passing, for Moravia's women are occasionally endowed with a sort of hulking secret, just as they are given personal names (Leda, Adriana, etc.) more consistently than are the men. Moravia's heroes are apt to be small, indistinct, ill-favored, and hesitant; and there is a portion of verisimilitude here that I will not labor, both in the portrayal of Italian women and men and in the exposure everywhere on the chosen scene of the sexual preoccupation. But what the men do acquire is the consolation of a rueful humor, a still faintly comic reflection of *This is the way things are;* how foolish, ultimately, is the human posture and the human destiny. For the price of failure is to be condemned to a second-class existence, a form of nonexistence, something that is to be suffered rather than enacted. Moravia's stories are therefore, and by design, pathetic rather than dramatic; pathos is the middle and the end of his characteristic narrative.

In *Luca*, a little sum of existence is actually retrieved: enough to give this excellent short novel a rarely positive and almost (but not quite) a hopeful quality. Luca, an adolescent of good family, undergoes a nervous breakdown and is brought back from the edge of nonexistence by a robust woman who nurses him, bathes him, and finally makes love to him; but his recovery is isolated and private, almost metaphysical; it relates him to existing things qua existing, but in no sense does it relate him to humanity. The suggestion of a Camus or a Silone, that the answer to the sense of nonexistence is companionship and compassion, has yet to appear in the pages of Moravia. Hence the dispirited, prematurely exhausted quality that so often pervades these pages: the absence, that is, of creative tension. Such tension as his fiction does manage to generate is elaborately exemplified in *The Woman of Rome*, in the contrast between the natural, inframoral bias toward life of Adriana, the Roman prostitute, and the bias toward death of her succession of lovers.

Adriana has a simple capacity for existence; and it is that capacity—rather that any rage to live—that is challenged, bruised, and seduced, but never destroyed in the course of her recorded experience. For along with a talent for existence, Adriana has a distinct taste for the deathly. Her lovers are death symbols, symbols of antiexistence, recognizable variations on deadliness: and the drama they engage her in is an antic, sensual, and highly traditional *danse macabre*. Then men in her life cavort ominously before her, beckoning and grinning: Astarita, the police administrator, who looks like a death's-head and who speaks of himself as a "garbage-can for rubbish" and curses the day he was born; Sonzogno, the murderer, in whose embrace Adriana "felt a pleasure made sinister and atrocious by fear (so that) I could not restrain a long wailing cry in the dark, as if the final clasp had been the clasp of death, not of love, and my cry was life departing from me"; Mino, the hapless revolutionist, who is faithless to his calling and who tells Adriana in bed that he has "died—just died. Died forever." For her part, on her side of the bed, Adriana acknowledges the deeply seductive appeal of nothingness in a meditation of singularly erotic detail:

> I began to think about the sea again and was overcome by the longing to drown myself. I imagined it would only be a moment's suffering, and then my lifeless body would float from wave to wave beneath the sun for ages. The gulls would peck my eyes, the sun would burn my breast and belly, the fish would gnaw my back. At last I would sink to the bottom, would be dragged head downwards towards some icy blue current that would carry me along the seabed for months and years among submarine rocks, fish and seaweed, and floods of limpid salt water would wash my flesh, smoothing and refining me continually. And at last some wave would cast me up on some shore, nothing but a handful of fragile, white bones . . . and perhaps someone without noticing it would walk on my bones and crush them to white powder. With these sad, voluptuous thoughts, I fell asleep.

But Adriana survives the self-annihilating impulse of her lovers; and while Mino commits suicide and Astarita and Sonzogno deliberately get themselves killed, Adriana's tribute is the only pregnancy I can recall in Moravia's fiction.

The Supremacy of Sadness

The Woman of Rome is, on balance, a distinguished piece of fiction; but it is distinguished, I suggest, in the terms proposed above, as an image of Eros moving between being and non-being. To speak of its affinities with French realism, as some readers have done, or to identify it as an Italian *Moll Flanders*, is to miss its real quality by extracting the subject matter from the texture. The tone of Daniel Defoe and the world it informs (hard, dry, virile, and epiphenomenal) have almost nothing in common with the lyrical reflectiveness, the muffled nostalgia, that modify the happenings in *The Woman of Rome*, or any other work by Alberto Moravia. That tone is most effectively rendered, perhaps, in *Conjugal Love;* over which we may briefly linger, by way of conclusion, since it seems to me his most elegantly wrought romance of existence.

Conjugal Love has a kind of subdued perfection; and it illustrates memorably Moravia's personal sense of the poignant foolishness of human aspiration and illusion. It tends, too, to confirm the suspicion aroused by *Agostino* and *Luca* that Moravia is usually happier with the short novel (and the short story) than with the novel proper; his resources and his themes appear to lack the variety and the inward momentum that novels require. *Conjugal Love* seems aware of these limitations, and never seeks to extend itself. The husband's narration gives the impression of some tidy person leafing through his private scrapbook. For what happens in the book—more important than its plot, which is a reshuffle of Moravia's theatrical stock in trade—is the creation through the arts of narrative of a feeling or a mood: the sense of existence as suffering.

The story introduces us to a married couple of independent means, enjoying the graceful leisure of a Tuscan villa. The wife, Leda, is a fastidious and affectionate person, marked however by an observably ambivalent attitude—a combination of attraction and disgust—toward the sordid and ugly in human experience. The husband is marked by the sort of taste, intelligence, and fussy kindness—all genuine, but when taken together, pathetically inadequate—that characterized Lambert Strether, whose unlucky fate it was also, in James's *The Ambassadors*, to stumble upon an adultery that his very kindness and taste had prevented him from guessing at. Like Strether, the husband is a man of mild literary pretensions; and when we meet him, he is settling down to the composition of a story—a small work of art that will be called, of course, *Conjugal Love*. Creative power and sexual power are established in the familiar but always fertile tension of similarity and hostility: the husband's brief fit of artistic energy demands from him a marital abstinence, as his entire fund of potency is given over to his writing. We are not left in doubt over the outcome, for the tone from the beginning has reduced drama to pathos; and we foresee, without the need for bracing, the evening when the husband will discover at once his wife's infidelity and his own irrevocable failure as a novelist. But the moral of the book—and perhaps it is the moral of Moravia's fiction in general—has been reached several chapters earlier.

The husband has been puzzled by some elusive quality in Antonio, the barber who comes to shave him daily and who will eventually cuckold him—dragging from his wife the full physical expression of her fascinated revulsion. The barber's secret, the husband learns, is simply that his demure and courteous exterior masks an indefatigable Don Juan, an erotomaniac. But the husband goes on to realize that the discovery answers nothing; and his mediation at this point is almost a personal apologia of the author.

> The mystery I had noticed when I knew nothing about him survived even now when I thought I knew everything. That mystery had been pushed backwards into a less accessible zone, that was all. It was a little, I began to think, like the mystery of all things, the big and the small; you can explain everything except their existence.

The perception of the enigma of existence beneath the puzzle of devouring sexuality shapes the husband's final attitude and hence the feeling diffused through the book. The disasters, such as they are, do not spring from vicious or chronically self-willed deceitfulness. They are due to an impersonal fraudulence in the nature of things, the way things ineluctably are; and so the book closes on a note of simple acceptance—not with anger or bitterness, but with rue for remembrance and sadness for all the imaginable future. The husband confides at the end his acceptance of a second class existence, a shrunken assignment to perpetual mediocrity; he will become "a much more modest man."

Sadness is thus the supreme emotion in the Moravian universe. It is the one emotion that transcends indifference—as indifference itself is an achieved condition that transcends the vulgar credulity, the unexamined faith in human debasement, of the Antonios and the Leos. Indifference is the final response to the world in its sexual aspect; but sadness is what a man feels when he has "pushed [the mystery] backwards into a less accessible zone"; it is the only sentiment remaining to those who have arrived at the condition realized at a stroke by Moravia in the first of his novels, *The Time of Indifference*. This is why, as some Italian critics have complained, there is not much "story" to Moravia's career: his themes, his characters, his devices, his moral range were all exemplified by the time he was twenty. His story is the story of an endeavor to move beyond indifference, and for reasons of art as well as morality. Sadness is as far as he has been able to get. For what Moravia is unable to portray—because in all honesty he is unable to detect it—is a moral world in which his characters glumly move: a more remote machinery, even if it turns out to be infernal machinery, at work behind the stage machinery so prominent in the middle distance.

The absence of such a counterworld means the absence, too, of any sharply defined vision of evil; for the betrayals Moravia describes are not flanked by the persuasive imagery of innocence and conscience. There is consequently only a slight and shadowy moral tension, little actual resistance and no tragedy. At most, the minds of his characters are fleetingly troubled, not by a sense of sin, but by a sense of having forgotten something that might once have been a sense of sin. "The fault was Carla's as well," muses Michele, ". . . and his mother's, too. The fault was everyone's; impossible to discover its source, the original cause of it." And behind that, a sense, fainter than perfume in an empty room, of a lost paradise: "a paradise of reality and truth," as Michele vaguely tells himself; "a paradise where everything—gestures, words, feelings—would have a direct connection with the reality in which they had originated."

The memory of this paradise appears as an occasional mirage in the stories of Moravia, something to serve as the basis for resentment but not strong enough to promote rebellion. The representative hero of Moravia, like modern man himself in Camus's definition, feels himself a stranger "in a universe suddenly emptied of illusion and light," an exile fatally deprived "of the memories of a lost home country or the hope of a promised land." In the world of Albert Camus, revolt has gradually emerged as man's only dignifying act; but Moravia's is a world in which revolt is improbable. It lies dormant, a painless hell, undisturbed by the expectancy of a fresh revelation, a larger conversion: the conversion, perhaps, of existence into life. The contents of that world are fairly indicated in the very language of Moravia's titles (especially in the original), with their invariable allusion to indifference, contempt, sickness, weariness, poor judgment, equivocation, deceit, crime, smallness, ugliness, conformity, bitterness, unhappiness, or solitude. The word "hope" or anything like it has never appeared except once, and then in the title of an essay rather than a narrative: La Speranza. But La Speranza is not an affirmation of hope, it is a skeptical analysis of its phenomenon, and an analysis that—by defining hope as the illusory impulse that spurs men on in the endless pursuit of the impossible—permits Moravia to identify The Castle of Franz Kafka as the very type of hope-filled book.

The aspects of Moravia stressed in this chapter are the ones which ought to be stressed at this reckoning of him; they have been the defining aspects of his work over nearly three decades. But his estimate of the world has grown increasingly complex. In his most recent novel, Two Women, Moravia concludes by a clear sounding of the themes that mark him unmistakably as a central participant in the novelistic "world of discourse" of the second generation. They are the themes which will especially concern us during the rest of our discus-

sion—the radically simple interlocking themes of human compassion and of the motion from death to life which compassion
may stimulate. *Two Women* is the detailed account of life in
a refugee hideout in the mountains during the long months
between the Allied invasion of Italy and the liberation of Rome.
The experience of Cesira (the lower-class woman who tells the
story) and her daughter Rosetta—the confusion and danger and
discomfort, the singularly brutal violation of the daughter and
her subsequent moral collapse, the shocks and betrayals: all
this seems to the mother in retrospect to have been an experience of death itself. But returning to Rome at last, she remembers the reading by a heroic young neighbor-in-hiding of the
Bible story of Lazarus, the man raised from the dead by Jesus.
In the book's final words, Cesira seems to find in Lazarus a
symbol for herself and her daughter.

> Now I understood that Michele was right; and that for some
> time we had been dead, Rosetta and I, dead to the compassion we
> owe to others and to ourselves. But grief had saved us at the
> last moment; and so, in a certain sense, what had happened to
> Lazarus was true for us also; since, thanks to grief, we had come
> out of the war which had shut us up in its tomb of indifference
> and cruelty. We had begun once again to go forward in our own
> life, a poor life full of uncertainty and error, but the only life we
> had to live. . . .

It was not by accident that Ignazio Silone, as we shall see,
chose the name of Lazarus for the Italian peasant-farmer who,
in *A Handful of Blackberries*, would represent the possibility
of rebirth through the force of compassion. Both Silone and
Moravia were drawing on one of the greatest recorded symbols
of human resurrection; and both are associating the event symbolized with the sharing of pain. Nor is it, as I shall suggest, a
mere coincidence that Graham Greene's most recent work, *The
Potting Shed*, should turn on another instance, not less miracu-
lous than that of Lazarus, of a man actually and physically

restored to life. An involvement with that extraordinary event, whether it be seen as literal or metaphorical, is a determining feature of second generation writing.

But Moravia's last sentence should not be overlooked, either: "a poor life, full of uncertainty and error. . . ." No gay and splendid triumph has been envisaged or described. The human reality Moravia looks upon and delineates for us remains soiled and it remains stunted; for that is the way it does look to a writer of courage, tenacity, intelligence and very considerable talent. There is a measure of gallantry in Moravia's picture of things, and in his resolute refusal to make his picture any handsomer, or to draw on sustenance from afar. We find in his work little evidence of that larger human heroism, the sacrificial devotion to the miseries of mankind that characterizes betimes the fiction of Camus and Silone, of Faulkner and Greene and to which the word "saintly" so ambiguously applies. In this respect, too, we acknowledge Moravia's stubborn gallantry. Not everyone who says to him, "Lord, Lord," will persuade Moravia that the waiting reality is, or in any manner resembles, the Kingdom of heaven.

NOTES

1. *La Terza Generazione*, initiated in Rome in 1953, and dedicated to "solutions," other than political, of the cultural crisis of our time. The magazine was discontinued in 1957.
2. I should acknowledge here a sensible review of Moravia's career by Aldo Paladini, in the Milanese periodical *Settimo Giorno*, December 2, 1954.
3. The very form and the peculiarly haunting music of Elio Vittorini's brilliant *Conversazione in Sicilia* (1937) were a necessary and happy response to the Fascist challenge.
4. A collection of sixty-odd "short short stories" or anecdotes, published originally in newspapers and dealing with the comic or seedy side of the city of Rome. They have not all been translated into English. The one referred to here is "Il Mediatore."

5. Interview in the *New Yorker*, May 7, 1955.

6. In a review of Moravia's collection of articles, "Un Mese in URSS"; *L'Espresso* (Roman weekly), April 13, 1958. Milano continues: "For the massive facts of history . . . Moravia has the same dark respect that the phenomena of nature excite in others. This is one of the forms of Moravia's pessimism, on which his vigor as a novelist depends, as well as his analytic acumen and his antirhetoric." The book under review, incidentally, is the first collection of Moravia's journalistic writings to be published.

7. For this and for several other references, I am indebted to *Introduzione a Moravia* by Euralio de Michelis (Florence, 1954).

8. *Hudson Review*, Summer, 1951.

9. Paladini, *loc. cit.*

10. *Sentirsi vivo. Vivo* is only partly rendered by "alive"; it contains the note also of making one's presence felt, of being recognized and acknowledged.

11. After reading this chapter, which was published as a separate essay in *Modern Writing No. 3* (1956), Moravia addressed a letter to me, in English. I have permission to quote the following (dated April 13, 1957):

> It is quite true that sex has been for me the key to open many doors. The fact is that I started to write in 1925 . and in that time there were very few or no values at all which, after the terrible crisis of the so-called twenties, resisted a close examination. Everything in this faraway time seemed tottering, inconsistent, contradictory and false. There were only a few things which seemed to me solid and true and these things were connected with nature and with the less objectionable and analysable and ineffable sides of the human soul. Among these things no doubt was sex, which is something primordial and absolute. I have said the word: absolute. Looking for the absolute, it was impossible to find it then in the upper spiritual world but only in the depths of the unconscious and of the lowest and most obscure instincts of man.

12. In the letter addressed to me by Moravia, and already quoted in part, he adds the following:

> Ten years before Sartre's *Nausée*, I wrote *The Time of Indifference* which was an existentialist novel avant-la-lettre. From existence to

being it is very difficult to pass; there is a big gap between the two.
I tried hard to fill the gap, to cross the line between existence and
being. Maybe I didn't succeed.

The present chapter is clear, I hope, in its conviction that the failure
to cross the line in Moravia's novels is a failure of the characters
and not of the author; that Moravia is dramatizing a failure, but
not himself failing. In this respect, he may be compared with
Chekov. The failure of will and nerve in Chekov's plays is a quality
of his dramatis personae, and not of himself; hence Chekov may
aptly and ironically call *The Cherry Orchard* "a comedy," as I
would call most of the stories by Moravia.

8

ELIO VITTORINI:
THE OPERATIC NOVEL

Donald Heiney

The novelistic language of Vittorini is not essentially a realistic one. In a 1933 article he distinguishes between two kinds of writers: those who make you think, "Yes, that's the way it is," and those who make you think, "I had never supposed it could be like that," and in this way suggest a new mode of experience, a new "how" to existence.[1] The experience communicated in a work of fiction is of course specific, fixed to a single place on the map and a single point in time; in this at least Vittorini is a realist. But the effect on the reader (and Vittorini is as much interested in the psychology of the reader as he is in the creative process) must not be bound to or limited by this specific. "Poetry is poetry for this reason: because it does not remain tied to the things from which it originated and can be related, if it is born out of pain, to any pain."[2] This approaches the aesthetics of Mallarmé and the Symbolists; poetry is concerned not with things but with the general emotions generated by things. For the Symbolists, in fact, the poem itself is the thing, more comprehensible and more aesthetically satisfying than the imperfect world of objects.

Reprinted by permission of the University of Michigan Press from *Three Italian Novelists*, adapted. Copyright, 1968, by The University of Michigan Press.

But Vittorini does not go this far. His fiction remains tied to a world of sunshine, melons, wine, rain, human voices. Yet one of the points of his method is to demonstrate that melons and sunshine are the same for all men, to affirm the universality of sensory experience. Underlying this is a notion of solidarity, of the resemblance that links all men together in the human condition. Men feel heat and cold in much the same way, and this is a reminder that all men hunger and suffer in their lives, feel love and hate, and finally die. This concept of the community of experience is the connecting link, a tenuous and not very satisfactory one, between Vittorini's aesthetics and his politics. The sensations of the novelistic hero, which are also those of the author, are projected as possibilities for the reader and for all men. (It is important to note that they are "possibilities"; Vittorini's fiction does not so much evoke the reader's own experience as suggest new things that might happen to him.) The solidarity of feeling thus becomes the solidarity of politics; or at least Vittorini attempts to bring the two together. The difficulty is that, while all men feel heat and cold in the same way, they may not necessarily feel the same about such political questions as freedom and the artist's relation to the state. The relative failure of Vittorini's later fiction turns around this difficulty. In *Conversazione in Sicilia* (*Conversation in Sicily*) this fundamental tension is resolved more successfully than it is in any of the rest of his work. The reason is that at the point where he began to conceive this novel, in late 1936, he had finally grasped the aesthetic principle that his whole career was to turn around. And, paradoxically, the existence of censorship helped him by rendering abstract or "poetic" the overt political element that was to weaken later novels like *Uomini e no* (Men and Not-Men) and *Le donne di Messina* (The Women of Messina). Obliged to be vague and general, Vittorini turned vagueness and generality into an emotional device of great power.

Conversazione in Sicilia opens with the well-known reference to furies: "That winter I was prey to abstract furies. I won't say which, that's not what I want to tell about. But I have to say they were abstract, not heroic, not alive; some sort of furies connected with the doomed human race."[3] The furies are both inside the narrator and out. They have something to do with the newspaper placards (the Spanish war, the chest-pounding of fascism) and yet the narrator implies that he is quite privately responsible for them. Instead of an impulse to counter-attack he feels a kind of passive anesthesia. "That was the terrible part: the quietude of hopelessness. Believing the human race to be doomed and yet feeling no fever to do anything about it, an impulse, for example, to share the doom myself."[4] Did all men feel this? How to convince all men that they ought to feel this, or might feel it? "Putting the reader inside" implies at least some degree of universality, if not in the experience itself then at least in the work of art that reflects it. This is the basic task of his writing in the middle period of his career: to objectify the subjective. *Conversazione in Sicilia* is not a travelogue of Sicily, and it is not really a portrait of regional manners in the style of Verga, even though there are certain resemblances. For Verga the important events of the narrative happen to the fisherfolk who are the real characters of *I Malavoglia;* for Vittorini the events happen to the protagonist, a visitor who sees the train-travelers and Sicilian villagers from the outside, as much as he may empathize with them. These secondary characters are important, in fact, only insofar as they provoke impressions, emotions, and inward processes in the narrator. Vittorini's mature style, the style of *Conversazione in Sicilia,* is an effort to find the verbal equivalent of certain emotions. The narrator's disclaimer that the furies are "not what he wants to tell about" we may take as an artistic feint, a tactic to direct the reader's attention to the surface of the narrative before it is led to what is underneath.

This is the real meaning of Vittorini's statement that poetry "does not remain tied to the things from which it originated" and "can be related, if it is born out of pain, to any pain."

Yet the view that Vittorini is a regionalist is not entirely unsound. Sicily is used as a major setting in only two of his novels, *Conversazione in Sicilia* and *La Garibaldina*. But underlying his whole work there is a matrix of personal experience: the abandonment of primitive Sicily for an urban north, and a later attempt to recover this innocence and primitivism of his youth. The finest tale of the early collection *Piccola borghesia* (Lower Middle Class) is about a Sicilian boy who, in the middle of the war in Gorizia, plays with his northern cousins at games of the Wild West and Matto Grosso. *Viaggio in Sardegna* (A Trip to Sardinia) five years later is a slightly ironic search for the primitive, the poetic, in another island resembling Sicily; in fact when he reissued the book in 1952 he retitled it *Sardegna come un'infanzia* (Sardinia Like a Childhood). This search is simply objectified, fictionalized, in *Conversazione in Sicilia*. In Vittorini's work there is always the implication of a kind of geographical polarity: on the one hand the north, cities, civilization, white collars, books, intellectualism; on the other hand the south, the land, wine, sunshine, the basic and primitive elements of existence. Fascism he associates with the north, even though fascist policemen and bureaucrats (Mustache and No Mustache in *Conversazione in Sicilia*) are often southerners. The "screaming newspaper placards" are of the city; fascism is made out of paper, it takes over the apparatus of the city and civilization and uses it as a weapon against the country. Vittorini's origins were small-town and petty bourgeois, and in spite of his youthful experience as a construction worker he never quite made the transition to the proletariat. The workers are ostensibly the heroes of the Resistance novel *Uomini e no* and of the "Autobiografia in tempo di guerra," but his deepest emotions are always tied to childhood, to Sicily, to the sea and sun. This is precisely the difficulty with his later leftist or "collectivist" fiction: the tension between the outward political apparatus and his innermost emotions is unresolved. In *Viaggio in Sardegna,* an extremely revealing book, he begins what is ostensibly a travelogue by confessing, "I know the joy of spending a summer afternoon reading a book of adventure half-naked in a chaise-longue, by a house on a hillside overlooking the sea. And many other joys as well: of being hidden in a garden and listening to the wind barely moving the leaves (the highest ones) of a tree; or of hearing in the sand infinite sand-existences crumble and fall; or of getting up before dawn in a world of chickens and swimming, alone in all the water in the world, by a pink beach."[5] These are not precisely the joys of a dedicated revolutionist. Vittorini's retreat into primitivism is analogous to Pavese's; and like Pavese's, it is a retreat that the political part of him regarded as a kind of betrayal. The tension is especially apparent in the badly unresolved conflicts of *Le donne di Messina,* his most pretentious and yet in many ways his least successful work. In short, Vittorini's career as a writer is in some respects an unfortunate case of mistaken identity. At a certain point in his life, regarding himself as a poet in the most technical sense of the term and addressing himself to purely poetic problems, he produced a single novel that transformed the Italian literary scene to a greater degree, probably, than any other book of his generation. But he was able to maintain this purity only during a brief period of his life, the ten years or so that came to a climax in 1942. The years before 1932 are apprentice years, devoted to learning his craft against the tremendous handicaps of his lack of education. And with *Uomini e no* in 1945, and perhaps even earlier, with the "autobiographical" fragments written during the war, he turned from this poetic vocation to the problem of *littérature engagée,* to the attempt to make a "collective novel" that would reconcile the individual and political elements in his own nature. By 1946 he had practically abandoned fiction to devote himself to political questions as

editor of *Politecnico*. But the true artist is "engaged" only with
the problems generated by his own nature as an artist. If these
are political, as in Malraux, or metaphysical, as in Kafka, then
pursuing such problems is a necessary condition of his own
fulfillment. But if the artist's innermost nature is not political
then it is impractical to impose a political framework on his
talent; abstract furies are difficult to collectivize. This is the
reason for what every reader feels: that *Conversazione in Sicilia* is his only fully resolved and totally successful work of
fiction.

Vittorini has left us a record of his struggle to construct the
aesthetic framework of this novel. In the 1948 preface to *Il
garofano rosso* (*The Red Carnation*), a key document for any
serious student of his development, he describes his emotions
on seeing his first opera, a performance of *Traviata* at La Scala
probably in the fall of 1936. The Spanish Civil War had begun
a few months before.

> In those days there was a special way of going to the opera, with
> your heart full of anxiety for the news from Spain, much as I
> imagine Verdi's contemporaries were full of the Risorgimento as
> they listened to his music, and as Verdi himself must have felt as
> he composed it. But the opera itself, along with the modern con-
> ditions under which I saw and heard it, had the effect of making
> me realize that the musical drama has the power, denied to the
> novel, of expressing through its complexity some splendid gen-
> eral emotion, indefinable by nature and independent of the action,
> the characters, and the emotions portrayed by the characters.
>
> Is it music that does this? Music is for the opera what *some-
> thing* should be for the novel. Why should the novel be denied
> what the opera has in music?[6]

In a completely fresh way, bypassing the history of literature
he had never systematically studied, Vittorini had arrived at a
useful discovery about the origin of the novel. The discovery
had been made by others before him, but for him personally it
was an important one, and it was important that he worked it

out for himself. For Homer narrative and poetry had been one; likewise with Virgil, Dante, and Milton. Then came the "separation of styles," approximately in the seventeenth century. The novel, an outgrowth of biography and letter-writing, headed off in one direction and poetry continued in another. The novel became vernacular, bourgeois, factual; poetry moved increasingly toward the subjective and esoteric.

> The opera began in pure music just as the novel began in pure poetry. The opera has taken on, in its formation, a something else that is not music, just as the novel has taken on something that is not poetry. But the opera has remained music, while the novel has not remained essentially poetry. The opera has assimilated and reabsorbed into music, then reexpressed in music, all its originally nonmusical elements; the novel has not done the same for its nonpoetical elements. The opera has knitted together and the novel has split apart.

And he concludes, "To me, it is not that the novel enriched and magnified poetry by adding something to it, but that prose (the classic prose of antiquity) was more or less enriched by the poetry. So the novel marked the birth of a new kind of prose rather than a new kind of poetry."[7]

This is Vittorini's version of the "crisis in the modern novel." Naturally he was not the only one to object to the prosiness and flat factualism of modern fiction; the whole tendency of experimentalism in modern narrative, from Joyce to Proust to Pavese, can be regarded as an effort to "put the poetry back in the novel." Vittorini's particular contribution was to attack the problem with the freshness of an autodidact, and to apply to it a particular framework of rhetoric: that of the opera. When he speaks of opera it is Italian opera that is meant, and particularly Verdi. The chief impression made by operas of this kind on a person lacking in musical sensibility (e.g., Tolstoy) is the imbecility of the plot and the completely unnatural behavior of the singers on the stage. A chorus lingers singing "Andiamo, andiamo!" over and over instead of simply

leaving for the place it is so imperative to go to. Violetta, dying
of consumption at the end of *Traviata,* moves every heart with
her superb aria before she collapses. In *Rigoletto* the murdered
Gilda emerges from a sack and sings a duet with her father
as she dies. But Tolstoy misses the point that the opera is
freed from the necessity of realism through the effect of the
music. When the "something" provided by music is added to
the libretto the result is the total technical effect that Vittorini
calls *linguaggio:* ". . . that which results from the action and
the music together, as the unified language of the composer."[8]
It was a "something" comparable to music that he sought to
add to prose fiction. His new concept of the novel, at the point
where the partly unsatisfactory *Il garofano rosso* and the unfinished *Erica* lay behind him, was a form that achieved its
effects through pattern and rhythm, emotion-provoking in the
diffuse and unspecific way that opera provokes emotion, "poetic" without being bound by the conventions and limitations
of verse.

The manner of telling of *Conversazione in Sicilia* balances
two more or less antithetic elements: on one hand its generality, the Dantesque element of allegory, and on the other
hand the quite specific setting and circumstances of the action.
The narrator Silvestro is a typographer by trade and lives in
Milan even though he is Sicilian by origin; he has a "girl or a
wife" who waits for him at home, the massacres of the Spanish
War shrill at him from the headlines. The opening paragraph
is a stylistic model or matrix of the whole novel. Beginning
with the word "I," it is simultaneously vernacular and rhythmic, more intricate than it appears. As in a musical composition certain motifs or images are introduced, set aside for the
moment, and then repeated with variations; in the first paragraph furies, abstract, rain, water, shoes, recur in an inter-
mittent refrain. The paragraph ends with "a mute dream,
hopelessness, quietude." The following passage, like an aria
continued by another singer, takes up these images from where

the first has left off ("This was the worst: the quietude of hopelessness") and continues with other images which it adds in turn: blood, wine, bread, Sicilian figs and sulphur, the "lost human race." This catalog of concrete objects is an important clue to the nature, or more precisely the effect, of the abstract furies. "It meant nothing to me that my girl was waiting for me; go to her or not, or thumb through a dictionary, was the same for me; and to go out and see friends, other people, or stay at home was the same for me." The numbness of alienation extends from words (thumbing through a dictionary) to sexual experience and even to simple acts like drinking coffee and eating bread—"as though," he concludes, "I had never struck anybody, or believed this possible"—the first suggestion of a political theme, of the idea that one's relations with others can take the form of antagonism as well as friendship. This opening chapter—the novel is divided into sections averaging two or three pages each—ends with a banal and almost Chaplinesque detail, the water leaking into the narrator's broken shoes.

Like Dante's despair in the darkling wood, the spell of his isolation is broken by a message: a letter from his father. Silvestro's relationship with his family corresponds exactly to Vittorini's. At fifteen he has run away, at thirty he returns. His father is a minor railway employee who plays Macbeth in amateur theatricals—the role is a particular irony, since ambition is exactly what he is lacking in. Now he has left his wife— according to his own statement in order to run away with another woman—and asks Silvestro to keep the mother company in the Sicilian village on her name-day (which happens to be the eighth of December, the Feast of the Immaculate Conception, the first clue that her name is Concezione). Silvestro writes a conventional greeting card to his mother, takes it to the station to mail, and instead impulsively boards a train to deliver it himself. He makes the long journey to Sicily, meeting on his way various sympathetic and antipathetic people, and is reunited with his mother in a scene dominated by sensory reawakening (cactus, wood fires, the smell of a roasting herring). Quite literally his homecoming involves the ascent of a Purgatory; his mother lives at the top of a hill and he has to climb a stairway to reach her.

> There were bundles of firewood on the stairs, in front of some houses, and I climbed, and now and then there was a patch of snow, and in the cold, in the morning sun, almost noon now, I arrived finally at the top overlooking the immense country of mountains and valleys spotted with snow. There was no one to be seen, only barefooted children with feet ulcerated by chilblains and I made my way through the houses around the large Mother-Church that I also recognized as something out of my forgotten memories.[9]

The sensory and the Divine unite. Even earlier his reconciliation with other men has begun. On the train-ferry from the mainland to Messina he tries to make friends with the Sicilians who are traveling third-class—workers, laborers in the orange groves, railwaymen. "There's no cheese like our own,"[10] he tells them, munching away at the Sicilian cheese that tastes of goats and wormwood. But they are wary, taking him for a northerner even though he speaks dialect. Finally Silvestro achieves a somewhat unsatisfactory communication with one of the Sicilians, the smallest and darkest of the lot. They discuss New York and unemployment. But the Sicilian contends that unemployment is not the root of the problem. He himself is not unemployed; like the other Sicilians he works all day long in the orchards. Yet something unmentioned in the air is starving him to death. The "earth is offended"—one of the recurring images of the novel is *il mondo offeso*. And along with the offended earth goes the doomed humanity of the opening chapter. "I have to say the furies were abstract, not alive; furies connected in some way with the lost human race."[11] This "doom" is in one sense political, but the political is connected to everything else. It is because of fascism that

man can no longer enjoy bread and friendship, or is it because
he has forgotten how to enjoy bread and friendship that fascism has so easilly enslaved him?

The political thread of the narrative comes to the surface,
somewhat more overtly this time, in the following passage
dealing with the train journey from Messina to Siracusa. Taking his seat in a compartment, Silvestro hears two "baritones"
speaking in dialect in the corridor outside. These voices belong
to Coi Baffi and Senza Baffi (Mustache and No Mustache),
two fascist agents who conduct a kind of duet in which they
complain to each other the "lack of respect and consideration"
of people in general, and especially those they are obliged to
arrest. "In Lodi, my barber." "My landlord, in Bologna."
"They have no respect." "They have no consideration." The
words *police* and *fascist* never break through to the surface,
and this is not only because the novel was published under
censorship. The passage deals with an immediate and local
political phenomenon, and yet in another sense its implications
are general or universal. The effect achieved is something like
that of the Expressionistic drama: character is depersonalized
and turned to type, while at the same time retaining enough
surface detail to lend an impression of concretion. Mustache
and No Mustache are a piece of local color, "two Sicilians of
the carter variety," but they are also all men who become
policemen, sergeants, jailers because they like to bully others.
Naturally the threat of censorship that loomed over the book
is an important factor in setting the tone of this passage and
others. The effect of censorship was precisely to encourage a
style of ambiguity, a style which is vague on the surface but
speaks quite precisely to those who possess the key. This
tendency to abstraction, to a style of suggestion rather than
overt statement, is evident in a number of other writers who
developed under fascism, from Moravia to critics like Alberto
Carocci. Like the argot of prisoners, it is a language that proceeds on two levels, an overt surface and a concealed or semi-

concealed code. This "duplicity" or tendency to say two things at once, it goes without saying, is also characteristic of poetry itself.

On a simple level this technique is demonstrated by the passengers in Silvestro's compartment, who begin discussing the two fascists outside in veiled terms: "Don't you notice the smell?" "The smell? What smell?" "What? Don't you notice it? I mean that smell out there." The passengers really have no ideological objection to dictatorship in principle; their politics is simply a hatred of the police, which they connect, quite soundly, to the hunger that drives them to eat sour oranges. Mustache and No Mustache understand this even though they are not very bright, and recognize their fellow Sicilians as their enemies precisely because they are hungry.

> "Every starving man is a dangerous man," said No Mustache.
> "How could he not be? capable of anything," said Mustache.
> "Of robbing," said No Mustache.
> "That goes without saying," said No Mustache.
> "Stabbing."
> "Undoubtedly," said Mustache.
> "And of lending himself also to political crimes," said No Mustache.[12]

This might be a duet of two pompous courtiers in Verdi, for example from *Rigoletto*. In actual fact *Rigoletto* was censored because the Austrian regime suspected, probably correctly, that it contained a political message in code. In Vittorini's novel the political implications remain, for the most part, at this "operatic" level, a level that is emotional and aesthetic rather than ideological in any overt sense. In the train scene Mustache and No Mustache are balanced off by the Great Lombard, another abstracted or semi-depersonalized character who shares some of their physical qualities: ". . . a Sicilian, large, a Lombard or Norman possibly from Nicosia, a carter type like the voices out in the corridor, but authentic, forthright, and tall, with blue eyes."[13] He is one of the several Virgils of the novel, an encourager and guide to the uncertain traveler Silvestro. He ingenuously tells everything about himself: he is a landowner from Leonforte in the Val Demone, he has "three beautiful female daughters," and when he rides his horse about his estate he feels like a king. But he does not feel at peace with other men. "We are a sad people, we others."[14] The English translator Wilfrid David renders *noi* here as "we Sicilians"—but is it not as well all who suffer under tyranny, all the disenfranchised of the earth? The Great Lombard goes on to explain, or merely to remark calmly, that he believes man is ripe for new duties—not merely to rob and kill (the Abyssinian War?), not even to be a good citizen (conformity in a fascist state), but to do something "for the sake of our conscience in a new sense."[15] A naive passenger asks him, "Are you a Professor?" and this provokes general laughter. But if he is not a Teacher, or a Prophet, what is he? He is a man, but he is "more a man," *más hombre, più uomo.* This is another of the key phrases of the novel, and in order to define the exact implications of it, it is necessary to go back again to Vittorini's account of the writing of *Conversazione in Sicilia.*

> My thoughts came out of my needs, as my needs came out of the life I was living then, and the good will I felt toward the things of the earth and toward men. *Más hombre,* I thought. I believed I had caught these two Spanish words out of what was for me the Spanish War: the nights of listening to Radio Madrid, Radio Valencia, Radio Barcelona with my fellow workers; my thought was nothing more than *más hombre,* nothing more specific or rational. What does *más hombre* mean? "More a man," I suppose; this is what it meant to me as I wrote the book that was to be *Conversazione,* and my way of thinking about the novel I sketched above is a way that now, at last, I can explain—now that I have written other books and gone on seizing every chance I could get of seeing a good classic opera.[16]

It is necessary to be aware of this passage in order to grasp that, when the expression *più uomo* recurs in *Conversazione in*

Sicilia, there is a connection in Vittorini's mind to the Spanish War and all its political implications. The phrase is not very clearly defined either as a literary image or as a political concept; it is deliberately left diffuse. But the implication is clear that fascism is man-destroying—that Mustache and No Mustache have become dehumanized puppets, whereas the Great Lombard and the others of the novel who "feel the need of doing something for the sake of conscience" are reinforced and enhanced in their humanity. This is connected to Silvestro's own inability, in the early part of the novel, to feel or love anything in the world around him; fascism anesthetizes the feeling and desiring part of man, leaving him in the "quietude of hopelessness."

This metaphorical framework of the Great Lombard and *più uomo* recurs frequently in the remainder of the novel. Somewhat later Silvestro, in a conversation with his mother, inquires whether his grandfather was a Great Lombard. When the mother asks what a Great Lombard is, he merely replies, "a man." This leads to a kind of repetitive litany that continues for several pages: Silvestro cites one quality after another of the Great Lombard (large stature, much hair, blue eyes), the mother denies in turn that the grandfather had any of these qualities, and Silvestro insists that he was nevertheless a Great Lombard. The repetition is not syntactically rigid; there are backings and turnings, divagations in which the mother remarks that in Nicosia they make bread with hazelnuts on top or that she once had a pitcher from Aidone. But in its singsong return to the same refrain the passage is as invariable and monotonous as a children's chant. It arrives finally at the question for which all the other questions have been only preparation: "Didn't he say that our present duties are obsolete? That they are rotten, dead, and there's no satisfaction in performing them? . . . Didn't he say there was a need for other duties? New duties, not the ordinary ones? Didn't he say that?"[17] The mother doesn't remember whether he said this or not. But she

does remember that "basically" he wasn't content with the
world, but was content with himself. Clearly the grandfather
was *più uomo*, a giant who spoke straight and saw clearly; a
Great Lombard.

Technically this scene is an ingenious piece of indirection;
the innuendo of the dialogue is always present under the surface but never emerges, or emerges only in cryptic form in the
reference to "new duties." The logic it follows is that of a
submerged track of emotion, Silvestro's gradual realization
that there are other men who share his state of mind and are
capable of taking action against the "furies." In this process of
awakening the mother herself performs an important function,
although she herself is unaware of it. In the quasi-religious pattern of allegory underlying the novel she represents charity,
the Latin *caritas*. This has nothing to do with philanthropy
either organized or unorganized; it is simply the state of mind
of selfless love. It is the mother, first of all, who reintroduces
Silvestro to the lost sensory world of his boyhood: lentils,
dried tomatoes, rosemary, wine, melons, herring. Her *caritas*
begins with acceptance of the world, of the hard and vivid
sensations of existence. Together she and Silvestro recall a
playful ritual that she and the children used to repeat. She
would hide the melons in a place they could never find for all
their searching ("It was as though you were hiding them inside
yourself"[18]), then every so often, on Sunday, she would produce one as if by magic. It was for this that they called her
Mamma Melon. The melon and the fish, along with her name
Concezione, are three of the four motifs that define the mother.
The fourth is her function as a village nurse: she goes daily on
her rounds from one house to another giving injections to the
sick. The untrained or half-trained *infermiera* who lives by
giving injections is an Italian institution, but in the pattern of
the novel the mother is something a little more complicated.
In his manner of portraying her going from house to house
injecting health into the sick, encouraging them to eat, bring-

ing always light and warmth with her since a fire must be
made to sterilize her instrument, there is no doubt that Vittorini intended her as a quasi-religious figure. She even announces as she enters each house, "I have my son with me,"
and the reaction of the villages is one of a dignified and suit-
able respect ("You've made him big like yourself").[19] The
women who sit around the bed of the sick man are "like nuns,"
and the darkness of their huts is the mysterious darkness of
the church. There is no inconsistency here with Vittorini's
leftism and anticlericalism, or if there is a contradiction it is
only superficial. The mother herself explains this point in
speaking of the grandfather, who was "a great socialist, a great
hunter, and great on horseback when he rode in the procession
of Saint Joseph." When Silvestro asks how he could be a socialist and yet believe in Saint Joseph, she tells him scornfully,
"He had enough brains to do a thousand things at once. He
was a socialist because he understood politics. . . . But he could
believe in Saint Joseph." But, Silvestro objects, wasn't the
procession a thing of the priests? "You're an ignoramus! The
procession was horses and men on horseback. It was a caval-
cade."[20] The men rode on horseback and honored the saint precisely because they were men and not because the priests told
them to; in the same way the mother gives injections out of
humanity and not for the few pennies that, for the most part,
she does not even receive. Her *caritas* is a quality of character,
and consistent with, or even connected to, her quite human
fallibility. (She contradicts herself frequently, saying at one
time that it is worse if the man is sick and at another time it
is worse if the wife is sick, and she even confesses to Silvestro
a marital infidelity.) The mother personifies a concept basic to
the novel: that the religious impulse may exist outside the organized Church, and even, under conditions like those of
fascism, in opposition to the organized Church.

   These injection-rounds of the mother play an important
part in the change going on inside Silvestro himself, a change

that it would not be inappropriate to call a "conversion." The theme of the rediscovery of sensory experience assumes slightly comic overtones when the mother insists that he witness the injection of a shapely widow to "see how well-made she is." Silvestro is embarrassed, the widow struggles, and the mother finally unveils her perfections; in the end all three are flushed and pleased. The innocent eroticism of this scene is a pendant to the opening passage of the novel, in which Silvestro explains that going to bed with his girl or thumbing a dictionary is all the same for him. Furthermore this rediscovery of the sensory involves a rediscovery of the poor, of the emotional ambience of the poor. This thematic element comes to the surface particularly in the curious twenty-sixth chapter, a kind of abstract or depersonalized portrait of a Sicilian family in which the children out of hunger "devour chair-legs, and would like to devour their father and mother."[21] This in turn leads to a kind of essay or meditation by Silvestro on the subject of the humanness of humanity. The motif of *più uomo* is reiterated and reinforced, and the "operatic" repetition of motif reaches back all the way to the opening of the novel. The abstract furies are not specifically mentioned, but their attendant images—rain, broken shoes, the massacres in the headlines—come to the surface again.

> But perhaps every man is not a man; and the whole human race is not human. This is a doubt that comes, in the rain, when you have broken shoes, water in your broken shoes, and nobody in particular your heart is concerned with, no particular private life, nothing done and nothing to do, nothing to fear, nothing to lose, and you see, over there outside yourself, the massacres of the world. One man laughs and another man weeps. They're both men; the one who laughs has been sick too, he is sick; but he laughs *because* the other weeps. He can massacre, persecute, and if you, in your despair, see him laughing over the newspapers and the headlines, you don't go over to him but instead you weep, in your quietude, with the other who weeps. Not every

man is a man, then. One persecutes and other is persecuted; and the whole human race is not human, but only that part that is persecuted.[22]

This passage combines the operatic style (the repetition of the first sentence, the recurrence of laughing, weeping, water, broken shoes) with a technique something like that of the Elizabethan soliloquy, the essence of which is that the mind is seen in the *process* of working out its thoughts rather than presenting the thoughts in their final form. Beginning with the hypothesis that "perhaps" every man is not a man, the passage goes on to speak of doubts, of persecution, of laughing and weeping, and comes finally to the working-out of its logic: "Not every man is a man, then." All this is provoked in Silvestro's mind by the shabby and obscure sufferings of the poor, while the mother, that imperfect Madonna, injects them with healing medicines. When he asks his mother what she thinks of these people her reply is characteristic: "I think that perhaps they won't pay me."[23]

This whole development of political and religious emotion comes to a climax in Silvestro's encounter with the knife-grinder Calogero, a scarecrow-like figure who is half chimney-sweep out of Dickens and half a crazy kind of saint. He meets the knife-grinder immediately after another soliloquy in which the "offended world," impiety, slavery, and injustice are mentioned again. Chapter thirty-three, Silvestro's first dialogue with Calogero, is perhaps the most striking passage in the novel. Physical impressions of the knife-grinder (the blackness of his face and clothes, the light that gleams "from various parts of his person and his cart" are alternated with an "operatic" dialogue par excellence. "Sharpen, sharpen!" the knife-grinder repeats. "Haven't you got anything to sharpen?" For a time Silvestro fails to grasp what the conversation is about, exactly as he did earlier in the talk about the "smell" in the train compartment. Don't the people hereabouts give him anything to sharpen, he asks the knife-grinder? "Nothing much worth while. Nothing much worth the trouble. Nothing much that gives pleasure." But surely the people in the country-side have knives, scissors? The knife-grinder denies this. Then what do they give him to sharpen? "That's what I ask them," he cries back. "What will you give me to sharpen? Will you give me a sword? Will you give me a cannon? And I look them in the face, in the eyes, and I see that what they've got can't even be called a nail." Silvestro, and the reader, are drawn gradually into the innuendo. Skirting cautiously, the knife-grinder comes finally to his conclusion as Silvestro, in his soliloquies, comes to the working-out of his own thought. "Sometimes I think it would be enough for everybody to have their teeth and nails sharpened. I'd sharpen them into viper's-teeth and leopard-claws. . ."[24] They wink, speak secretly into each other's ears, and cry "Ah!" What they say to each other Silvestro does not reveal, just as Dante is taciturn over his conversation with the five great poets in Limbo: "Then we moved on toward the light, speaking of things of which to remain silent is well here, just as it was well to speak of them there." In this chapter the problem of the specific and the general is solved to perfection. The knife-grinder is a vivid concretion; the reader sees his "gleaming person" and hears his speech. But the political implications *remain* implications, remain abstract, and this lends them a universality that extends beyond the local and temporary problem of fascism. It is for this reason that *Conversazione in Sicilia*, while a "revolutionary" novel in a general and ethical sense, manages to transcend the limitations of a political tract, even so skilled a one as Malraux's *L'espoir*. It manages to do this because Vittorini, for all his concern with politics, is primarily an artist and relates to the writing of his novel primarily in artistic rather than politic terms. The concept of the autonomy of art recurs frequently in Vittorini's essay; like Moravia he rejects the Marxist concept of art as a "superstructure" explainable in terms of the economic and political conditions that produce it. We are no longer involved in Homeric politics in any direct way, in other words it does not really matter to us who wins the Trojan War, and yet we still read the *Iliad* with pleasure. This can only be because Homer, beginning from certain specific political events, has managed to generalize his narrative to the point where anyone who has ever experienced human emotions can associate himself with it.

Vittorini's problem is not precisely parallel to Homer's. For one thing several centuries intervened between the events of the Trojan War and the final form of the poem as we have it, and a number of different hands modified the poem in this long process of universalization. The Greeks of the Pisistratan period were hardly more involved in Homeric politics than we are. But Vittorini was involved in fascist politics; fascism interfered with his artistic development and had the power to deprive him at any time of his freedom or even his life. There is therefore a control, an irony, in his half-veiled allusions to political conditions, but there is no Homeric serenity. It is this pressure under the surface, in fact, that produces the characteristic and strangely powerful effect of the novel. As it progresses and passes its point of climax—the dialogue with the knife-grinder—the narrative becomes successively more personal; Silvestro develops from a passive narrator into the central figure of his own story. He gives a little penknife to Calogero to sharpen, and it is this negligible weapon that establishes a bond between them. Except for the train journey itself this is, significantly, his first overt action. For the rest of the novel pointed objects are equivalent to anti-fascist possibilities. Furthermore there is the unspoken implication that the novel itself —not only the novel as a form but the very novel we are reading —can be one of these "pointed objects."

This rather important connection is first suggested in the following scene in which Calogero and Silvestro go to visit the harness-maker Ezechiele, "someone who owns an awl,"[25] as Calogero describes him. Ezechiele asks Calogero whether, by chance, he has come to borrow the awl. But Calogero replies that there will be no need of it this evening, since he has found a friend who has a blade. The harness-maker comments that he is glad to hear this, and adds, "The world is offended, but not yet in here."[26] This somewhat mysterious phrase identifies him as one of the secret order of men of good will—an order that includes Silvestro himself, the little Sicilian on the train, the Great Lombard, and now the new friends who gather in the harness-maker's shop. Ezechiele—who has a prophet's name—is another in the succession of guides who help to free Silvestro from the abstract furies. "The world is big and beautiful," he tells Silvestro, "but it has been much offended. Everyone suffers for himself, but not for the offended world, and so the world goes on being offended."[27] There is no doubt that in the figure of Ezechiele the "possibility" of anti-fascism is specifically connected to writing, to the literary vocation. He has a "kind of notebook" on a little table, along with a pen and ink, and with these he "spends his days like an ancient hermit" writing the history of the offended world. If any further testimony is needed that a pen can be a blade, the knife-grinder immediately shouts, "Knives, scissors, pikes."[28] It is obvious that Vittorini has projected himself into Silvestro the linotype-operator, whose job it is to put letters together and who suffers from abstract furies. But there is no doubt that the abstract concept of Writer, or artist-as-revolutionary, is connected as well to this Ezechiele who records the history of the offended world, and who greets Silvestro in some mysterious way as a brother.

After his acceptance into the Calogero-Ezechiele group Silvestro returns to his mother's house and there encounters the last of the prophetic figures of the novel: the ghost of his brother Liborio, who has evidently been killed in the war. The dialogue tone, wry and ironic in the earlier conversations, now becomes genuinely tragic. "Do you suffer much?" "Millions of times . . . For every printed word, for every spoken word, for

every millimetre of erected bronze."[29] Silvestro is a typographer; in the air is the unspoken implication that it is he who
prints the words, who aids those who erect the bronze. Like
Aeneus trying three times to embrace Creusa only to have his
arms close on empty air, he tries three times unsuccessfully
to offer the ghost a cigarette, and finally shouts, "Take it,
then" into the night. In this final episode the motif of personal
involvement or commitment emerges unmistakably as the dominant note, one that, like the theme of an operatic finale,
gathers and assimilates the earlier motifs of the work. In this
involvement Silvestro, the author, and the reader are merged
into a single consciousness, a consciousness that becomes
"more man" in its recognition of the frailty and guilt of common humanity. There is no mistaking the skill with which this
is done. The conventional apparatus of the scene—the dream,
the ghost, the banal religious symbolism—are no more damaging to Vittorini's final effect than similar conventions are to
Verdi's. The narrative has been freed from the banality of its
events and devices by "something which does for the novel
what music does for the opera." The encounter with Liborio is
a moving, strange, and original scene; there are few passages
to match it in Italian literature or the whole of modern writing.
It is followed by a kind of epilogue in which the mother washes
the feet of a stranger who turns out to be the father: a prodigal
father greeted by a forgiving son. But even this rather banal
piece of allegory is saved by the oblique and poetic manner of
its presentation.

NOTES

1. *Diario in pubblico* (Bompiani, 1957), 58. All translations of this
and subsequent citations are my own.
2. Ibid., 198.
3. *Conversazione in Sicilia* (Bompiani, 1953), 8. Hereafter cited as
CS.

4. *CS*, 8.
5. *Sardegna come un'infanzia* (Mondadori, 1952), 9.
6. "Truth and Censorship: The Story of *The Red Carnation*," *The Western Humanities Review*, IX (Summer, 1955), 203. This American version of the preface to *Il garofano rosso* is based on a text revised by Vittorini himself for translation and differing in some respects from the original.
7. Ibid., 204f.
8. Ibid., 204. This passage has been retranslated for this present article.
9. *CS*, 51.
10. *CS*, 15.
11. *CS*, 8.
12. *CS*, 24.
13. *CS*, 27.
14. *CS*, 29.
15. *CS*, 31.
16. "Truth and Censorship," 205. Retranslated for present article.
17. *CS*, 85.
18. *CS*, 75.
19. *CS*, 107.
20. *CS*, 66.
21. *CS*, 120.
22. *CS*, 122.
23. *CS*, 123.
24. *CS*, 160–163.
25. *CS*, 167.
26. *CS*, 168.
27. *CS*, 172.
28. *CS*, 172.
29. *CS*, 200.

9 MYTH AND DEATH IN CESARE PAVESE'S
THE MOON AND THE BONFIRES

Gian-Paolo Biasin

On August 27, 1950, Cesare Pavese committed suicide in a hotel room in Turin. But today his work remains more alive, tender, and disturbing than ever. It is true, as Fulvio Longobardi says, that

> it is up to the living to bury the dead: they sometimes return at night, when work is finished or postponed, and the children are sleeping; and they threaten our solitude, the niche we have made for ourselves, they ask our reason for going on: we know why they are dead, but we don't know why we are living.[1]

On the other hand it is also true, as Roland Barthes says, that

> death has another importance: it denies the reality of the author's signature and makes the work a myth: anecdotal truth endeavors unsuccessfully to become symbolic truth. . . . By destroying the writer's signature, death establishes the truth of the work which is an enigma.[2]

Certainly, Pavese's work helps us to understand the human reasons for his need to write, for his suffering and for his death; yet it remains fundamentally enigmatic, rich in a

Reprinted by permission of Cornell University Press from *The Smile of the Gods*, trans. Yvonne Freccero. Copyright, 1968, by Cornell University Press.

symbolism, significance, and ambiguity, which are not concerned directly with the author, and which, perhaps, more directly concern us.

In analyzing the enigma of Pavese's work, his last novel, *La luna e i falò* (*The Moon and the Bonfires*, New York, 1954),[3] appears to be the *summa* of his poetical themes and achievements, the culmination of his search. After the universal and metaphysical experience of *Dialoghi con Leucò*, 1947 (*Dialogues with Leucò*, Ann Arbor, 1965), Pavese could finally understand the sub-lunar world; he was now able to understand man's true nature, see himself in relationship with others, judge his own position in history, lucidly and tormentedly, at first, in *La casa in collina*, 1949 (*The House on the Hill*, New York, 1961) and then peacefully and poetically in *The Moon and the Bonfires*. In the latter novel there is total comprehension of himself in a historical context, and, as a result, total acceptance of self and world. This acceptance and comprehension is expressed in Pavese's own poetic images. Thus the poetic myths of *The Moon and the Bonfires* are meant to signify not mystify. They express precisely and definitively the dichotomy of contemplative man cut off from the world of action—a fundamental theme in poetry and narrative from Leopardi to Pirandello, and from Svevo to Montale. They are no longer an "escape into metaphor" but a whole life made into word, memory, poetry.

Thus all the themes Pavese had put into his previous works and examined fragment by fragment with increasing depth are revived in *The Moon and the Bonfires* and encompassed in their totality, in a supreme effort to understand the "monolith." In this novel all Pavese's great themes are fused into a poetic whole and only the exigencies of analysis (and therefore of clarity and critical comprehension) can induce us to separate them in order to reveal their components: solitude, poised between inability to communicate and participation; love and violence; work and holiday; childhood and death; nature and history; myth and destiny; maturity. This unity of themes contains within it and concludes, like a cycle, all Pavese's work, and world vision. And since basically the cycle is a return we shall begin our analysis of *The Moon and the Bonfires* from the return.

As a preliminary we notice that the narrator "Anguilla" ("eel," a nickname which in itself is emblematic, though perhaps unconsciously, in that eels swim back up the mountain streams and return to their birth-place, "to the paradise of fertilization" as Montale says) has a tendency to escapism, a contemplative disposition fed and stimulated by his friend Nuto, and felt as a personal destiny preordained since childhood. There is a further indispensable element for the understanding of Anguilla's escapism: the desire for improvement, for confirmation that he could build his life, like Leopardi, who "would rather be unhappy than mediocre" and this we see when the adult Anguilla stands at the window of the *albergo dell'Angelo* and feels "like a mayor looking down from the balcony of the town hall." It is interesting to note that all Anguilla's activity is completely external to the novel: it precedes it or is introduced by means of memories or allusions, but it is not an integral part of the narative nor of the personality of the narrator.

In order to satisfy his longing for escape Anguilla, the dreamy contemplative boy, had to leave; but the years have merely taught him the need to return, and this sets the tone of the novel from the very first paragraph: "To find somewhere where you belong so that you are worth more than the usual round of the seasons and last a bit longer." It is clear that the need to return is a suffering and is profoundly linked to the awareness of its limitation: Anguilla is a bastard and therefore his return is not a return to family or ancestors (after the manner of Herodotus),[4] but rather a search for his own individuality, in perfect harmony with his own contemplative nature. The death or absence of the father of the protagonist who is

seeking self-affirmation is not a new theme either in Pavese
or in Italian literature in general; through the rediscovery of
the countryside, particularly, it reminds us of the childhood
memories of Rousseau and of George Sand's *François le
Champi*, and then of the rustic novel of Carcano, of Nievo,
right up to its various developments in Verga, Pirandello,
Tozzi, Svevo, Morante and Gadda. Thus the return signifies
the self taking root and becoming aware of human *durée* in
contrast to the impassive cycle of the natural seasons. A similar
antithesis is described in Pavese's diary in the following terms,
apparently only paradoxical in the context of this particular
problematic:

> In life, there is no return. As the seasons come around, the pass-
> ing years color the same theme in ever-different ways. The
> beauty of our own discordant rhythm—moderation and inven-
> tion, stability and discovery—is that age is an accumulation of
> equally important things, growing richer and deeper all the time.[5]

In life there is no return, because, even if one can return to the
scene of one's childhood, there is no going back in time: on the
one hand impassive nature repeats its vital cycles, and in this
sense one can say "among the hills time stands still" and the
narrator can delude himself into thinking he can find himself
in the natural cycle, return to the womb of the mother earth—
in brief, ecstatic, mythical moments. But on the other hand
time really does pass and in this sense the unchanging seasons
stand in opposition to the years which bring awareness, profundity, maturity:

> To make a long story short, I was a man too. I was someone else
> —if I had indeed found La Mora as I had known it the first winter,
> and the summer after, and then summer following winter again,
> day and night through all these years, I certainly wouldn't have
> known what to do with myself. Maybe I came from too far away
> —I didn't belong to this house any more, I wasn't like Cinto now,
> the world had changed me.

There come to mind the words which Verga puts in the mouth of 'Ntoni in *I Malavoglia* (*The House by the Medlar Tree*): "When someone leaves his home it's better never to go back, because everything changes while one is away, and even the faces with which they look at one are changed, and one seems to have become a stranger oneself." In fact time silently influences the aspect of people and things, their very existence; Anguilla, no less a stranger than 'Ntoni, or Clelia in *Tra donne sole*, 1949 (*Among Women Only*, New York, 1968) when she returns to her own district of Turin, recalls the old peasants who had brought him up and refers to them as being "like all the people who are gone now" as if there were no other people from his village. From the discordant rhythm of nature and time Pavese gathers the fundamental unity of personal experience: "It was strange how everything was changed and yet the same . . . Everything had the taste, the smell, the colour of long ago." Equality and change, immutability and innovation are intertwined and inseparable in things and persons. And so, rather than the myth of return, it is total comprehension of life and the world (in their mystery, ineffability, inseparability and contradiction) which is the basis of *The Moon and the Bonfires*. Without a doubt it constitutes its deepest and truest maturity and poetry, in figures and rhythms which are unforgettable.[6]

The environment of the novel is provided by the Langhe hills with America in the background. The "bitter America" of chapters III, XI and XXI (three key chapters in their symmetrical position in the novel, at the beginning, middle and end), apart from echoing Pavese's literary debut as translator from the American, has the precise function of revealing to the narrator and clarifying for him his own solitude: from the "lights of San Francisco"—an echo of all the city lights in *Lavorare stanca*, 1936 (*Work Is Wearying*)—and from the "din of the cicadas and frogs" in the hills of California, to the empty landscape of the desert seen in a hallucinating perspective,

America always seems to arouse a feeling of tremendous solitude which in itself immediately rouses fear, followed by
thoughts of violence.[7]

The hills, which have been the *leit motif* of Pavese's poetry
since *Work Is Wearying*, are inseparable, even in the novel,
from the human substance of the narrative: everything is dominated by Gaminella, "a hill like a planet," "all vineyards and
overgrown watercourses." It was in the hills that Anguilla first
discovered the world: work and the toil of the fields, the joy
of festivals with bonfires, the first vague feelings of love for
Irene and Silvia, violence and death, the lunar fixity of destiny.
As always Pavese is at his best when he is describing a "festival
night" or an "August holiday" in the hills, with the bonfires
which are lit at night for the feast of John-the-Baptist.[8] Even
the dichotomy work-holiday has been overcome in the description of the landscape in which vineyard and waste land coexist
harmoniously, evoking a feminine image; and the moon, the
symbol of destiny and atemporality, is linked to the vineyards
on the hills: "the vineyards lying white under the moon" often
appear in the novel, giving it a shudder of tragedy. There is in
fact a great deal of tragedy in the form of violence and death in
the novel. It is primarily concentrated in the figure of Valino,
"dark and thin, with eyes like a mole," who would beat his
women like Vinverra in *Paesi tuoi*, 1941 (*The Harvesters*, London, 1961), and like one of Vico's peasants. In Valino is concentrated, physically first and then emblematically, the failure
of the Resistance to shatter the *mezzadria,* a typical Italian
agricultural and bourgeois institution, which has only recently
been modified by the impetus of industrialization, and yet, even
after the Second World War, it was often synonymous with
exploitation and misery, especially in the not very fertile regions of the Langhe hills, and presented a continual source of
stifled bitterness among the social classes. "To divide out the
harvests with the scales" is not only unjust, but harmful on a
psychological plane. In the figure of Valino Pavese was able to

describe this situation with brief touches of resentment and emotion, connecting it in an unexpectedly poetic and intense movement to Anguilla's destiny and the failure of his return to childhood:

> [Valino] had never got out of the valley of the Belbo. Without meaning to, I came to a stop on the path and thought that if I hadn't run away twenty years before, this would have been my fate too. And yet I have gone on wandering about the world and he has wandered over these hills without ever being able to say, "This land belongs to me. On this bench I shall grow old. In this room I shall die."

Valino will disappear from the scene by hanging himself after having killed his women and burned his house out of desperation and misery—a tragic bonfire, not festive like those for John-the-Baptist.

But above all, when talking of violence we must notice how heavily the dead weigh on the narrative: the dead from the civil war, the Germans, the Fascists, and the partisans, all united in the same pity, starting with the final pages of *The House on the Hill,* and seeming a repetition of ancient sacrifices, a prelude to the idea of destiny, and yet a negative contrast since so many of the bodies found remain unidentified; the man who dies unidentified dies without achieving individuality and awareness at least of the act which seals his life (the episode of the gypsies is a good example of this). Moreover, especially in chapters XII and XIII, it is from the discovery of the unknown dead and the political speculation that the local priest weaves around them, that Pavese gets the impetus for one of the liveliest portrayals of our recent history, the transition from Resistance to peace with all its compromises and the political-social involutions involved in it, of which Valino is the most tragic witness. Finally it is the thought of the unknown dead whch provides the emotional and psychological impetus, half-way through the novel, for the re-evocation of all the narrator's other known and beloved dead: especially Irene,

Silvia and Santa. Thus an almost perfect fusion is achieved between individual and social datum, between the personal and the historic, between documentation and elegy.

At this point it would be best to concentrate on the three characters Anguilla, Nuto and Cinto in whom are embodied other Pavesian themes. As usual these characters are not immediately disclosed in their totality, they gradually acquire substance and their physiognomy is outlined bit by bit as we see them act and talk, in relation to things and people.

In Anguilla, the contemplative narrator, the bastard who "must be the son of a mountebank and a nanny-goat," the boy and the man coexist, almost like two characters, one of which explains the other. Here is the boy: "at La Mora I learnt a trade. . . . I was Anguilla and I was earning my keep"; his working life was calm, broken up by pleasant breaks like the hours spent naked with his companions on the banks of the Belbo (it will be remembered that in all the other references to nudism in Pavese, it was considered an effort at identification of self with nature and one's origins, whereas here there is no longer an effort or even a trace of decadentism: "we *were* the whirlpool" of life, as boys, without knowing it). As he grows older Anguilla gets to know the world, watching closely what happens around him; Nuto, his great friend, helps him to learn. It is Nuto, for example, who suggests that he take up music (but Anguilla doesn't succeed and thinks only about travelling): it is Nuto who pushes him to study, with the same attitude as Pablo's in *Il compagno*, 1947 (*The Comrade*, London, 1959): " 'They're books,' he said, 'read what you can of them. You'll never be anything if you don't read books.' " By reading this way, Anguilla learns a lot too about other people, their ideas, sentiments, relations. But fundamental to our understanding of Anguilla's character is his attitude to Irene and Silvia, with whom his relationship is primarily and quite literally an Hegelian one of slave and master (therefore an inferior's relationship to a superior, composed of timidity, embarrassment and fear); this relationship gradually evolves into one of mediation, composed of admiration, longing, and unconscious love; nothing henceforth can change it, not Anguilla's *education sentimentale* acquired from his experience in the world, nor his critical awareness. His attitude is expressed poetically in a sentence which seems a fragment of Sappho's: "When they walked past with their parasols, I eyed them from the vineyard the way you look at a couple of peaches too high on the branch." With the passing of time Anguilla understands the two girls more and more, their motives, their desires, their frustrations and caprices which he always compares with his own experience; but the two girls seem to have influenced his sentimental life in a decisive way, since the women he knew after he left home always reminded him, somehow, of the two girls of his adolescence.

A whole world, now dead, seems indeed to live still in Anguilla's mind, despite his newly acquired awareness, his experience. The small world which provided a faith and a security, however illusory, a model of judgement even more than behavior, is deeply rooted in the child's mind, as is seen in several passages in which the term of comparison is automatically the church: flowers, "real flowers like those in church," old books "in Latin, like the missal," or even the room at Il Nido "more beautiful than a church." With these comparisons Pavese underscores, consciously and with feeling, a whole spiritual condition, an education that had been given, precisely at the moment when he recognizes rationally' that it has been superceded and therefore lost.

Thus Anguilla's importance would seem to be in the embodiment of the contemplative, solitary side of Pavese's personality; Anguilla does not get stirred up, does not get involved, does not marry, just like the narrator of "The Langhe Hills"; and at the end of the novel, he is ready to set out again, like 'Ntoni Malavoglia: "But I'm maybe going on a ship. . . . I'll come back for the festa another year." He is left without roots, alone, distant; it is the price he must pay for the knowledge he has acquired of the world, for being the witness and the narrator—and Pavese has to pay a similar price for his own poetic vocation. At the end of 1938, he writes in his diary:

> Maturity is this, too; no longer seeking outside ourselves, but letting our inner life speak with its own rhythm—the only thing that matters. Then the outside world seems petty and materialistic, compared with the unforeseen, profound maturity of our memories. . . . Maturity is isolation that is sufficient unto itself.[9]

Nuto, instead, is just the opposite of Anguilla: sociable, active, involved, he is probably the calmest, most positive figure to appear in Pavese's work, one of the few characters who succeeds in "maturing and taking part in the human fray, assuming his responsibilities in it."[10] From the contrast between him and Anguilla originates a single vision of life and destiny which had never before been realized in one single figure. Nuto incarnates the difficult acceptance of humble, everyday reality, difficult because it consists of compromises, denials and limitations, intercourse with others, political faith, success in love and family life—all the things which were so difficult, problematic and full of torment for Pavese.

Nuto, as opposed to Anguilla, remains in the hills; in him work and holiday are united, tools and clarinet; "winter was Nuto's season," just as summer was Anguilla's. His house still gives the same feeling of strength, of serenity and security (and the geraniums which decorate it seem to echo those at Sandiana's window, in "Intimate History"—the longing for a paternal home). Besides, even as a boy Nuto had a strong attractive personality, he was Anguilla's guide and model (like Gallo for the narrator of the story "The City," and like Candido for the narrator of "The Sea"). Basically, Nuto remains the same after twenty years: "he was only a bit more solid, a bit less of a dreamer. That cat's face of his was quieter and more surly." Of course, he was less of a daredevil and had

learned to assume responsibilities: "after ten years of festas
he laid aside the clarinet on the death of his father," and not
"even for the Feast of the Assumption in August" did he want
to take up playing again, instead he dedicated himself to his
father's job of carpentering, to soothe the wounds of civil war,
to rebuild in a conscious fraternity (all of which cannot be
realized by playing in a band). Only he still had the habit of
putting his lips the way he would when he played every time
he was concentrating on expressing an opinion. Nuto has a lot
of ideas and he expresses them in a few, rough words: above
all he does not believe in violence, he doesn't like it, and tries
every way he can to stifle and overcome it, and it is true
he did not fight during the Resistance but

> had kept a wounded partisan hidden in a hole in a gully on Salto
> and carried food to him at night. . . . Only yesterday when he met
> two boys on the road who were tormenting a lizard, he took it
> from them.

Above all Nuto's ideas on destiny are important, his faith in
the possibility of improvement in the world (like Leopardi's
Timandro, when he says, "the human condition can improve
considerably over what it is just as it has improved more than
can be described over what it was"). In his conception of
human destiny Nuto is the exact (and complementary) opposite of Anguilla, as is seen in the discussion about the bonfires
which in his opinion "are awakening the earth:"

> Nuto said very quietly that a superstition is a superstition only
> when it does harm to someone and if anyone were to use the
> moon and the bonfires to rob the peasants and keep them in the
> dark, then he would be the backward one and should be shot in
> the square.

For Nuto, in short, "we are in this world to transform destiny
into freedom (and nature into causality),"[11] whereas Anguilla's
position is considerably more negative, on the practical level,
in that it is not a question of action but of comprehension and

evidence. Despite their different ideas, Nuto and Anguilla are able to find a common ground and can collaborate in their decision in common to bring up Cinto, when, after running away from Valino's massacre of his family and destruction of his home by fire, "he seemed to wake up suddenly" almost to a new life, the young Aesculepius with two Chaërons at his side.

Cinto is seen for the first time "wearing a shirt and ragged trousers held up by broken braces," "barefoot," with a "scab under one eye and bony shoulders," "one of his legs stretched out, kept apart from the other in a way that wasn't natural" ("to see him on that threshing-floor was like seeing myself," Anguilla remarks). Even more than Dino in *The House on the Hill*, Cinto is the *alter ego* of the narrator, whose very mediation by Nuto is repeated in reverse with Cinto: "I was speaking to him as Nuto had spoken to me." Moreover in Cinto Anguilla finds both the return and the impossibility of return, memory and hope; and, at a subsequent level of interpretation, Cinto is

> the young boy "bearing the sign" like an initiate (he is lame), in whom Pavese sees . . . the charming boy-god who is the guide in the kingdom of the dead; and in fact the "return to one's village" is always a *katàbasis* in Pavese.[12]

Certainly *The Moon and the Bonfires* is *katàbasis;* Anguilla does not refind his past; the old order is dead dragging into ruin with it those who best represent it, Irene and Silvia, and she who marked the necessity of its passing, Santa, as John Freccero has shown.[13] To understand the fascination of the three girls in the second half of the novel one must remember precisely that all three are dead, like so many other people whom Anguilla no longer finds in his impossible return: therefore their re-evocation is born precisely of the narrator's desperate awareness that time and violence have carried away his own youth. And so the re-evocation is carried out on two

levels: the present, with its cruel critical awareness, its rational
and practical logic; the past, with its tender, irrational myths,
its melancholy elegy. I shall confine my analysis here to Santa,
the third sister, who seems to combine the physical characteristics of the first two: "her hair was turning out golden like
Irene's, and she had Silvia's black eyes," like "the black heart
of a poppy" Nuto would say. Her temperament is clearly defined from the moment we meet her— "they were killing the
pig and the women had all run away except Santina, who was
just learning to walk then"—and she is constantly shown as
decisive and independent, a character like a destiny: "At the
wedding [of Irene] Santina was the beauty, all dressed in silk—
she was only six, but she looked as if she were the bride." And
her proud and foreboding words should be remembered:

> They'd burn me if they could. They don't want a girl to make
> anything of her life. They'd like to see me finishing up like Irene
> and kissing the hand that strikes me. But I'd bite the hand that
> strikes me. . . .

The last two chapters, among the most beautiful and most
moving of the novel, with Nuto's memories intertwined with
and superimposed on Anguilla's, are dedicated to Santa: "I
was thinking how everything happens again as it has happened
before—I saw Nuto in the gig driving Santa up the slopes to the
fair, as I had driven her sisters." Nuto then, as he climbs the
slopes of Gaminella with Anguilla, tells him about Santa's end,
about her playing a double game with the fascists and the
partisans without making up her mind for one or the other, as
was necessary:

> One morning Santa came back, under escort. She no longer wore
> the windbreaker and the slacks she had worn all these months.
> To come out of Canelli she had put on women's clothes, a light
> summer dress, again and when the partisans had stopped her up
> by Gaminella, she'd got a shock. . . . Then Baracca read out the
> sentence and told two of them to take her outside. They were

more bewildered than she was. They'd always seen her wearing her jacket and belt and they couldn't get used to the idea that now they had a hold on her, she was dressed in white. They took her outside. She turned round at the door and looked at me and made a face just like a child. But, once outside, she tried to run away. We heard a cry and someone running and a burst of tommy-gun fire which seemed endless. We ran out, too, and saw her lying on the grass in front of the acacias.

What strikes us most in Nuto's account is the luminosity of the images: "one morning," "a light summer dress," "dressed in white," "on the grass in front of the acacias." This luminosity gives a special emotive and lyrical power to the narration (or perhaps it would be more accurate to say re-evocation) particularly in that it fixes the temporal limits (a summer morning, the typically Pavesian time and season) and the spatial limits (the grass and the acacias in a field on a hill, near a vineyard, as we know from the context—the place too is a typical, mythical setting of Pavese's); and secondly, because it is contrasted with the "black ruined walls" of the farm, still existent and visible reminder of the tragic events of the past, of violence, war and death. But there is something else to notice, something that will not escape the attentive reader because it is repeated, emphasized and specified: Santa first appears in "a light summer dress" and then is described as "dressed in white." The lightness of the dress seen vaguely in the distance is seen to be white when it is thought about later more intently. Unequivocally the whiteness of the dress is the center of the scene and therefore has an exceptional importance in the death of Santa. But why this white?

For an exhaustive answer we must begin by remembering other passages of Pavese's where the color white seems to have an emblematic value. Generally the lunar light which suffuses so many of Pavese's landscapes gives an almost distorted vision of reality, so that it provokes a shiver of fear rather than a feeling of serenity, or it creates a tense, dramatic atmosphere. It is sufficient to remember the "lunar horror" of the poem "August Moon" or the story "The Field of the Dead" to see the truth of this. More specifically we think of the cynical Moro in "Summer Storm," with skin "as pale as the belly of a fish," and "a flash of ill-temper in his eyes;" of Nora in "The Leather Jacket" who was "as pale as the belly of a fish" (and when she is killed by Ceresa, the narrator was "still thinking of Nora's white skin"); but most of all we think of Gisella in *The Harvesters,* when she is dying ("I could see the Grangia and the moon. . . . Between the candles and the moonlight, there lay Gisella on the bed, all swathed in bandages, with a white dressing on her forehead, but her nostrils and her mouth were black"): in each of these passages white is used to emphasize scenes composed of violence, evil and death. Or we think of Clara in "First Love" who had "the dazzling white skin" and who was seen by the boy narrator when she was in the act of making love, "a white body lying at full length" in the darkness of a shack in the vineyard; or of Artemis in "The Lady of Beasts" in *Dialogues with Leucò* who looks, to Endymion, in the moonlight like a wild girl dressed in a (white) tunic which "barely reached her knees": in these examples white emphasizes feminine beauty and the mystery, evil and tragedy which derive from it. Or again, we remember the dialogue "The Mares" in which the light of the Bright One "cruel, blinding," exposes everywhere "sadness, wounds, the vileness of things."

If then we turn to the beginning of Pavese's career, we remember the cousin in the poem "Southern Seas," "a giant dressed in white" who introduces the myth of return for the first time in Pavese's work, a theme which is constantly restated and culminates in *The Moon and the Bonfires.* There are obvious echoes in this poem of a work which Pavese had been translating, Melville's *Moby Dick,* and there are many passages of *Moby Dick* which concern our present examination; the whole chapter XLII is dedicated to "The Whiteness of the Whale," to the white color "mystical and well nigh inefrable," inspiring a "vague, nameless horror." It is one of Melville's very learned dissertations between encyclopedia and bible, in which Ishmael asserts among other things that:

> Though in many natural objects, whiteness refiningly enhances beauty, as if imparting some special virtue of its own, as in marvles, japonicas, and pearls . . . and though in other mortal sympathies and symbolizings, this same hue is made the emblem of many touching, noble things—the innocence of brides, the benignity of age . . . yet for all these accumulated associations, with whatever is sweet, and honorable, and sublime, there yet lurks an elusive something in the innermost idea of this hue, which strikes more of panic to the soul than that redness which affrights in blood.

In fact Ishmael asserts, with many examples which are not specifically interesting for the present purpose, that nature numbers among her powers white, "this crowning attribute of the terrible," and that humanity cannot help but recognize in some cases "the supernaturalism of this hue" as in the pallor of the dead. Ishmael concludes that "though in many of its aspects this visible world seems formed in love, the invisible spheres were formed in fright," as whiteness shows us, because when we consider that

> the great principle of light for ever remains white or colorless in itself, and if operating without medium upon matter, would touch all objects, even tulips and roses, with its own blank tinge —pondering all this, the palsied universe lies before us a leper.

So for Melville the color white is symbolic of grace and beauty, and of a vague feeling of mystical, puritanical, awesome religiosity, and most of all of evil, grief, of the tragedy of the universe, in the life of man and things. Melville's affirmations appear to be echoed (and transformed by a sensibility which is different from Melville's) in the passages of Pavese we mentioned. But to return to *The Moon and the Bonfires* and Santa's death scene, how much of Melville did Pavese find in himself, in his own "reflected culture," to be in agreement with his own poetic and human sensibility, and with his own myths?

Above all the color white is certainly a symbol of noble and moving sentiments: it is an image of innocence, underscored by the face that Santa makes "like a child" and confirmed by the memory of the time when Santina, at Irene's wedding, "looked as if she were the bride," a child of six dressed in silk —very much Melville's "the innocence of brides." As for religiosity, in Pavese it is not so much mystic, puritanical and awesome, as it is in Melville, but rather mythical and secular: if we think about the name of the girl, *Santa,* then the white of her dress becomes the color of the sacrificial victim who will be burned on the final, ritual and propitiatory bonfire, like those of the primitive peoples in *Dialogues with Leucò.* [14] Finally the tragic quality of white: on the literal level, Santa puts on women's clothes, a white dress, almost as if she foresees her death; but Pavese shows her dressed in white almost as if he sees in her a much greater tragedy than that of the character. On the one hand, in fact, he has become "aware of history" (the war, the Resistance, the after-war period; the passing of people, the changing of the social classes and of ideologies); on the other hand he has realized the impossibility of his own return, the impossibility of regaining childhood and therefore the impossibility of attaining the absolute in the sublunar world ("the palsied universe lies before us a leper," empty and meaningless as it is for Rosetta in *Among Women Only*): the "burst of tommy-gun fire which seemed endless" would seem to suggest and fix cruelly, as one bullet after the other penetrates the tender and proud body of Santa, in its white dress, the inevitability of history and death, the double awareness of Pavese. Thus, even though in Pavese there is not the same powerful inspiration, eloquence and grandiosity as in Melville, yet he as created an image which is hard to forget, an image all his own, inserted in the texture of his themes and myths—an image which concentrates elegy, judgement and symbol.

In fact the white figure of Santa seems to stretch even into the last scene of the novel, constituting the premise for it in the richness of its meaning. It is precisely in relation to Santa that Anguilla (like Corrado at the end of *The House on the Hill*) in a pause in Nuto's account, can express his elegy and also his judgment, his feelings of grief, his pity for all those who are no longer: "Rather than Nuto, I saw Baracca—he had been hanged, too, until he was dead." And it is thanks to the white dress of Santa's that the end of the story can achieve its mythical meaning which is completely immersed in Pavese's poetic world: this dress, because it makes Santa more beautiful, makes her desirable even though she is dead, and to avoid any possible necrophilism—with all the morbidity and obscurity there are in such a thought—Nuto and Baracca decide to burn the body of the woman they loved, and without knowing it consecrate her:

> Nuto had sat down on the wall and looked at me with his obstinate eyes. "No, not Santa," he said. "You won't find her. You can't cover a woman like her with earth and leave her like that. There were still too many men who wanted her. Baracca saw to that. He made us cut a lot of twigs in the vineyard and we piled them on top of her until we had enough. Then we poured petrol on the pile and set fire to it. By midday, everything was burnt to ashes. Last year the mark was still there, like the bed of a bonfire.

Thus Santa really becomes "earth and death," like Gisella in *The Harvesters*, but with a difference. By making a mistake, she finally transformed her destiny into freedom: she betrayed both fascists and partisans, but only in an effort to understand, to be herself, disregarding and transcending historical contingency. Like Coronis in the dialogue "The Mares," Santa "walked through the vineyards and played with the Bright One till he killed her and burnt her body," but at least "she found herself as she died." Moreover, like an echo of the ancestral human sacrifices in the dialogue "The Guest," her ashes in the bed of the fire contribute to the earth's fertility—to the fertility of the hill Gaminella green with vineyards and thickets, "like a planet" which shelters all of humanity; and again, as in that other mythological dialogue "The Bonfires," we can think of her sacrifice as serving "to bring some justice back to the world"—the aim which the Resistance had not been able to achieve in entirety. We think in fact of the desperate fire set by Valino, the last whisper of violence, the last protest against injustice; and we see Cinto, who escaped from that fire, appearing like a young Aesculepius born on the funeral pyre of his mother: thus Santa, on her bonfire-funeral pyre, culminates, within the novel's time, all the violence of the war, and can be considered the mother-symbol for Cinto, the uncertain yet hopeful future. But for Anguilla, the narrator who is not interested in that future, as is seen by his ending the story there, Santa is the final term, the seal of his *katàbasis*.

Thus Pavese's last novel ends with Santa's death and the image of the bonfire, and it can truly be said that in it "myth is linked directly to poetry without passing through theory or action," and Pavese has achieved a style which can be so identified with things that "it destroys every barrier between the ordinary reader and the most dizzying symbolical and mythical reality."[15] *The Moon and the Bonfires*, in fact, contains, even in the title, various symbolical references embedded in the two images which compose it: the moon as cycle of nature and the seasons, the bonfires as moments of human time, as an echo of escapism, joy and festivals (already mythical) for the young narrator, and as a sacred part of human activity and work (in that they serve to awaken the earth, they are also the ancient propitiatory rites); the moon as an impassive force of destiny, the bonfires as man's acts—of destructive violence (Valino burns his own house in rebellion against an unfair destiny), and of compassionate love (Baracca and Nuto burn Santa consecrating individuality in the face of destiny); the moon as immanence, the bonfires as transcendence. In the words of John Freccero, who is emphasizing primarily the mythical roots of Pavese's world, especially in reference to *Dialogues with Leucò*:

> To propitiate the gods is in a sense to manipulate them, to answer their crushing force. If the victory of such a revolution seems pale, and the fire a little thing against the moon, it is nevertheless all that man has, the only weapon against fate that he has been able to fashion from the gift given him by Prometheus.[16]

Finally there remains the need to underscore the novel's epigraph, taken through F. O. Matthiessen from Shakespeare's *King Lear:* "Man must endure /his going hence e'en as his coming hither. /*Ripeness is all.*"[17] This epigraph contains the hidden meaning not only of *The Moon and the Bonfires* but of all Pavese's work: total comprehension of human life, from birth to death; virile acceptance of the mystery behind life; the maturity which derives from understanding and acceptance. On the artistic plane, ripeness is realized both in the lyrical expression of *durée* and in the epic surpassing of it: individual destiny in time, self-recognition, elegy; destiny as seen in history, recognition of others, compassion. All the elements which remain separate and opposed up to the end of *The House on the Hill* are blended into one in the last novel.

Unfortunately the epigraph becomes tragic on the human plane: Pavese kills himself right at the time of his greatest maturity as author, perhaps because that maturity was not sufficient in an absolute sense for himself as man.

The idea of maturity had always interested Pavese greatly. Beginning with some of the poetic images of *Work Is Weary-ing* (such as those in "Grappa in September"), again in the essay on Matthiessen entitled "American maturity," and even in his last critical essay "The Art of Maturing," his preoccupation becomes clearer, increases, becomes more profound and wider. By nature, Pavese was always attracted to "angelism"

and tended to look on childhood as the real world, but at the
same time was always able to resist the temptation and inte-
grate it consciously into his literary and civic duty. That he
grew into "a tragic hero, aware of history,"[18] is fully proved
by his narrative works; so much so that Natalino Sapegno,
defining him as "a character in a tragedy," wrote:

> No one more than he, in a closed culture such as ours with its
> tendency to easy and soothing solutions, has expressed that basic
> reluctance for life, that internal laceration and anticipated ruin of
> all the feelings and ideals that go towards its composition, that
> primordial vocation for death which is at the root of so much of
> our civilization.[19]

And since our civilization basically goes back to romanticism
(of which decadentism is only one aspect), it is to romanticism
that we must refer if we are to understand it—especially "that
passive availability for experiencing life,"[20] which is fundamental to the contemplativeness and introspectiveness of so
many greater writers, the last of which is Pavese. One of his
lucid earlier pages should be reread in this connection, as it is
ingenious and extremely valid for the categorical quality of his
affirmations:

> I am one of the many decayed sons of the nineteenth century.
> That century was too great in thought, feeling and action; and
> by the laws of history, equally great must be the dejection of
> those who can no longer believe in its ideals and cannot reso-
> lutely find new ones. That's the way I am.[21]

The figure of Carlo Michelstaedter comes to mind, a man who
had much the same experience as Pavese, at the beginning of
the century. In a note written in 1905, five years before he
committed suicide, Michelstaedter described himself as a person who "sees too much," in whose "embittered mind the
source of feeling has dried up" nor is it possible "to reacquire
the lost spontaneity, past enthusiasm."[22] In Pavese, as in Michelstaedter (apart from their differences) the inability to ad-

here to romantic ideals, the sterility, the frustration, the falling back on himself, led him to an examination of existence and the absolute which could not be satisfied.

There is no doubt therefore that Pavese, in his "reluctance for life," in his "passive availability for experiencing life," reached his own artistic maturity in the sense he himself indicated: in his works, especially *The Moon and the Bonfires*, man and history, nature and destiny are seen with a "monolithic" total comprehension, as "symbolic reality."[23] Pavese reached this comprehension gradually and combined in his last novel all that he had accumulated in his years of research (poetics, style, psychology and mythology).

Thus in his work Pavese succeeded in interpreting contemporary exigencies, exigencies which are also universal and permanent. In his feeling for what is beautiful he was a part of the tradition which started with Foscolo and Leopardi, developed through Verga to D'Annunzio and Pascoli (not to mention Baudelaire and the symbolists), and with the aid of American writers widened into an extremely rich, subtle, nuanced prose which is both lyrical and essential, concrete and symbolic, classical and familiar. Certainly the same cannot be said of many other styles: it is in fact a prose in which are fused the best aspects of classicism, Italian *verismo*, American realism and European decadentism to form a very individual whole.

With his examination of existence Pavese made a completely original contribution to the literary currents of the twentieth century which range from psychoanalysis to German expressionism, from Pirandello's irrationalism to ethnology, currents which can be traced back to the childhood of Rousseau and the myth of Vico. Pavese drew these currents together and continued them with a constant, determined, integral effort at depth and clarity. He absorbed and went beyond whatever experience had convinced him of, in his constant anxiety to acquire more knowledge. Thus, the decadent and sensual images inspired by D'Annunzio's *superuomo* are to be found in Pavese but in a more tormented, psychoanalytical form, as if depleted by his anticipated awareness of failure; we find too the myth of childhood, but dramatically, of a problematic rather than consoling childhood; we find that nature does not offer shelter and peace as in Pirandello and Michelstaedter, but is rather divided between order and chaos, between civilization and the wild, containing the mystery of human origins.

Furthermore, Pavese knew how to express man as a social creature. His characters are the mouthpiece of his own irresolute but spontaneous political engagement, his own incapacity for action of which he was ashamed, his own populist feelings resolved in a watchful and lucid historicism. But primarily he dealt with the asocial side of man, the crisis of the individual torn from society and contemporary reality: solitude, the inability to communicate which is suffered and yet at the same time self-determined, the contemplativity of the writer isolated in his ivory tower yet tormented by awareness and remorse that this tower of his (as Virginia Woolf wrote) would henceforth overlook burning fields on all sides.

Pavese therefore was able to lift himself out of the lucid and painful individual portrait to the universal framework of the contemporary epoch, expressing it in his myths and images even more than in his critical reflections. Although perhaps his teaching remains limited by the lack of a precise ideology which would enable him to find a sure route through the sea of contemporary contradictions which he interpreted so well, precisely because of this, since even we have not resolved and overcome these contradictions, Pavese is so close to our affections that in the years to come he will be the voice of our gneration and of our consciousness. And he will be so because of his recognition of our limitations, as when he wrote that "we in Italy today are provincial:"

> Italian culture *today* does not exist: there is a European, and maybe even a world culture; and one can only say something valid if one has digested the whole of contemporary life.[24]

Pavese's characters and writing reflect tragically the conditions of a culture which is precisely "provincial" (or peasant, or archaic) which is tending to become "European" or "world" (or civic and modern) and which nevertheless does not succeed in surpassing its own origins but maintains them in constant tension with present developments.

There can be no doubt, however, that the tragedy of Pavese's maturity is to be found in his own life and not on the cultural plane. His yielding to the "primordial vocation for death," to the *vizio assurdo* which had always pursued him can be traced during the period between the conclusion of *Among Women Only* and the beginning of *The Moon and the Bonfires* "when his myth has become *figura*, and he, unoccupied, can no longer believe in it but cannot yet resign himself to the loss of that good, of that authentic faith which kept him alive, and he makes another attempt at it, turns it inside out and becomes disgusted with it."[25] We read in fact in the diary: "Probably this is your most intensive period, and it is getting past its best."[26] Perhaps Pavese felt that his most intense and mature season could not have lasted. After *The Moon and the Bonfires*, in fact, he only wrote some essays and the poems of *Verrà la mort e avrà i tuoi occhi* (Death Will Come and Will Have Its Eyes), and these too, like the novel, are dedicated to "C.," the woman who reminds him of the years of his youth, and renews for him the torment of a love that has failed ("All is the same / time has gone by"). Moreover he felt perhaps he was to blame for not being capable of political engagement. Remember that Pavese, in an obvious allusion to Peter's betrayal, gave the title *Prima che il gallo canti* (*Before the Cock Crows*) to the volume containing *Il compagno* (*The Comrade*) and *The House on the Hill*, the premise and the conclusion of his disengagement.[27]

However it was not failures, or apparent failures, such as these which drove Pavese to suicide; if anything they were the fortuitous cause of it, in that maybe they confirmed the relativity and imperfection of the sublunar world (remember, again, the anguish and disgust of Rosetta in *Among Women Only*, re-echoed in the penultimate sentence in Pavese's diary: "All this is sickening"); so that death, deliberately chosen and determined, signified for him the act that opens the way to the absolute, so long sought after in childhood and in love, pursued in myth, longed for in the smile of the gods. Dominique Fernandez writes:

> Suicide is not a break but the ultimate point of maturity, the moment when subjectivity—after having fought long with moral and social laws, and having fought also with its own desire to know and love the world, its adversary—abandons the world to itself and retires within itself to realize itself to the full.[28]

Since even the word is part of the world, Pavese finally commits the act which will negate the word and destroy the relationship between literature and life which till then had been held in a difficult balance: the ultimate maturity, for him, will not be a book but silence. The relativity of books and days is succeeded by the absolute of silence outside time. A silence which seals the enigma of Pavese's work, its authenticity, its myth.

NOTES

1. Fulvio Longobardi, "Ancora Pavese," *Belfagor*, vol. XX, n. 6, November 1965, pp. 693–716. The quotation is on p. 693.
2. Roland Barthes, *Critique et vérité*, Paris, Aux éditions du seuil, 1966, pp. 59–60.
3. Cesare Pavese, *La luna e i falò*, Turin, Einaudi, 1950, translated into English as *The Moon and the Bonfire[s]* by Louise Sinclair, London, Lehman, 1952, and Penguin, 1963; there is another translation by Marianne Ceconi, New York, Farrar and Straus, 1961. The quotations are taken from the Penguin edition.
4. Cf. Dominique Fernandez, *Le roman italien et la crise de la conscience moderne*, Paris, Grasset, 1958, p. 198: "The family would

still be the hateful 'other' and the return to one's home country would not be that return purely to oneself which it must be."

5. Cesare Pavese, *Il mestiere di vivere (Diario 1935–1950)*, translated as *The Burning Brand* by A. E. Murch, New York, Walker and Co., 1961, March 30, 1948, p. 322. Pavese's comprehension of time in its contrasting aspects can be linked to his interest in ethnology, and actually seems to be in line with recent conceptions of anthropologists such as E. R. Leach: see his "Two Essays Concerning the Symbolic Representation of Time" in his *Rethinking Anthropology*, London, London School of Economics, and New York, Humanities Press, 1961, then 1966, pp. 124 ff.

6. A similar aspect of total comprehension is shown too in the sensory details which accompany descriptions, memories, and feelings; thus smells, colors, flavors, sounds reveal the real with a richness which goes beyond ordinary impression, because "undesired things, multiplied by perceptive subtlety provided an ever more abundant source of symbols" (Cesare Pavese, *La letteratura americana e altri saggi*, [American Literature and Other Essays], Turin, Einaudi, 1959, p. 183.)

7. On the meaning of the American chapters in the structure of the novel, see Peter M. Norton, "Cesare Pavese and the American Nightmare," in *Modern Language Notes*, Vol. 77, n. 1, Jan. 1962, pp. 24 ff.

8. For the mythical significance of the festivals which are mentioned frequently in the novel (as on pp. 42 and 104, with the bonfires on the Feast of John the Baptist), see *La letteratura americana*, pp. 345–346: "The myth is that which happens and rehappens endlessly in the sublunar world and yet is unique, outside of time, like a recurring festival, each time it takes place it is as if for the first time, at a time which is the time of the festival, of the non-temporal of the myth."

9. December 6 and 8, 1938, pp. 140–141.

10. Cesare Pavese, *La letteratura americana*, p. 361.

11. Cesare Pavese, *The Burning Brand*, Jan. 17, 1950, p. 356; and on the following page, Feb. 1, 1950: "Will power can be applied to myth in order to transform it into history. Destinies which become freedom."

12. Furio Jesi, "Cesare Pavese, il mito e la scienza del mito," in

Sigma, special issue dedicated to Cesare Pavese, Dec. 1964, n. 3/4, p. 112; his affirmation is closely related to the German poetics of the expressionists. Jesi also makes a very sharp appraisal of the differences between Thomas Mann and Pavese regarding myth. On the subject see Armanda Guiducci, *Il mito Pavese*, Florence, Vallecchi, 1967.

13. John Freccero, "Mythos and Logos: *The Moon and the Bonfires*," in *Italian Quarterly*, vol. 4, n. 16, Winter 1961, pp. 3–16.

14. Santa as a sacrificial victim seems to conclude the progress of Pavese's characters "from the myth of festival to the myth of sacrifice," as outlined by Furio Jesi in his introduction to the latest edition of Cesare Pavese's *La bella estate*, Turin, Einaudi, 1966, pp. vii–xx.

15. Cesare Pavese, respectively in the diary, Feb. 9, 1950, p. 357, and in *La letteratura americana*, p. 180.

16. John Freccero, *op. cit.*, p. 16.

17. The meaning of this epigraph can be clarified by a passage of György Lukàcs, *Die Theorie des Romans* (The Theory of the Novel), Italian edition *Teoria del romanzo*, Milan, Sugar, 1962, p. 178, which almost seems to repeat the words in a general context: "The novel is the form of virile maturity. . . . This is how time becomes the vehicle of the noble epic poetry of the novel: time is inexorably made to exist, and no one is in a position any longer to be able to move back along its current. . . . And yet there remains alive a feeling of resignation: all this must come from somewhere, must have been directed in some place; the direction of the flow certainly shows no sense, and yet it is always a direction. And from this feeling of virile resignation emanate the temporal experiences, which are legitimately noticed from an epic point of view in that they arouse actions and germinate from actions: hope and memory; temporal experiences, which at the same time are the surpassing of time: a complex vision of life as inspired unity *ante rem*, and the panoramic intuition *post rem* of life itself."

18. Cesare Pavese, *La letteratura americana*, pp. 360 and 363.

19. Natalino Sapegno, "Pavese, personaggio di tragedia," in *La stampa*, May 22, 1963, p. 7.

20. György Lukàcs, *A lélék es a formàk* (The Soul and Forms), Italian ed. *L'anima e le forme*, Milan, Sugar, 1963, p. 108.

21. Cesare Pavese, *Lettere 1924–1944*, Turin, Einaudi, 1966, p. 40; letter to Tullio Pinelli, Oct. 12, 1926.

22. Carlo Michelstaedter, *Opere* (Collected Works), Florence, Sansoni, 1958, p. 630.

23. Cesare Pavese, *The Burning Brand*, pp. 346–347, Nov. 26, 1949.

24. Cesare Pavese, *Lettere 1945–1950*, Turin, Einaudi, 1966, (letter to Nicola Enrichens, July 26, 1949), pp. 404–405.

25. Cesare Pavese, *La letteratura americana*, p. 351, italics mine.

26. June 22, 1949, p. 340.

27. Cesare Pavese, *Prima che il gallo canti* (Turin, Einaudi, 1948), containing *Il carcere* (1939) and *La casa in collina* (1948). Cf. his diary, May 27, 1950, p. 363, and Davide Lajolo, *Il "vizio assurdo."* *Storia di Cesare Pavese*, Milan, Il saggiatore, 1960, p. 368: "He was convinced that everything was useless, that he had nothing left to write, that he wasn't suited to politics, that he was worthless for women, for his friends and for himself."

28. Dominique Fernandez, *op. cit.*, pp. 147–148. See also Davide Lajolo, *op. cit.*, p. 375: "He decided to carry out the supreme act like a human sacrifice, not so much to escape from men as to go back into himself"; and Natalia Ginzburg, "Portrait of a friend," in her *Le piccole virtù* (Small Virtues), Turin, Einaudi, 1963, pp. 31–33.

10 THE ITALIAN RESISTANCE NOVEL (1945–1962)

Frank Rosengarten

In the context of strictly literary history, there is no such thing as a subgenre of the novel in Italy called "the Resistance novel," but only a large number of novelists who have dealt with the theme of the resistance against fascism from diverse points of view and with different stylistic methods. The title "The Italian Resistance Novel" is therefore meant to suggest only a common subject matter of deep interest to certain Italian novelists who have worked independently of each other. To be sure, a few of the novelists whose works I shall discuss, notably Vasco Pratolini and Elio Vittorini, were identified in the immediate postwar years with "neorealism." But neorealism was not a literary school: it issued no manifestos and was basically a term applied rather loosely to a group of Italian writers, artists, and film-makers who attempted to deal directly and honestly with the problems of war-ravaged Italy.

It is necessary to stress the fact that the theme of anti-fascism appeared in the Italian novel before World War II. In *Fontamara*, 1933, and *Pane e vino*, 1937 (*Bread and Wine*), Ignazio Silone wrote powerful stories of Fascist oppression and of heroic if unsuccessful efforts to struggle against Mussolini's regime. Carlo Levi's famous book *Cristo si è fermato a Eboli* (*Christ Stopped at Eboli*), although not published until 1945, was written in 1936 and 1937 while Levi was under police confinement in a remote Southern Italian village. Elio Vittorini's *Conversazione in Siciliu* (*Conversation in Sicily*) appeared first in serial form in the magazine *Solaria* during the latter part of the 1930's. In its humane concern for all the oppressed peoples of the world, in its search for a moral basis on which mankind might construct a better, more dignified and fulfilled existence for all, *Conversation in Sicily* is an anti-Fascist novel of great value and influence. Alberto Moravia's *Gli indifferenti*, 1929 (*The Time of Indifference*), and Carlo Bernari's *Tre operai*, 1935 (Three Workers), although not explicitly anti-Fascist, present bleak descriptions of bourgeois and proletarian life under Fascist rule and can be justifiably regarded as protests against the official optimism of Mussolini's regime. The chronological limits of this essay therefore indicate simply that I shall concern myself with a group of representative Italian novelists who were inspired chiefly by the ideals and accomplishments of a specific event in recent Italian history: the armed Italian Resistance movement of the years 1943 to 1945.

The Italian Resistance from 1943 to 1945 was a movement that engaged the energies not only of a minority of dedicated anti-Fascists but also of thousands of previously uncommitted or even pro-Fascist Italians who were shocked into political awareness by the unprecedented disaster to which the Fascist regime had brought their country. It was a collective struggle involving intellectuals and students, workers and farmers, ex-Fascist soldiers and militiamen, lawyers, and businessmen. The Italian partisan brigades were composed of men and women belonging to all social strata. The Committees of National Liberation, formed in most of the principal Italian cities after September 8, 1943 (the day on which the Italian government, headed by Marshal Pietro Badoglio, announced Italy's surrender to the Allies), were organized and led by men representing all of the Italian anti-Fascist political parties, from the Communists to the Christian Democrats.

It is generally recognized that the events that sparked the armed resistance in Italy were the strikes staged in March 1943 by the industrial workers of Turin, Milan, and other northern Italian cities. The strikers called for "the liberation of our comrades who have been arrested, the expulsion of police guards from the factories, the right to elect real workers' representatives."[1] Almost immediately after these strikes, protests against the Fascist regime and demands that Italy withdraw from the war poliferated throughout the country. On July 25, 1943, the ouster of Mussolini by dissident members of the Fascist Grand Council was carried out partially in response to the mood of discontent and rebelliousness sparked initially by the March strikes. Most Italians greeted Mussolini's ouster with enthusiasm. They thought that the war would soon be over for them, that the Fascist era had ended. But they quickly realized how wrong they were when, after September 8, the German Army carried out a full-scale occupation of Italy and began stubbornly to resist the Allied offensive.

Faced by the terror of Nazi military authorities, caught between two opposing armies, the Italian people were also confronted with a reborn Fascist movement initiated in late September 1943 by Mussolini after his rescue from prison by German parachutists. It was in this situation that the armed Italian Resistance movement took shape. By the end of 1943, Italian partisan brigades were already harassing German troops in guerrilla operations, saboteurs were blowing up enemy trucks and installations, and a growing number of anti-Fascist undergound newspapers were being circulated.[2]

Thirty thousand Italian partisans lost their lives in the Resistance struggle; tens of thousands were imprisoned and tortured. The partisans' contribution to the Allied victory was substantial if not decisive. It is not surprising, therefore, that in many cases Italian Resistance novels should stress the valor and virtues of Italians engaged in combat against the Nazis and Fascists. Nor is it surprising that many Italian Resistance novels should have as their protagonists men and women of the working classes. This class, and its political representatives, the Italian Socialist and Communist Parties, had, after all, provided an example of commitment to the anti-Fascist cause that made possible the success of the Resistance. To be pro-working class and pro-Communist, as well as anti-Fascist and antibourgeois, were prevalent attitudes among many Italians immediately after World War II. Antibourgeois feelings were endemic among Italian writers and intellectuals at that time, and quite understandably, since all segments of the bourgeoisie had made decisive contributions to the triumph of fascism in Italy. Italian big business and industrial interests had given generous amounts of financial assistance to Mussolini from 1921 on. Powerful landowning families in central Italy financed the first Fascist "squads," which, from 1921 to 1925, carried out brutal "punitive expeditions" against Italian working-class institutions in both urban and rural areas.

Nothwithstanding the heroism and political achievements of the Resistance, most Italian Resistance novels are not merely polemical denunciations of fascism and celebrations of the virtues of anti-Fascist Italians. They are also inquiries into some of the political, moral, and psychological causes of fascism. They do not simply glorify the valor of the partisans; they also seek to probe the factors that led originally to the destruction of freedom in Italy. In 1945 (as in 1969), thoughtful, politically conscious Italians were also compelled to ask themselves the questions: How did it happen? How, for more than two decades (1922–1943), did Benito Mussolini succeed in seducing the majority of Italians into believing that his will was their will; that his ambitions were their ambitions; that his regime, his hierarchy, his concept of Italy's national destiny were their regime, their hierarchy, their concept? The reading of Italian Resistance novels is a rewarding experience not only because of what they say about human courage and the will to resist oppression but also because of what they reveal about the de-

ficiencies of character, the social and political inequities, and
the general state of moral corruption that form the breeding
ground for fascism. As far as many Italian writers were concerned, fascism could not be dismissed as a mere accident of
Italian history. There was a cause-effect relationship between
the weaknesses of Italian society and the triumph of fascism
that had to be dealt with, and the Resistance novels that I shall
discuss show that this relationship has very much preoccupied
Italian men of letters from 1945 to the present day.

But the Resistance novel is also linked with several other
important phenomena of Italy's recent literary and political
history.

In the nineteenth and early twentieth centuries Italy had
produced a number of novelists whose work constituted a
precedent for the realistic confrontation of social and political
conflicts. Nineteenth century Italian naturalism, called *verismo*,
as exemplified especially in the works of the Sicilian Giovanni
Verga, was a basic point of reference for Resistance novelists
in the sense that *verismo* decisively broke through the barriers
of class prejudice and rhetorical traditions that for centuries
had prevented the majority of Italian writers from concerning
themselves with the immediate, everyday problems and conflicts of life.

Another literary precedent for the Resistance novelists was
established by certain American writers who, during the
1930's, enjoyed great prestige and popularity in Italy due principally to the labors of Elio Vittorini and Cesare Pavese, both
of whom devoted themselves to translating Dreiser, Steinbeck,
Hemingway, Caldwell, and other American novelists into Italian. American fiction, by reason of its preoccupation with violence, its probing of social problems, its concern for the lives
and destinies of ordinary people, its raw, straightforward
language, was probably the most important foreign influence
on the subsequent development of the novel of political conflict
in Italy.

For Fascist "civilization" never produced a literature of its own. During the 1920's and 1930's, with the few notable exceptions mentioned before, Italy's most sensitive and sophisticated men of letters engaged in a kind of conspiracy of silence. Those who did publish in those years often neglected to mention fascism at all and devoted themselves instead to nonpolitical and exquisitely private themes. The decade of 1930 to 1940 witnessed the appearance of an extremely large number of books—both prose and verse—in which nostalgic reminiscences of childhood were described in oblique or impressionistic language that was the very antithesis of the vigorously masculine prose advocated by Fascist critics. The 1930's was also the heyday of hermetic poetry, whose chief exponent, Eugenio Montale, expressed a vision of life whose basic assumptions had nothing to do with Fascist ideology. Montale became a culture hero for many Italians who repudiated fascism. His pessimism, his awareness of the principle of decline and decadence in all forms of life and his sense of man's finiteness, were so far removed from the official optimism of Fascist civilization that one cannot help but attribute his prestige during the 1930's to moral and political as well as aesthetic factors.

Still another significant cultural development during the 1930's was the large number of literary and political magazines published in Italy by groups of so-called left-wing Fascist intellectuals. The young men who contributed during the mid-1930's to *Il Bo* in Padua and to *Campo di Marte* in Florence, for example, were all theoretically committed to fascism. Yet their writings often reveal a sharply critical attitude with regard to the regime's lack of intellectual dynamism, its failure to effect basic social and economic reforms, and, above all, its continued alliance with Italy's most reactionary forces: the Catholic Church, the Monarchy, the Army, the industrial monopolies, the agrarian landowners. Without the prior experience of having struggled against the most reactionary features of the Fascist system, it is doubtful that young left-wing Fascist writers such as Pratolini and Vittorini would have moved so decisively into the anti-Fascist camp in 1943 and subsequently written novels in which the resistance against fascism is so dramatically depicted.

It should also be noted that the spirit of militant antifascism was never completely crushed at any time during the Fascist era. During the 1920's and 1930's, the sacrifies of renowned anti-Fascists such as Giacomo Matteotti, Piero Gobetti, Giovanni Amendola, and Antonio Gramsci were not forgotten. In fact, many of the partisan brigades that distinguished themselves in guerrilla action from 1943 to 1945 were named after these men. Nor were Mussolini's Fascist "volunteers" the only Italians who fought in the Spanish Civil War. More than three thousand Italians fought on the side of the Republic in the famous "Garibaldi" brigade, about six hundred of whom died on the battlefields of Spain.

Among the scores of novels published in Italy since 1945 that deal with various facets of the Resistance, seven works stand out as representative of the main problems and themes that have most deeply concerned Italian anti-Fascist writers. These are Elio Vittorini's *Uomini e no* (Men or Not); Vasco Pratolini's *Cronache di poveri amanti* (*A Tale of Poor Lovers*); Italo Calvino's *Il sentiero dei nidi di ragno* (*The Path to the Nest of Spiders*); Renata Viganò's *L'Agnese va a morire* (Agnese Goes to her Death); Cesare Pavese's *La casa in collina* (*The House on the Hill*); Carlo Cassola's *Fausto e Anna* (*Fausto and Anna*); and Mario Tobino's *Il clandestino* (*The Underground*).[3]

The political backgrounds of these writers are quite varied. Vittorini and Pratolini were both left-wing Fascists until the period of the Spanish Civil War, when they began to evaluate their political ideas in a new light and subsequently swung over to militant antifascism. Calvino, born in 1923, was an anti-Fascist partisan during World War II. Renata Viganò belonged to a Communist partisan brigade from 1943 to 1945; during the 1930's she was an intrepid anti-Fascist conspirator. Pavese was always an intransigent enemy of fascism, underwent several years of confinement and imprisonment in the latter half of the 1930's, and remained opposed to every form and manifestation of fascism until his death by suicide in 1950. Carlo Cassola was an "unpolitical" school teacher throughout the 1930's, but his sympathies and general world outlook were incompatible with Mussolinian sham heroics. Mario Tobino served as a doctor with the Italian armed forces in North Africa, but was never a Fascist, and after Italy's surrender to the Allies in September 1943 he participated actively in the Italian Resistance movement.[4]

Vittorini's *Men or Not* (1945), Pratolini's *A Tale of Poor Lovers* (1947), Calvino's *The Path to the Nest of Spiders* (1947), and Viganò's *Agnese Goes to Her Death* (1949) reveal that in the immediate postwar years the Resistance inspired fervently hopeful and equalitarian feelings in many Italian writers and intellectuals.

In *Men or Not*, Vittorini uses the struggle waged in 1944 and 1945 by a group of Milanese resistance patriots against the Nazis and the Fascists to dramatize his belief that World War II was a conflict between men and nonmen, between humans and nonhumans. In this work antifascism is an assertion of humanity much more than a political program; to resist means to struggle for the redemption of mankind, to affirm the right of men and women throughout the world to love and live in peace. Vittorini's anti-Fascist characters are simple, peace-loving people who respond not to doctrinaire appeals from party organizers but rather to a moral imperative that demands that they act against the horrendous debasement of life perpetated by the Nazis and their Fascist henchmen. The Nazis, and to a lesser extent the Italian Fascists, are portrayed in one of two ways: either as stupid, mechanized individuals in whom every trace of spontaneous human concern has been obliterated

or as sadistic fiends for whom violence and terror are sources
of the most intense pleasure.

For Vittorini, a moment of love and intimacy between two
human beings becomes itself an act of resistance against fascism in much the same way that sexual intercourse consummated in privacy is described in George Orwell's *1984* as being
ultimately a political act in a world in which every word and
gesture is supervised by a faceless, bureaucratic authority. The
protagonist of *Men or Not*, known only by his partisan code-
name N2, enjoys only fleeting moments of communion with a
young woman he had loved earlier in his life, yet it is precisely
these pathetically brief encounters that give him the courage he
needs to carry on the dangerous activities in which he is engaged. Without the comfort of friendship and intimacy, without the knowledge that there is someone who cares about him
as a man, as an individual, N2 would be deprived of the one
component of human experience that, in Vittorini's view, truly
distinguishes men from beasts. In their incapacity for love, in
their roles as sadistic wielders of power, the German Nazis and
Italian Fascists definitively repudiate their humanity.

Vittorini's purpose in this novel—to dramatize the division
of mankind into men and nonmen, humans and nonhumans—
is somewhat marred by the fact that none of the characters
are very well delineated, so that they often seem to be stereotyped abstractions. Certain stylistic characteristics of the novel,
such as its deliberately simple, obsessively repetitive dialogues,
reveal the influence but lack the impact of Ernest Hemingway,
whom Vittorini translated and admired intensely. Yet the
humane and compassionate spirit of the book is effectively
communicated despite the above-mentioned flaws. The motives
that inspired some Italians to risk their lives as Resistance
fighters, as well as the defects of character and moral obtuse-
ness that allowed other Italians to serve the Nazi-Fascist cause,
are vividly depicted.

Unlike the other novels discussed in this essay, the action of

Pratolini's *A Tale of Poor Lovers* does not take place during the years 1943 to 1945 but rather during the mid-1920's, when the Fascist regime was firmly in power and was already stamping an indelible imprint on the character of Italian political and social life. Yet there can be no doubt that this novel was directly inspired by the Resistance movement of World War II, and that Pratolini's own participation in the Resistance in Rome was a necessary spiritual precondition for the elaboration of anti-Fascist themes and attitudes that had long lain dormant within him.

A Tale of Poor Lovers is set in Florence in 1925 and 1926. Its downtrodden but amazingly resilient characters, over fifty in number, are almost all inhabitants of via del Corno, a narrow, obscure, impoverished street not far from Palazzo Vecchio. The central conflict of the novel is the struggle between the representatives of the newly established Fascist regime, of which a young insurance salesman named Carlino Bencini is the main spokesman on via del Corno, and the spirit of anti-Fascist resistance, represented on via del Corno mainly by a blacksmith nicknamed Maciste. Via del Corno is in fact a microcosm of the Florentine and possibly even the entire Italian world at the moment of fascism's conquest of power.

Carlino and Maciste are both Italians, they are both Florentines, and they are both residents of via del Corno. They see the same grime and dirt each day, they breathe the same air, and they know the same people. Yet they are as different in their personal conduct and especially in their political opinions as two human beings can be. How is this possible? This is a question that fascinates Pratolini and is one of the problems he seeks to unravel in his novel.

Carlino is not a doctrinaire Fascist. Ideas matter little to him. For Carlino, what counts in life, what has enduring meaning, is power backed by force and violence. He senses instinctively that in an Italy governed by sensible, moderate men devoted to parliamentary procedures, he stands little chance of ever becoming an important person, since he is intellectually mediocre and has no particular talent for business, politics, or any of the professions. As a matter of fact, his fondness for gambling and whoring automatically preclude a conventionally successful life as a respected member of his community. But in an Italy ruled by fascism, in a country governed by a regime that prizes violence and terroristic methods of acquiring and wielding power, he can become someone. It is for this latter reason that he associates himself so passionately with the Fascist movement. In short, Carlino is a Fascist because fascism provides him with a political rationalization for his deep-rooted craving for power and violence, which in turn derive from a gnawing fear of personal inadequacy. In Carlino, Pratolini depicts a character who typifies large numbers of petty-bourgeois Italians who did not merely allow fascism to take power in Italy but who actively seized upon fascism as a political movement that would give meaning to their otherwise drab, mediocre lives.

Resistance to fascism, on the other hand, is incarnate in the figure of the blacksmith Maciste. Like so many other protagonists of Resistance novels, Maciste is a Communist, a trusted and loyal member of the Italian Communist Party. But he is a Communist who has never read Marx, Engels, or Lenin. The only names of prominent Communists that are familiar to him are those of Amadeo Bordiga and Antonio Gramsci, leaders, respectively, of the extremist and moderate factions of the Italian Communist Party at the time of its founding in 1921. Gramsci in 1924 had passed down the word to party cell-leaders that the strategy of opposition to fascism must be based on careful planning and organization, that individual acts of terroristic resistance must be discouraged. Maciste dutifully follows Gramsci's instructions. He attends party cell meetings, carries out party orders, and helps to organize a clandestine apparatus in Florence.

Yet it is not in his activities as a party organizer that Maciste essentially differs from Carlino. Pratolini does not see the difference between fascism and communism primarily in political terms. What truly distinguishes the two men is that for Carlino every action is motivated by a lust for power, while for Maciste the motive is always his sense of personal dedication to specific individuals and ideals. As in *Men or Not,* one discovers that the capacity for love is the genuinely dynamic factor in the personalities of Maciste and other of the novel's anti-Fascist characters. He seeks to create and sustain life, not destroy it. He is a Communist because to him communism represents the political expression of a universal human desire for brotherhood and solidarity. It is significant that most of the individuals he attempts to save from Fascist violence (in doing so he loses his life) are not Communists. All, to be sure, are anti-Fascists, and this factor certainly contributes to Maciste's decision to help them. But fundamentally they are men in danger, and his primary commitment is to the sanctity of life.

One other character deserves mention in connection with the conflict between fascism and antifascism as described by Pratolini: the unnamed "Signora." Like the dictator "Lui" who rules the nation, to whom she is explicitly compared, the Signora has a compulsive need to place herself at the center of the universe. The Signora, with her spies, her unearned wealth, her cravings and keen intelligence, is the ruler of via del Corno. She is malicious, hypocritical, and extraordinarily clever. A sexual pervert, she rationalizes her lesbian lusts by claiming that her love creates, while that of a man destroys. She is dominated by her appetites, which are insatiable, and by a feeling of vengeful wrath toward the whole world. She is alternately enfeebled and full of animal spirits, states of being that depend on the responses of the young woman or women unlucky enough to fall into her clutches. She worships power, money, and things—but, above all, power. From a political and moral standpoint, she is completely opportunistic.

A massive stroke combined with a series of personal defeats

finally reduce the Signora to a state of blubbering idiocy, yet
even after her downfall (as after the downfall of Mussolini
himself), one is left with the uncomfortable feeling that her
spirit still hovers above via del Corno (and above all of Italy).
In fact, Pratolini is probably suggesting that the grasping for
power, the hypocrisy, the vindictiveness, the rationalizations
and meanness that characterize her behavior represent ever-
present threats to the well-being and happiness of human com-
munities everywhere. In any case, the Signora and Carlino are
among the characters in *A Tale of Poor Lovers* who function as
symbolic representatives of those aspects of human psychology
which, in Pratolini's interpretation, permitted fascism to take
root and to thrive in Italy.

In Italo Calvino's *The Path to the Nest of Spiders* and
Renata Viganò's *Agnese Goes to Her Death*, the scene of action
is once again Italy during the years 1943 to 1945. In both
novels, as in *Men or Not* and *A Tale of Poor Lovers*, anti-Fascist resistance is depicted as the spontaneous expression of
generous, humane sentiments that are counterposed to the
predatory cruelty of the Nazi-Fascists.

Calvino's novel deals with the development of the partisan
movement in the mountainous region around Genoa, but its
protagonist is not, as one might expect, the political commissar
of a Communist-led guerrilla brigade, nor any of the numerous
workers and peasants who have gone to the mountains to fight
the Fascist enemy. The novel's hero is a fourteen-year-old boy
named Pin, an outcast from society, a rootless ragamuffin (his
mother is dead; his sailor father had abandoned him many
years earlier), whose principal occupation is petty thievery and
whose chief delight is singing ribald songs to the unemployed
winos of the slums of Genoa.

At the outset of the novel, which begins in September of
1943, the adolescent Pin is unable to see any essential difference between the German sailor who fornicates with his prosti-

tute sister and the Italian sots whom he entertains in the local taverns—they are all grown-ups whose constant mockery of him force him into an attitude of defiance and bravado. But then civil war between Fascists and anti-Fascists breaks out in Italy, and Pin accidentally falls in with a group of men (including a few of his drunken friends) who are in the process of organizing a partisan brigade. In these men Pin discovers qualities of warmth and generosity he had never known before. Although always on guard against possible betrayal, although still full of suspicion, the boy begins to identify himself with this group of bedraggled partisans, who like him are largely outcasts from society thrown together by fate and circumstance. The concluding episode of the novel, which pictures Pin walking trustfully, arm in arm, with a partisan nicknamed "Cousin," is undoubtedly meant to communicate the idea that the Italian Resistance movement marked the birth of an era in which even the most degraded people of Italy were able at last to find a reason for being that transcended the brute struggle for survival, in which love and trust could overcome hatred and deceit.

Calvino does not idealize his partisans. They are not stalwart Sir Galahads, but ordinary flesh-and-blood people who are quite prone to vulgarity, lust, and cowardice. Yet when they speak of the motives that prompted them to join the struggle against fascism, they sound authentic, they express thoughts and feelings that one readily accepts as genuine. Fundamentally, the outcast Pin is caught up in a movement that offers him at least the possibility of redemption. One of Calvino's characters, a student whose *nom de guerre* is Kim, describes the Resistance in Italy as "an elementary, anonymous struggle for human redemption from all our humiliations: for the workers from exploitation, for the peasant from ignorance, for the petit-bourgeois from his inhibitions, for the pariah from corruption."[5] A messianic fervor permeates this novel, a great hope for redemption animates its humble characters. When Pin links his arm to that of "Cousin," he performs, in his way, an act of faith in the men of the Italian Resistance.

The main character of Renata Viganò's *Agnese Goes to Her Death*, like Pratolini's Maciste and some of the partisans portrayed in *The Path to the Nest of Spiders*, is a dedicated Communist who knows nothing about the teachings of Marx, Engels, and Lenin. She is a peasant woman whose obscure heroism and steadfast devotion to the rebellion against tyranny recalls the protagonist of Gorki's *Mother*. Agnese's involvement in the Resistance begins in the fall of 1943, when Italy's surrender to the Allies provoked the German occupation of the country and subsequently led to the civil war between Italian Fascists and anti-Fascists. Her hatred is directed mainly against the Germans, since it is they who deport her aging husband to a forced labor camp, where he dies of malnutrition.

Like her husband, Agnese is a person of few words; profound loyalty to the Italian Communist partisans, whom she regards as the redeemers of her land; and a human being who acts in accordance with elementary standards of good and evil. Good means to be left in peace, to enjoy friendly rapport with one's neighbors, to earn a decent livelihood. Evil means to be hounded by spies and informers, to see innocent people taken as hostages and shot, to suffer cold and hunger while others who collaborate with the Nazis and Fascists live in luxury. For more than a year Agnese obediently and stoically carries out every order given to her by the partisans with whom she is associated. The subtleties of ideological disputation are of little interest to her: she knows that she has a job to do, and she does it with inflexible determination. Her death at the hands of an enraged German soldier brings the novel to an abrupt and tragic end.

Viganò makes no effort to philosophize about the significance of the characters and events she describes. Her narrative is consistently concrete; her style, terse and direct. From a thematic point of view, Viganò doubtless intended to create in Agnese a character who represented the thousands of obscure people who, prior to the period of Resistance, had abandoned all hope of playing a decisive role in Italian national life, but who, finding themselves suddenly immersed in struggle, were starkly confronted with the need to make a decision and to begin to shape their own destiny. In this sense, Agnese's sacrifice can be seen as a necessary precondition for the redemption of the Italian working class.

Standard Marxist dogma? Willful proletarian partisanship? Yes and no. Viganò wrote her novel in 1947 under the influence of her own personal experiences as a Communist partisan, and her work reflects the powerful current of pro-Communist feeling that swept over Italy during and immediately after World War II. Yet there is nothing abstract or willful about the way she handles her theme. Agnese's allegiance to the Communist-led partisans grows out of her daily experiences; it is a natural part of her way of living and thinking. It should not be forgotten that it was the Italian Communist Party that from the beginning of the Fascist era possessed the most effective and durable conspiratorial apparatus and that paid the heaviest price in terms of personal sacrifice. The Communist Party also played a decisive role in the Resistance movement of 1943 to 1945, and organized some of the most combative partisan brigades. For these historical reasons and because of her own personal experiences, Viganò quite naturally saw fascism and communism as antithetical movements, and not, in accordance with the point of view of many people in the Western world, as two forms of substantially the same political evils.

The fervently hopeful attitude toward the Resistance that pervades the four novels just discussed did not last for long, however. By the late 1940's Italians who had participated in the Resistance were already beginning to take a long critical look at the new Italy that had emerged from the war.

What aroused the resentment of Italians who believed in
the values of the Resistance was that in Italy the same conservative and reactionary forces that had "coexisted" with
fascism were once again ruling the country. The fall of the
Parri Government on November 24, 1945, had been an omi-
nous symptom of restoration politics for all persons who believed in the Resistance as a regenerative force in Italian
society. Ferruccio Parri, a prominent member of the Action
Party—which contributed so magnificently to the Resistance—
and an intransigent anti-Fascist, had been unable to cope
effectively with the charges of "vacillation" and "incompe-
tence" levelled against his government by the Liberal and
Christian democratic parties. The result was that his government fell, to be succeeded in the following years by a series of
Cabinets headed by the Christian Democrat Alcide De Gasperi.
De Gasperi was also a distinguished anti-Fascist, but the era
that began with his assumption of power was certainly unfa-
vorable to the furtherance of the ideals of the Resistance. In
fact, as noted by the historian Giuseppe Mammarella in his
study *Italy after Fascism*:

> After a period of disorientation the forces that traditionally had
> controlled the economic power began to react to what appeared
> to them as an emergency situation, attempting to retake the
> initiative lost to the popular classes. In this case the industrial
> haute bourgeoisie, who desired a rapid reconstruction of industry
> in order to defend its privileged position, allied its interests with
> those of the petit and middle bourgeoisie, whose traditional
> control of the administration was strongly endangered by the
> political purges and the powers assumed by the Committee of
> National Liberation. Such a state of affairs bred a reactionary
> spirit with its traditional class hatred.
>   The growing attitude of hostility was directed not only against
> the popular classes and the parties which defended their demands
> but inevitably also against the Resistance movement, considering
> the great part the popular classes and left-wing parties had
> played in it. Its values were discounted with the result that the

Resistance came finally to be denounced as a great communist conspiracy for the conquest of power; conversely, the old regime and its defense of the "traditional values" was remembered with nostalgia.[6]

The men and women of the Resistance had hoped that the purifying "wind from the north," that is, the combative spirit of antifascism that had pervaded northern Italy from 1943 to 1945, would also "clear the Roman political atmosphere, liberating it from inertia and fear, and also clarifying the objectives for a renovation of the base of Italian society."[7] But restoration, not renovation, was to be the key element of postwar Italian political life; and despite the continued mass following enjoyed by the left-wing parties, the Socialists and Communists, Italy moved gradually and almost inexorably toward a rather grey, uninspired, conservative normalcy. True enough, the Italian people had voted on June 2, 1946, to transform Italy from a monarchy into a democratic republic, but institutional changes were no guarantee of basic internal reforms within the structure of society itself.

Carlo Levi's novel *L'orologio* (*The Watch*), written between 1947 and 1949 and published in 1950, expresses the frustration and resentment felt at that time by thousands of people who had hoped that the spirit of the Resistance would continue to inform Italian life in the postwar years. Levi refers to "that active and creative freedom" symbolized by the Resistance, a spirit which, unfortunately, "like all miracles, last a very short time." He writes mournfully about the left-wing Resistance intellectuals who were destined to failure because of their inability to emerge from the rarefied atmosphere of pure abstract ideas and ideals. He denounces the new bureaucrats swarming all over Rome, laments the rapid "Americanization" of Italy in the immediate postwar years, describes the dreadful poverty of the Roman masses, and, in one tragicomic chapter, speaks of post-Fascist Italy as again, as always, divided between a vast horde of "Luigini"—those who live off the labor of others and idle away their time in pretentious displays of wealth and pseudoculture—and the "contadini"—the "peasants" or people who really produce something worthwhile and make life possible for the rest.

Three important Resistance novels that reflect some of the discouraging limitations and failures of the Resistance are Cesare Pavese's *The House on the Hill,* 1949, Carlo Cassola's *Fausto and Anna,* 1952, and Mario Tobino's *The Underground,* 1962.

Pavese, Cassola, and Tobino are not entirely devoid of that faith in the fundamental goodness and capacity for sacrifice of the Italian common man that sustained Pratolini, Calvino, Viganò, and Vittorini. They, too, see the Resistance as a liberation, as a collective struggle for justice and freedom. Corrado, the protagonist and narrator of Pavese's *The House on the Hill,* although aware that he himself is too reflective, too fearful and indecisive to take an active part in the Resistance, has great confidence in the revolutionary capacities of his working-class companions. The common people of Italy, he says at one point, "are not angry with the Germans, not only with them: they are angry with their former bosses. This is not a war of soldiers, which could end tomorrow; this is the war of the poor, the war of the desperate against hunger, misery, prisons, disgust."[8] At another moment he exclaims optimistically that the Resistance marks the beginning of an era that belongs to the working classes, since "the future is in the factories," he says, with those who work and produce. Similar thoughts are expressed on occasion by the befuddled intellectual protagonist of *Fausto and Anna* and by many of the persons who form part of the partisan movement described in Tobino's *The Underground.*

Yet despite this optimistic component in their works, Pavese, Cassola, and Tobino present us with a more complex and at the same time less hopeful view of the Resistance. Pavese's *The House on the Hill* is much more the story of an alienated, nostalgia-ridden man than it is an account of heroic exploits performed by guerrillas intent on redeeming their country from oppression. For Corrado, a forty-year-old school-teacher who spends most of his time reminiscing about his lost childhood and wondering whether he is the father of a boy born to one of his former sweethearts (he never finds out), all of human history can be summed up in the expression *plus ça change, plus reste la même chose.* Corrado is a deeply pessimistic man whose sadness, with respect to the Resistance, is conditioned mainly by his inability to find a satisfactory answer to the questions: why have so many innocent persons suffered and died in this war? Why do the dead faces of even our bitterest enemies evoke in us feelings of pity and compassion and compel us to seek more than merely human justification for our violence? But there are also less spiritual reasons for Corrado's pessimism. He recalls the frivolous, stupid comments some of his colleagues at school had made to the effect that Mussolini's regime was not to blame for the tragedy that befell the Italian people in World War II. When his former sweetheart Cate asks him if he is a Fascist, he replies: "We are all fascists, my dear Cate. If we are not, we ought to revolt, to throw bombs, to risk our skins. Anyone who lets things happen and is content, is already a fascist."[9] Indeed, Corrado makes many disparaging observations about the Italian people that tend to attenuate one's sense of identification with Fonso, Nando, Tono, and other characters in Pavese's novel who do risk their lives fighting the Fascists. "We Italians," says Corrado, "obey force alone. Then, with the excuse that it was force, we laugh about it. Nobody takes anything seriously."[10]

Carlo Cassola, who in some respects is very close in spirit to Pavese, published his *Fausto and Anna* in 1952, when it was abundantly clear to many Italians that, although the Resistance had helped to liberate Italy, it had not solved some of the social, moral, and political problems that had plagued the country both before and during the Fascist era. Certain of these problems are embodied in the characters of Cassola's novel, which spans a period of eight years, from the latter half of the 1930's to the end of World War II.

Fausto Errera, the novel's protagonist, is the incarnation of the kind of moral confusion and political ineptitude which many observers, both foreign and Italian, have found to be all too common among Italy's middle-class intelligentsia. The son of a well-to-do provincial lawyer, Fausto is portrayed in the first half of the novel as a bored, irascible youth who affects antibourgeois tastes, has unfounded literary ambitions, and suffers intensely from a sense of inner emptiness. His two redeeming traits are his distaste for the sham heroics of the local Fascist hierarchy, coupled with a genuine desire to find some purpose in life other than that prescribed by his respectable, conformist parents. The outbreak of civil war in Italy gives Fausto the opportunity he is seeking. He returns from Rome to his native town of Volterra, and there joins forces with a group of hard-core Communists who are laying the groundwork for a partisan movement in Tuscany.

But various factors prevent Fausto from participating wholeheartedly in the Resistance. First of all, his impossible love for Anna Mannoni, who had once returned his affections but finally rejected him when she discovered how shallow and unreliable he was, keeps him in a constant state of anxiety. Often, instead of concentrating on his responsibilities as a member of the partisan movement, Fausto (like Doctor Zhivago, to whom he has been sometimes compared) prefers to daydream about Anna. For a brief period, Anna almost consents to go back to him; but, unfortunately, during the time Fausto was in Rome, she had decided to enter into a loveless but secure marriage which she is now unwilling to break. Anna's justified rejection of Fausto is not, however, the most serious obstacle to his total involvement in the Resistance movement. Even more important is his discovery in himself of the very religious impulses which he had mercilessly mocked only several years earlier. Suddenly the sanctity of life, the Judeo-Christian injunction against killing takes complete possession of him, and he begins to talk about man's indestructible soul. By reason of this newly-found belief, he cannot, of course, share the materialistic convictions of the Communist intellectuals and workers who form the backbone of the partisan movement in Tuscany. When a poor working-class partisan exclaims: "When they come to carry me away, I want a red flag on my casket, because that's my faith, and that's all," Fausto replies: "In the presence of death, communism doesn't count for anything."[11]

Cassola's novel is filled with precise, realistic descriptions of guerrilla warfare, of tedious periods of waiting, of crises and heroic deeds, of lengthy if inconclusive discussions about war, fascism, religion, and communism. Few, if any, postwar Resistance novelists have succeeded so well in conveying the atmosphere of tension, conflict, and expectancy that pervaded Italy in those years. But the central problem of his novel— which hinges on the reasons behind Fausto's repudiation of communism and his search for an alternative way of justifying the Resistance—is not effectively developed, precisely because Fausto himself is such a mediocre and colorless personality. After becoming acquainted with him in the first sections of the novel, the reader is not prepared to accept as legitimate Fausto's posture of moral superiority with respect to the supposedly cynical Communists who execute their enemies without benefit of trial and who, in the person of Claudio, a "Nazi-like" Italian partisan commander, are motivated by a thirst for blood and revenge.

Another aspect of Cassola's novel that leaves one with a deeply ambivalent feeling about the Resistance is the story's ending, which depicts the arrival of American forces and the subsequent disbanding of the partisan organization, now under Allied jurisdiction. Cassola describes the dramatic moment in which the partisans, flushed with the joy of victory, were peremptorily ordered by an Italian-speaking American lieutenant to hand over their weapons to Allied authorities and to remove the red bandanas from their necks. No sooner had the Americans arrived, Cassola notes, "than the partisan organization was in complete disarray. . . . In the town there were still soldiers coming and going, and in the street automobiles were continuously passing by, but without arousing curiosity any more. Life was gradually returning to normal, the people were resuming their usual occupations. The peasants had returned to the fields to reap the grain."[12]

This sudden return to normalcy, coming as it does after the intense excitement of guerrilla warfare and the hope for renewal, is depressingly anticlimactic. In the final pages, Anna is talking with her husband Miro. She is resigned to her loveless marriage; he is contentedly puffing on a Camel cigarette given to him by an American soldier. It is nighttime. Anna looks out of her window, still searching rather aimlessly for Fausto. "It was completely dark. Nobody was there." And so *Fausto and Anna* comes to an end. Anna's life will take its normal loveless course, just as Italian life in general will resume its normal pattern and rhythm. For Cassola, the Resistance helped to restore Italy to a relatively dignified normality and accomplished no more and no less than this.

Exactly a decade passed between the appearance of Cassola's *Fausto and Anna* and the publication of Mario Tobino's *The Underground*, which won the Strega literary prize for 1962. A psychiatrist by profession, Tobino worked intermittently for several years on this Resistance novel, basing his narrative not only on oral reports and various historical documents but also on direct personal experience as a resister during the years from 1943 to 1945.

The Underground is written with unusual precision and thoroughness. Doubtless no other Italian Resistance novelist comes as close as does Tobino to achieving what the German historian Ranke meant when he exhorted his colleagues to strive for exactitude, to reconstruct the past *wie es eigentlich gewesen*. One is convinced that *The Underground* describes the Resistance "as it really was," from the first crude and awkward organizational efforts carried on by a minority of dedicated anti-Fascists to the final collective movement that involved ever more massive numbers of Italians from all classes and walks of life. Yet exactitude and attention to detail, although essential to the historian, are not the basic ingredients of fiction. As literature, as a novel dealing with the Italian Resistance, *The Underground* is a somewhat tedious work. Very few of its fifty-odd characters are delineated with sufficient depth to provoke in the reader a feeling of close involvement and identification with the fictional world created by the author.

Tobino emphasizes the collective character of the Italian Resistance by refusing to accord to any single person the role of protagonist. The Italian Resistance, he implies, had no indispensable leader like General de Gaulle, no essential motivating force other than the need felt by men and women of all types to redeem themselves and their country from twenty years of servitude. But Tobino, unlike the Resistance novelists of the immediate postwar period, does not confine his narrative within specific urban or regional limits. He devotes considerable attention to showing how the conspirators of the Tuscan town of Medusa establish political relations with other Italian centers of resistance and with the Allies. In addition, he gives us a direct view of Italian Fascist activities during the years of civil war, particularly with respect to the renewed effort made by Mussolini's followers in 1944 and 1945 to restore the confidence of the Italian people in fascism's democratic and equalitarian intentions. The result of this multifaceted description is a remarkably complete picture of the Resistance period.

The Underground offers a fundamentally favorable interpretation of the Italian Resistance. The tenacity of the anti-Fascist conspirators and the stocism and capacity for self-sacri-

fice of many of the characters are given due attention and recognition by Tobino. Indeed, Anselmo, a young doctor, dies at
the end of the novel in an attempt to save the lives of several
English and Russian soldiers trapped in a cave, and Saverio,
an ex-admiral of the Italian navy, boldly defies his Fascist in-
terrogators and pays for his courage with his life. Nor is brav-
ery only a masculine virtue in *The Underground*. Teresa, the
sister of an anti-Fascist philosophy professor, transforms her
home in the countryside into a hideout for the partisans, and
Rosa, a schoolteacher, risks her life by crossing over the German lines to deliver a message from the partisans to the Allied
military command in Naples. But this favorable description of
the Resistance is somewhat attenuated by several less hopeful
aspects of the novel. In the opening section of *The Underground*, Tobino states in no uncertain terms that the majority
of Italians were guilty of the crimes committed by the Fascist
regime and responsible for the outbreak of the Second World
War. With the exception of a slim minority, he writes, "all
Italians were responsible for the war. The distinctions between
ordinary citizens were minor. Many during the twenty years
of dictatorship had, within themselves or among trusted
friends, uttered imprecations or joked about facism, but it was
a fact of no importance, they were only words. Very many
had applauded later on, they had officially cheered victories;
during street demonstrations they had put on the masks of in-
vincible warriors."[13]

This unflattering observation, although intermingled with
some other comments about the human virtues of the Italian
people, recalls the pessimistic appraisal of the Italian character
offered by Corrado in Pavese's *The House on the Hill*, as well
as certain of the negative character types who appear in Cassola's *Fausto and Anna*. Tobino refers to the political prisoners released by Marshal Badoglio, Mussolini's successor in July
1943 as head of the Italian government, as "the only true anti-
Fascists." These and other similar remarks, coupled with vari-

ous episodes interspersed throughout the novel, give one the feeling that the Italian Resistance was only a brief and brilliant chapter in an otherwise slow-moving, repetitive history whose main themes would remain unchanged by the war and by the partisan struggle. For example, nowhere in Tobino's novel does one sense that the Resistance might possibly renew and revolutionize Italian society. The differences in caste and class that separate the rich from the poor, the privileged from the downtrodden, are taken for granted and accepted by almost all the characters, including most of the supposedly militant Communists.

The Resistance novels discussed in this essay have much to say to Italian and non-Italian readers alike. Each in its own way brings us into direct contact with a period in recent Italian history that ought not to be ignored by anyone interested in understanding some of the crucial political and moral problems of our time. Although not without artistic flaws, these novels have far more literary merits than defects. They effectively illuminate aspects of the human condition even if their setting, characters, and themes grow out of a specifically Italian reality. Each represents a *prise de conscience* with regard to a conflict whose dimensions were and remain universal, whose impact on today's world cannot be overestimated. Each contains characters who embody a wide range of traits and values which, when actively expressed in the arena of political struggle, assume large significance for the future of mankind.

NOTES

1. The strikers' demands were circulated in a series of clandestine manifestoes that have been published by the historian Giorgio Vaccarino in his essay "Gli scioperi del marzo 1943—contributo per una storia del movimento operaio a Torino," *Aspetti della Resistenza in Piemonte* (Turin, 1950).

2. Readers interested in the historical development of the Italian Resistance Movement should consult: Charles Delzell, *Mussolini's Enemies: The Italian Antifascist Resistance* (Princeton, Princeton University Press, 1961) and Frank Rosengarten, *The Italian Anti-Fascist Press 1919–1945* (Cleveland, Case Western Reserve University Press, 1968).

3. I have used the following Italian editions of these novels: *Uomini e no*, 1st ed. (Milan, Bompiani, 1945); *Cronache di poveri amanti* (Milan, Mondadori, 1966); *Il sentiero dei nidi di ragno*, 3rd ed. (Turin, Einaudi, 1954); *L'Agnese va a morire*, 4th ed. (Turin, Einaudi, 1954); *La casa in collina* in *Prima che il gallo canti*, 2nd ed. (Turin, Einaudi, 1954), pp. 135–311; *Fausto e Anna*, 5th ed. (Turin, Einaudi, 1964); *El clandestino*, 6th ed. (Milan, Mondadori, 1962). All English translations of passages taken from these editions and cited in this essay are mine.

The English translations of these novels are as follows: *A Tale of Poor Lovers* (New York, Viking Press, 1949); *The Path to the Nest of Spiders*, trans. Archibald Colquhoun (Boston, Walker, 1957); *The House on the Hill*, trans. W. J. Strachan (New York, Walker, 1961); *Fausto and Anna*, trans. Isabel Quigly (New York, Pantheon Books, 1960); *The Underground*, trans. Raymond Rosenthal (New York, Doubleday, 1966).

4. For additional information on the writers discussed in this essay, see the appropriate bibliographical notes at the end of the chapter.

5. Italo Calvino, *Il sentiero dei nidi di ragno*, p. 146.

6. Giuseppe Mammarella, *Italy after Fascism* (Montreal, Mario Casalini Ltd., 1964), p. 99.

7. Ibid, p. 94.

8. Cesare Pavese, *La casa in collina* in *Prima che il gallo canti*, p. 229.

9. Ibid, p. 184.

10. Ibid, p. 206.

11. Carlo Cassola, *Fausto e Anna*, p. 164.

12. Ibid, p. 307.

13. Mario Tobino, *Il clandestino*, p. 28.

11 GADDA, PASOLINI, AND EXPERIMENTALISM: FORM OR IDEOLOGY?

Olga Ragusa

The subject of this essay is threefold—threefold precisely in the sense which the title implies of simply juxtaposing the names of two writers and a concept rather than relating them more closely at a deeper level. To do full justice to the complex development of Carlo Emilio Gadda, to the equally complex but entirely different development of Pier Paolo Pasolini, and to the multiple aspects of linguistic and structural experimentation in Italian literature, three distinct and quite extensive studies would be required.

The connection between Gadda and Pasolini is not genetic. Although to the hasty reader the two are united by their rejection of the traditional literary language and their tapping of the dialect resources of Italy, it cannot truly be maintained that the older writer is a necessary premise for the younger, as Virgil was for Dante, Mallarmé for Valéry, or Shakespeare for Manzoni. Pasolini's work, which ranges from lyric to philosophical poetry, from political to literary journalism, from travel reports to film scenarios, is not patterned on the example—the Italians would say "the lesson"—of Gadda, who made his debut in 1926 in the pages of the review *Solaria* with literary essays and narrative fragments that owe much to the hermeticism of that time.

But though the connection is not a genetic one, it exists. And it exists primarily by virtue of the concept of experimentalism. The term was first used by the Romance philologist Gianfranco Contini in his studies of early Italian literature.[1] It was then chosen by Pasolini to describe an important, and to him determining, aspect of the poetic production of the Fifties. And finally it was adopted by the new avant-garde, the so-called *Gruppo 63*. This group of writers—this "new literary generation," as their mentor Luciano Anceschi called them—first gathered together in 1963 at a noisy literary congress in Palermo which reminded many of the participants of the fuss and fanfare raised half a century earlier by the futurists. The writers of *Gruppo 63* were convinced that, as one of their exponents put it, the literature of the future would be marked by experimentation with form and not with subject matter, that is, by a new use of the means of expression rather than by raising to literary dignity—as was done in naturalism, for instance—subjects that had formerly been avoided. Angelo Guglielmi, one of the theoreticians of the group wrote:

> Up to now language has tried to reflect reality as in a mirror. Henceforth language must take its place at the very heart of reality and instead of being a mirror must become a faithful recording machine. Or, as a second solution, language must remain outside and look in at reality as through a filter, so that objects will appear in distorted, surrealistic, or hallucinatory images and forms, and thus once again be capable of revealing their hidden meanings.[2]

In the new literature, then, and in the experimental novel, as it was soon to be called, language would no longer state and describe, but mimic and express. Pasolini made a similar distinction in the 1956 article "Il neo-sperimentalismo" referred to above, when he opposed the "stylistic syndrome of the new 'committed' writers" to "pathological, expressionistic neo-experimentalism."[3] But while both uses of language, the mimetic and the expressionistic, appear true and revolutionary innovations with respect to its conventional use in narrative to reflect the chronology of events in terms of logical discourse, only the second, the expressionistic, actually represents a total subversion of the accepted social and psychological structures. Only the expressionistic use of language, in the words of another critic, concerns itself with "the perceptual level, with the way in which time and space are conceived, how objects are seen, how feelings are recognized and designated, how syntax is articulated."[4] Or to return to the connection between Gadda and Pasolini, only Gadda—for reasons that I hope will become clear in the course of this essay—is recognized by the new avant-garde, whether it thinks of itself as politically committed or uncommitted, as a true and authentic forerunner.

There are certain obvious differences between Gadda and Pasolini, a consideration of which will, I believe, place the discussion of their work in a better perspective. The first—and it is no mean one—concerns the generation to which each belongs. Gadda was born in 1893; Pasolini, in 1922. Both, upon reaching manhood, found themselves on the threshold of war. But though some historians like to link the two World Wars, seeing in the second merely a continuation of the first, they were in fact quite dissimilar, both in the manner of fighting and in the changes which each brought to the social environment. Gadda fought in the First World War; he was captured and spent a long time in a prison camp made famous in the history of Italian literature because he had as barracks mates Ugo Betti, destined to become Italy's most important playwright after Pirandello, and Bonaventura Tecchi, who became a writer and scholar of repute and held the chair of German literature at the University of Rome until his death in 1968. During his early years Gadda witnessed and lived through that collapse of old and well-established values which characterizes the transition period between the nineteenth and early twentieth centuries. The world that is reflected in most of his works is that of the stable *fin de siècle* bourgeoisie, specifically of the Milanese upper classes—whose children were taken to play in the park of the Castello; who were concerned with keeping their houses in immaculate order; who built summer villas among the hills of the Brianza, the gentle countryside north of Milan immortalized by Manzoni; and whose family memories included the still vivid recollections of Hapsburg rule, felt not so much finished and done with as simply removed in time.

Pasolini, instead, spent his childhood following his army officer father from one military post in northern Italy to another. In 1943 while he was studying at the University of Bologna, he was evacuated, as were thousands of other civilians all over Europe. He was sent to Casarsa, the village in the Friuli from which his mother came. There, in that northeastern corner of Italy close to the Yugoslav border, he watched the Partisan warfare, which was as distinctive of the later years of the Second World War in occupied Europe as trench warfare had been of the First. Pasolini's earliest works were poems in Friulian, inspired by his love for the simple, instinctive peasant life of a rural region that progress had bypassed, the same region that a century earlier served as the setting for Nievo's wonderful *contes champêtres*. But Pasolini's interest in dialect poetry was not limited to his practice of it. A number of essays attest to his broader view, and in 1955 he published an important anthology of Italian dialect poetry, *Canzoniere italiano*. Its long introductory essay combines scholarly competence with a Marxian interpretation of the relationship of folk and art poetry, dwelling on the reasons for the progressive disappearance of folk poetry in the awakening class consciousness of the backward peasant populations on their way to urban proletariat status. Marxism, of course, is a doctrine that played no role in the formation of Gadda, whose whole orientation was away from the political and economic problems of society and toward those of the individual and collective psyche. Indeed, in the figures of Freud and Marx, we have as good symbols as any to epitomize the historico-cultural differences in the situation we have been discussing.

The second difference between Gadda and Pasolini concerns their temperaments. There seems to be something eternally young in Pasolini, and this impression is borne out by his restless seeking for always new avenues of expression: from poetry to militant journalism, from the novel to cinema. Gadda, by contrast, was born old, old and weary, with a tendency to pessimism, to bitter humor, to foreseeing catastrophes and therefore treading lightly. In the self-portrait which Pasolini contributed in 1960 to a volume of autobiographies by contemporary Italian writers, he speaks of his daily routine, and especially of his tireless wanderings through Rome, the city to which he moved in 1950:

> I spend the greater part of my life beyond the edges of the city, or as a bad neo-realist poet imitating the hermetics would say, beyond the city's end-stations. I love life with such violence and such intensity that no good can come of it. I am speaking of the physical side of life: the sun, the grass, youth. It is an addiction more terrible than cocaine. It doesn't cost anything, and it is available in boundless quantities. I devour it ravenously. . . . How it will all end, I don't know. . . .[5]

In his contribution to the same volume, Gadda wrote:

> By temperament I am rather inclined to solitude, incapable as I am of chattering vivaciously, uninterested in mundane social life. I approach my fellow-men and associate with them with a certain amount of difficulty and hesitation; the hesitation and difficulty increase, the more virtuous they are. In the presence of another human being I feel like a student at an examination. Instead, in my leisure hours I take pleasure in clarifying some "algebra" to myself. This tires me less than a drawing-room conversation where I am forced to appear witty and intelligent without being either.[6]

The juxtaposition of the two passages suggests that we are dealing with two personalities that would have manifested opposite characteristics even if the external circumstances of their lives had been identical. Gadda and Pasolini were not only born into different historical times; they were born as two completely different psychological types. The two facts that psychoanalytically inclined critics would pounce on and magnify—that Gadda and Pasolini both lost a dearly loved and not easily forgotten older brother through war, and that each had a typically ambivalent relation to his parents—turn out to be insignificant and nondetermining in the light of the broad attitudes toward life which make the one man a misanthrope and the other—if I may be permitted to give the word its etymological meaning—a philanthrope. This divergence in basic personality traits is of necessity reflected in the manner in which each faces his task as a writer.

During a recent trip to the United States, the novelist Italo Calvino told of a radio talk on the building industry which Gadda was once asked to give. It seems that he spoke first, with scientific precision, of houses built of reinforced concrete and how it is impossible to insulate them against noise. He then went on to the physiological effects of noise on the nervous system. And finally in a display of verbal fireworks he burst forth against the noises of city life themselves.[7] A similar mounting progression is recalled by Gadda in the self-portrait from which I quoted earlier. He speaks there of the many "philosophical meditations," all written in excellent prose (i.e., conventional style), which he has stored away at home and which are survivals of a time when he had not yet devoted himself to narrative writing. He then mentions the effects the experience of the war had on him: how because of it he turned from philosophy to the vicissitudes of human life and found himself torn between a strong predisposition to give expression exclusively to his lyric and satirical veins and an equally strong desire to understand his fellowmen by "noting down events." Finally he acknowledges that for him writing is often a means of "seeking vengeance" for the injuries inflicted on men by fate: "So that my storytelling often manifests the resentful tone of the person who speaks while holding back his wrath, his indignation." The anecdote and the self-analysis reveal that Gadda did not choose the narrative style which is most closely associated with his name because he was incapable of expressing himself in any other way. Rather he chose it —or it chose him, a formulation closer, as we shall see, to his view of the polarization of tensions which determines the relationship between the writer and his subject—because it alone could give shape to the noumenal reality, that "algebra" of the universe, which he pursues. On this last point, it might be fruitful to consider carefully the answer Gadda gave when in 1950 he was asked for his opinion on the then triumphant school of neorealism. He voiced his lack of sympathy for its basic assumptions in these terms:

> It is all well and good to tell me that a volley of machine gun fire is reality. But what I expect from the novel is that behind those seven ounces of lead there be some tragic tension, some consecution at work, a mystery, perhaps the reason for the fact, or the absence of reasons. . . . The fact by itself, the object by itself, is but the dead body of reality, the—pardon the expression—fecal residue of history. I would therefore want the poetics of neorealism to be extended to include a nouminous dimension.[8]

The search for the nouminous dimension is what gives its peculiar form to *Eros e Priapo (Da furore a cenere)*, 1967 [Eros and Priapus (From Frenzy to Ashes)], Gadda's most recently published work. In spite of what the jacket blurb claims, this is not an antinovel—except if we are ready to make of this expression a catchall for everything that we cannot define otherwise; nor is it a piece of historical writing, history being the complement to fiction as a narrative mode. *Eros e Priapo*, an indictment of the Fascist era, might be called a psychoanalysis of history, conceived as a scientific research problem with theorems and propositions, but conducted with a virulence and an emotional involvement which allow for no other conclusion than the one already implied in the premise. Specifically, it is an *exposé* of the pathology of exhibitionistic narcissism and its effects on an audience (in this case the Italian people under fascism), seen with the devastating clarity and single-mindedness of an individual who could never be a consenting and participating member of that audience. Early in the book Gadda states that his purpose in writing it is to induce self-knowledge, for "only an act of knowledge can bring about the resurrection of the Italian people, if indeed resurrection can even be attempted from so horrendous a ruin."

The two novels of Gadda's I am about to discuss also deal with knowledge. The first is a detective novel *manqué*, which means that the quest for the specific knowledge which is its objective is eventually foiled. The second proclaims by its very title that knowledge is its subject, and it is in fact a *meditation* on anguish and not the dramatization of that feeling through a story. Both novels can also be said to deal with ruin, "frenzy and ashes." In the first, crime upsets the social order and allows all the baseness and vileness that usually lies hidden under the mantle of convention to rise to the surface. In the second, it is mental disease, *il male oscuro* (the dark evil), which muddies the waters and breaches that moral order which appeases the savage drives in man and makes civilized living possible. In neither novel do we reach the stage of "resurrection," that is, of catharsis. They are both unfinished, perhaps unfinishable.

The German avant-garde writer, Günter Grass, has described *Quer pasticciaccio brutto de via Merulana*, 1957 (*That Awful Mess on Via Merulana*) as "the only crime novel I enjoyed and admired." Although I consider the book less interesting and powerful than Gadda's other novel, *La cognizione del dolore*, 1963 (*Acquainted With Grief*, New York, 1969), I shall discuss it first and at greater length because its setting is Rome, a city which is familiar to the foreigner and which can thus serve as a point of orientation in an otherwise labyrinthine and surreal representation of a particular social reality. As I have already said, *Quer pasticciaccio* is a murder mystery whose author fails to give the reader the satisfaction of telling him what really happened and of identifying the criminal. Actually there are two crimes involved: a jewelry theft, which is the occasion for high comedy, and a horrible murder, which opens the gates to the nether world, represented simultaneously as the social underworld and the psychological abyss of uncontrolled passion. The two crimes are related externally because they both take place on the same third-floor landing of the apartment house at 219 via Merulana, a building which is known to the neighboring proletariat (and try translating even as simple a phrase as "la gente der popolo" without losing its full flavor!) as the palace of gold. The internal connection between the crimes is that they both lead to the same group of suspects. These individuals, all mysteriously associated with one another, belong to the rural population of Latium, the countryside of Sabine fame surrounding Rome, a unique kind of *sub*urbia which appears in the opening pages of the book as the luxuriant home of a prolific people and is seen in the final pages as a gray landscape of abject hovels housing the lowest kind of vice and deception.

There is no central character in the novel, although readers in search of the accustomed "hero" may think they discern him in Francesco Ingravallo, familiarly known as Don Ciccio. Ingravallo, a police officer assigned to the homicide squad, is on hand in the first and last scenes of the book and is otherwise omnipresent as the man in charge of the investigation. But on closer scrutiny it becomes apparent that though Gadda represents him in all his human complexity, he is actually using him as a screen through which his own, Gadda's observations and ideas are filtered. The information we are given about Ingravallo's background and inner life, although revealed in a kind of running inner monologue which taps the depth of his consciousness, is of the most generic sort. His idolization of Liliana Balducci, for instance, the murdered woman whom he had known, is no more than the respect felt by the social inferior for gentility of manner and of being. His gift for intuition is the indispensable detective's flair for discovering what is hidden. His sensual appreciation of the physical attractions of the Balduccis' bevy of "nieces" and maids is the typical reaction of a youngish man of thirty-five living amid the sensual seductions of Rome. Like the "new" French novelists, Gadda eschews psychological analysis, while he dwells on the "atoms" of mental activity. Much of the action of *Quer pasticciaccio* is seen through the eyes of Ingravallo—a familiar procedure in the modern novel—but Ingravallo himself is not an object of observation for the author. His portrait and his story are never finished. He is essentially a filtering consciousness, an instrument of knowledge.

The instrumental use of the principal character and its importance for the structure of the book become even clearer in the light of two statements made by Gadda in two very different contexts. The first is an exposition of Ingravallo's theory of crime. It comes at the beginning of the novel, but only in retrospect do we realize how strategically it is placed, for only in retrospect do we see it as the necessary, if camouflaged, direction signal that it is.

> He [Ingravallo] sustained among other things that unforeseen catastrophes are never the consequence or the effect, if you prefer, of a single motive, of *a* cause singular; but they are rather like a whirlpool, a cyclonic point of depression in the consciousness of the world, towards which a whole multitude of converging causes has contributed. He also used words like knot or tangle or muddle, or *gnommero,* which in Roman dialect means skein.

The second passage deals with the personality in general and Gadda's personality as a writer in particular. It occurs in an article, "Come lavoro" ("My Method of Writing"), which Gadda contributed to a literary periodical in 1950 and which is now part of his important collection of essays *I viaggi la morte,* 1958 (Voyages Death). Expressing himself in terms which are curiously reminiscent of and at times identical with those of the passage above, Gadda writes:

> Each of us seems to me to be a lump or knot or tangle of physical and metaphysical relationships (the distinction is merely operational). Every relationship is kept suspended and in equipoise, within the "field" that is proper to it, by a polarity of tensions. . . . The act of self-expression—of writing—is the result, or better the symptom of that polarization which occurs between the "I" that judges and the thing judged, between the "I" that represents and the thing represented.

It is obvious on the strength of the passages just quoted that Gadda rejects both the traditional notion of the logical coherence of the personality and the equally traditional (Romantic) image of the artist as a creator. The result of this position is that in telling his story Gadda cannot pursue an overall linear development in which events are related to one another consecutively and logically. Instead, he will pursue each event in depth, each one being, as he has said, a juncture of causes which are in their turn tangles of other causes, large and small, whose relative significance it is impossible to extricate. Thus Commendatore Angeloni's preference in food—the hams, marinated herring, or jellied chicken mold he has delivered to his door—assumes at one point the same importance as Signora Balducci's ambiguous attachment to the girls she befriends or her equally ambiguous relationship to her nephew, or so at least the latter seems to the suspicious Ingravallo.

But how can we, readers who are outside the story, determine here and elsewhere how much of what Ingravallo "observes" is actually a fabrication of his "intuition" and how much of what Gadda tells us is actually essential to the plot—if plot indeed there is? In *Quer pasticciaccio,* though the reader is never directly addressed, he is constantly drawn into the story as a participant. Over and over again, the pieces of the puzzle are placed in his hands and he is left to do with them what he can. If only he were able to free himself of the inveterate habit of "reading on," of letting scenes passively unroll before him! For what he should be doing at every turn is "sink into" the page, pursuing each fact, each phenomenon through all the associations available to him, just as the author is doing on his part and Ingravallo (standing for the whole corps of detectives) is doing in exemplary fashion on his. It can readily be seen that no subject is better suited to this kind of storytelling than the murder mystery. The green scarf of the delivery boy (but was he a delivery boy?), the punched tram ticket (when and by whom was it lost?) seem to urge the plot on. But the investigation bogs down and the plot breaks off. Tired, hungry, and stupefied, Ingravallo sits at police headquarters, sunk in his musings. The "mystery" is all about us. Gadda, being a scientist (he worked for many years as an electrical engineer), belonging to the race of post-metaphysical man, rejects the mystical and the supernatural. But the irrational, the *sub*natural or *super*natural, takes its revenge and presents him with an epistemological problem. And so he creates Ingravallo, a detective whose business it is to ferret out knowledge and whose fate it is to remain ignorant.

It is legitimate at this point to ask whether *Quer pasticciaccio*, in addition to being read as a metaphor—a giant emblem for the human condition, similar in this to the *Divine Comedy*, for instance—also lends itself to a naturalistic reading as the depiction of a particular society at a well-established moment in history. The book's ready success, its translations in spite of the linguistic difficulties posed by its stylistic texture, would appear to point in the direction of an affirmative answer. There is no doubt, for instance, that the setting is conceived realistically, even though as in *The Magic Mountain*, for instance, it can easily be turned into symbol. In *Quer pasticciaccio* we are

in Rome, in February 1927, amid the *nouveau riche* created by
the First World War. The financial success of these "sharks,"
to use a favorite expression of that time, has whet the appetite
of the lower classes, who, as in the building at 219 via Merulana, surround and enviously watch them. Every once in a
while a choice morsel falls from the table of the rich: Liliana
Balducci's childlessness (a fault in nature) leads her to heap
gifts on the young and healthy who can be presumed to bear
children. We are in Rome also because we recognize the
familiar landmarks: the basilica of Santa Maria Maggiore, the
elephant on Piazza della Minerva, the open-air market in
Piazza Vittorio, the Collegio Romano, the Villa Borghese . . .
and on and on. There is hardly a page without a place name;
although we must note that because Gadda does not favor
description, these words remain ends in themselves, evocative
simply because words are magic formulas, incantations. We
are in Rome because of the peculiar quality of its air, its lumi-
nous sky, the strolling of its citizens at dusk, the marketing
housewives with their bulging shopping bags—how delighted
Gadda is by the leafy celery and the broccoli that stick out of
them! The humble, everyday life of the Urbs, quite unique in
the world. And finally we are in the Rome that is the paradise
of bureaucracy, ruled over by the hated "Lantern Jaw, the
bowler-hatted Death's Head, the Emir with black fez, and with
plume,"—by Mussolini in short, to note only a few of the
epithets with which Gadda heaps scorn on him.

Much has been made of the violence of Gadda's attacks on
Mussolini, of the ferocious inventiveness with which he fixes
on always new features of the Duce's personality. This is taken
to be an indication of the book's firm location in a definite
political environment. I do not question Gadda's antifascism,
but am inclined to attribute it, more than to political idealism
and thereby applicable to a specific historical setting, to the
reactions of a highly individualistic, self-centered man, who
feels his jealously guarded inner life *constantly* in danger of

being impinged upon. It is this fear, which often reaches the proportions of a persecution complex, that triggers passages such as the three-page footnote in the original version of the novel (later omitted), where Gadda lashes out at the regime's desire to see everyone married and busy contributing to the demographic campaign. With an explosion of historical, often very amusing, references to famous men who remained bachelors (Beethoven, Petrarch, Saint Augustine, Stendhal, Kant—he names at least fifty) and to other equally famous men who married to their discomfiture and eternal regret (Agamemnon, Napoleon, Shakespeare, Stalin, Peter Petrovich, who was strangled on orders from his wife Catherine the Great, etc., etc.), Gadda makes his plea for being permitted to remain what he elsewhere calls "a solitary glutton, unmarried and melancholy, and subject to fits of cyclothymia."

We are back then where we started. For all its being rooted in historical and geographical reality, *Quer pasticciaccio* is a novel that has left naturalism behind. Not that Gadda's imagination is not nature-bound, as is attested by his strongly concrete and sensual vocabulary. As a matter of fact, he seems to take contact with the world almost exclusively through the senses. His verbal ingenuity, his creative facility, remind one often of the physical pleasure of "mouthing" words, an extension of the joys of the palate, of his self-confessed gluttony. There is a magnificent passage to be mentioned in this connection, an unforgettable episode in *La cognizione del dolore* which shows the principal character gorging himself on an enormous lobster. It is carried off with such Rabelaisean gusto that it reveals the hand of the man both attracted and repelled, but essentially fascinated, by "oral" excess. Excess of this kind leads inevitably to deformation, and the world Gadda writes about is deformed by his singular, eccentric—I am tempted to say, in this connection, artistic as opposed to moralistic—vision. In this sense Gadda has gone well beyond naturalism in its literary-historical definition. Like the expressionists in the very years when he began to write, he must have felt at one time that it was senseless to set about "reproducing" the world as it is, that it is indeed impossible to do so, given the absence of any permanent rapport between the individual and reality.

Much of what we have said about *Quer pasticciaccio* also holds true for *La cognizione*, but generally to a more concentrated degree. *Quer pasticciaccio* is an unfinished work; *La cognizione* is not only unfinished but also fragmentary. In *Quer pasticciaccio* the creation of suspense inherent in the detective story is constantly undercut by the author's pursuit of the verbal and other associations that come his way. In *La cognizione* the story line at one point breaks down completely. (It is taken up again in Part Two, both parts of the book dealing with the same subject matter in a manner somewhat reminiscent of Faulkner's *The Sound and the Fury*.) *Quer pasticciaccio* goes deep into the amalgam of petty crime, violence, and unspoken wrongs; *La cognizione* adds to these the horror of unresolved guilt. In *Quer pasticciaccio* the setting is not only recognizable as Rome, it actually is Rome; in *La cognizione* the setting is recognizable as Lombardy, but is actually, within the fiction of the book, the imaginary South American country of Maradagàl. In *Quer pasticciaccio* the principal character, who is searching for the nouminous reality of life, is a stand-in for the author; in *La cognizione* the principal character is even closer to being the author himself (he is a war veteran, has lost a brother in the war, and suffers from a mysterious malady which renders life bitter and unendurable), although he hides under the fictional identity of Gonzalo Pirobutirro d'Eltino, hidalgo and engineer of Maradagàl. *La cognizione* has one quality which *Quer pasticciaccio* lacks: it is a book about suffering, and its vehemence is therefore frequently softened to elegy. It is a more human book, built around a truly tragic if monstrous character.

More even than *Quer pasticciaccio* it is a book for connoisseurs, with hardly a word in it that is not intended to call to

mind another word, to refer to some cultural or literary experience of Italian history. While the ordinary reader can approach
the Rome of *Quer pasticciaccio,* find his way in it, and move
among familiar monuments, only a learned and sophisticated
reader will be able to identify in the landscape of Maradagàl
not merely the landscape of the Brianza, but the landscape of
the Brianza as seen in Manzoni's *I promessi sposi.* Failure to
note connections such as this one would seriously impede not
only the comprehension but the enjoyment of the book. It is
essential, for instance, that in the passage which describes the
mountain Serruchòn[9] the reader be able to detect beneath
Gadda's words the counterpoint of Manzoni's description of
the same—or is it another?—mountain, the Resegone. Gadda
plants an open clue by referring to the Resegone by name; but
it is not sufficient to recognize the source intellectually, it must
also be savored esthetically by "close" and expert reading. *La
cognizione del dolore* is a book that clamors for an annotated
edition, to make explicit its wonderful richness of references,
its extraordinary abundance. The English translator of *Quer
pasticciaccio,* William Weaver, has done something of this in
his edition of *That Awful Mess.* Unfortunately, his explana-
tory notes are limited almost exclusively to historical and
political references, thus magnifying the element of anti-Fascist
satire which is present in the book, but which by this treatment
receives undue emphasis at the expense of the subtler, more
literary aspects of the work of this most literary, most idio-
syncratic and socially alienated of contemporary Italian writers.

In reviewing *Quer pasticciaccio* in 1958,[10] Pasolini recognized in it a stylistic versatility which, he said, would make a
critic like Spitzer as exhilarated—and the comparison is his—as
a mouse in a chunk of cheese. Pasolini analyzed briefly four
basically different uses of dialect in the book; pointed to the
extraordinary range of its syntactical forms, even coining the
word *hypertaxis* to place beside the more usual *parataxis* and
hypotaxis for describing Gadda's "monstrous syntactical jun-

gle"; and compared Manzoni's and Gadda's use of tenses as a key to their respective narrative techniques. As can be seen, his is a most competent and expert approach, a far cry from the run-of-the-mill practice of journalistic reviewing, which looks for little more than a novel's relationship to everyday reality. As a reader of Gadda, Pasolini certainly ranks with the best. In an earlier review of a collection of Gadda short stories, *Novelle dal Ducato in fiamme*, 1953 (Stories from the Duchy Aflame),[11] he had surveyed, again with economy and concentration, the nineteenth and twentieth century literary precedents to which Gadda owes aspects of his style: the "art prose" movement of the Twenties, which treated prose as though it were poetry and against which specifically the neo-realists reacted; Verga's "narrated interior monologue"; Manzoni's continuing orientation to the Lombard components of his culture, even under the surface aspiration to national unity; the social satire and irony of the Roman dialect poet Belli; and the post-Romantic avant-garde movement of the Piedmontese and Lombard *scapigliati*, whose truly revolutionary experimentation with linguistic and literary forms is barely beginning to be studied. In view of the breadth and depth of Pasolini's understanding of Gadda and of his admiration for what he calls "that very great mind and heart," it is all the more interesting to note his formulation of the latter's shortcomings. I pass here from the context of esthetics and literary craftsmanship to that of ideology and from the novelist Gadda to the novelist Pasolini.

Speaking of Pasolini earlier, I referred briefly to the role played by the partisan movement in the formation of his basic sympathies and convictions. The struggle for liberation from fascism during the later stages of the War was felt by the more idealistic and committed of its exponents as the beginning of a new era in Italian history, the harbinger of a social revolution which would finally wipe out all class and regional inequalities. This feeling of buoyancy persisted in spite of many disappointments and delays until roughly the time of the Hungarian uprising, an event which seriously shook confidence in the Communist solution to Italy's problems. Pasolini's political optimism, nurtured in the successful defeat of fascism, combined with his personal responsiveness to others and his acceptance of Marxism as a unifying ideological structure for judging progress, enabled him to focus on what he sees as the reactionary side of Gadda's position. In the review of *Quer pasticciaccio* already mentioned, Pasolini presents Gadda as simultaneously accepting and rejecting the social reality of Italy as created by the middle classes in the wake of the *Risorgimento*. The resultant ambivalence caused that feeling of despondent anguish and that "tragically mixed and obsessive style" which are the marks of Gadda's helpless and ever renewed fury at finding institutions which are potentially good turned into organizations which are actually bad. "Gadda belongs to an historical time," Pasolini concludes, "when it was impossible to see the world—this magma of disorder, corruption, hypocrisy, stupidity, and injustice—in a perspective of hope."

The full significance of this statement becomes apparent when we examine Pasolini's two novels, *Ragazzi di vita*, 1955 (*The Ragazzi*, New York, 1968) and *Una vita violenta*, 1959 (A Violent Life). In both Pasolini would like to see the world "in a perspective of hope" but both of them fall short of being true documents, the first of the "magma of disorder . . . and injustice" which must be destroyed, the second of the awakening of the social consciousness through which this destruction will be effected.

Ragazzi di vita is a novel because it deals with a group of fictional characters, the course of whose life we follow during a determined period of time. But it could just as easily be conceived of as a series of vignettes or episodes only loosely related to one another, whose main function is the representation of a milieu rather than the construction and revelation of a character. *Ragazzi di vita* came out at the height of the neo-

realistic vogue and was read at first as a document of the
desperate conditions of the Roman subproletariat in the dis-
consolate slums springing up with unbelievable rapidity on the
outskirts of the city.

The documentary aspect of the book appeared to be underlined by the glossary of dialect terms and underworld jargon
which Pasolini provides at the end. To some readers the list
seems incomplete and insufficient, although it is true, as Pasolini claims in his covering note, that comprehension of the
story or of any one episode of it is not really impeded by the
inability to translate into standard Italian every one of the
rude, vulgar, obscene expressions which occur in the speech of
its protagonists. Pasolini feels that no reader coming upon
these words for the first time could fail to grasp their meaning
through intuition of the context in which they are used. And
indeed the dialogue which makes up so much of the book is
little more than a string of curses, cries, expletives, urgings,
exclamations—the typical "conversational" exchanges which
occur when people do not *speak* to one another but simply,
almost by the accident of propinquity, share common
experiences.

Dialogue in novels has often been used to discuss important
philosophical problems or to introduce the author's personal
convictions. Nothing could be further from Pasolini's practice.
His message is never entrusted to the words of his characters.
Rather it is implicit in his representation of selected conditions,
or, in some rare cases, in his own narrated third-person comment on what he is telling. Thus, for instance, there is an
episode toward the end of *Ragazzi di vita* in which one of the
protagonists returns to the factory area which had figured in
the opening pages. Almost everything is changed: the buildings
and grounds are now shining with cleanliness and order, and a
new, unbroken wire fence surrounds them. Only the watch-
man's hut is still the same: it continues to be used as an abusive
public latrine. "That was the only spot that Riccetto found

familiar," Pasolini unobtrusively comments, "exactly as it was when the war had just ended."

The time span covered by *Ragazzi di vita* goes from the liberation of Rome in 1944 to the early Fifties. Riccetto, who might be considered the principal character if for no other reason than that he is most frequently on stage, lives through the years of his adolescence: he is eleven and receiving his first communion when the story begins, eighteen and having served a three-year term in jail when it ends. In noting with precision the exact limits of the historical situation which serves as background, Pasolini is fulfilling one of the desiderata of the esthetics of neorealism, which calls for the concrete rooting of fiction in a definite and verifiable reality. But *Ragazzi di vita* is in no sense an historical novel. It has nothing of Pratolini's *Metello* (1956) where historical events are made part of the plot. Nor do historical events shape its story as they do, in however muted a manner, in Verga's *I Malavoglia,* for instance. *Ragazzi di vita* gives back the "color" of a time only in an episodic, allusive manner. Thus we have in the early pages of the book the description of the pilfering of food and other necessities characteristic of day-to-day existence in occupied Rome. There is reference to the emergency housing of the homeless and the destitute—as a matter of fact, Riccetto's mother is killed in the collapse of an old school building which had been turned to this use. And there is the endless stream of "things," objects of all sorts from sewer lids to automobile tires to articles of furniture, which at one time or another fetched a good price on the market of stolen goods. We have, in other words, the landscape made familiar by films such as *Bicycle Thief* (1948), but without the underlying ethic of that film which dealt with a man's effort to make good, to find his place in society through his work. The protagonists of *Ragazzi di vita* do, from time to time, work. They sometimes have money, not necessarily honestly come by. And that money quickly slips out of their fingers again, for they do not consider it as a means of insuring security, of building a place for themselves in society—witness the amusing episode at Ostia, where the fifty thousand lire that Riccetto had just stolen from swindlers for whom he was working are with a Boccaccioesque twist in turn stolen from him.

The truth of the matter is that Riccetto and his friends are outsiders, typical juvenile delinquents unable and unwilling to make the compromises necessary to find their way into a social order, and that it is therefore difficult to consider their stories as representative of a socio-historical condition. Though *Ragazzi di vita* can be read as a Marxist indictment of the capitalist society which makes lives such as it describes possible, it is in no way an example of socialist realism, for it sets up no exemplary hero who through his awareness of the dynamics of social change can become the potential founder of a new order. *Ragazzi di vita* is the representation of a nether world no less absolute than that of *Quer pasticciaccio*. No broad and happy roads leads out of this world, toward that triumph of reason which Marxist writers, mindful of their Enlightenment origins, like to prognosticate.

But if the vision of the road leading to the transformed society is missing in *Ragazzi di vita*, it is not because Pasolini, as we have seen in his review of *Quer pasticciaccio*, does not consciously believe in its existence. It is simply that he has lost sight of it while telling his story, while exploring with loving attention the teeming life of the Roman underworld. For that underworld has a vitality for him, a gay insouciance, a forceful optimistic *élan*, a *joie de vivre*, that obscures its horror. As one of the gang exults, referring to the company that finds itself associated in petty crime one epic night at the Villa Borghese: "Two from Tiburtino, one from Acqua Bullicante, two from Primavalle, one deserter, and Picchio here from Valle dell'Inferno: why, we could band together and found the League of the Wicked of the Suburbs of Rome!" One hears echoes of the exploits of the Three Musketeers, of the Chevaliers de la Table Ronde of ballad fame, of all the merry bands that have roamed the face of the earth, recklessly following where adventure called.

For the Rome of *Ragazzi di vita* is the great scenario of adventure, a new *carte du tendre* without the tender sentiment of love but with similarly compulsory stops. To ride the street-cars of Rome, having just spent your last pennies for a ticket, is the beginning of adventure, for you do not know with whom you will be rubbing elbows nor with what you may end up in your pocket. To go for a swim in the yellow waters of the Tiber is the beginning of adventure, for you do not know whom you might meet nor what debris the sluggish water may bring your way—perhaps only a bird on the verge of drowning, which on an impulse you will save (a truly amazing episode at the end of chapter one). To help an old man steal a couple of cauliflowers from a sodden field is the beginning of adventure, for he may invite you home to meet his daughters. . . . And over and above it all, the sky of Rome with its pastel shades at sunset and its brilliant moon at night. Pasolini's landscape descriptions are extraordinary, shocking the reader as some preromantic landscapes do, with their feathery trees, their majestic ruins, and a ragged beggar half hidden by a broken column:

> By now, behind the low wall which overlooks the Tusculanum neighborhood like a terrace, beyond tennis fields and trodden tracts of land, the sun was setting, warm and red, making the windows shine on the pile of bluish buildings so that they looked like some Martian landscape. On this side of the wall against which Alduccio and the others were slouching indecently, the grounds of San Giovanni with their little flower beds and trees spread out equally melancholy, touched by the last rays of the sun which knocked up against the loggias and the huge statues on the cathedral, giving a border of gold to the red granite of the obelisk.

The first reviewers of *Ragazzi di vita* singled out its social nihilism and its literary estheticism for special criticism. Pasolini's insistence on a monotonous and unrepresentative segment of the Roman subproletariat seemed to them a deformation and a stylization of reality which went counter to the fundamental documentary intention of neorealism. Moreover, an episode such as the one in which the thoughts of a couple of mongrel dogs during a fight are recorded as though spoken in the same dialect used by the human protagonists of the book was cited as a clamorous instance of that flight from naturalistic objectivity to decadent self-indulgence which was also underlined by the picaresque aspects of the novel.

In an essay on Italian dialect poetry which he had written some years earlier,[12] Pasolini had already implicitly defended his narrative approach in *Ragazzi di vita*. In speaking of the Roman poet, Gioacchino Belli, the nineteenth century interpreter of the feelings and opinions of the city's unruly populace, he emphasized, as many other observers had done, the uniqueness of the Roman citizenry, those descendants of the *plebs* of antiquity, who in the midst of splendid testimonials of their past have always lived and continue to live outside of history, that is, outside the awareness and the dynamics of change. To the ideal of progress conceived in terms of social betterment, these people substitute the excitement of life lived exclusively for the moment, the happy-go-lucky acceptance of whatever opportunities, however slight and brief, chance offers them. To represent this "aristocratic Roman proletariat"—the expression is Pasolini's—in their saga of roguish adventure is thus, Pasolini claimed, to reflect the "real" Rome, the Rome that rebels against the political and economic structures of bourgeois society *not* by taking a conscious position against them but by simply ignoring them. And to use the Roman dialect to record the inner content of the fictional lives of these people (dialect is used only in the dialogue parts of the book and in some rare cases of stream of consciousness) is to apply the general rule later formulated by Pasolini in his answer to a questionnaire on the novel sponsored by the periodical *Nuovi argomenti*: "If the character and milieu chosen by the novelist are proletariat, let him use dialect in part or wholly; if they are middle-class, let him use the *koiné*. In this way he cannot go wrong."[13] By *koiné* Pasolini means the uniform, nondialect Italian usage of the petite bourgeoisie as formed by the unification of Italy, or, to use Gramsci's description, the language of the bureaucrats who effectively united the new state at the administrative level but left the Italy of regions and city districts virtually untouched. *Ragazzi di vita*, it should be remembered, was written and is set in the period immediately preceding the new levelling and cohesive forces of Italy's "economic miracle," which were to do so much to destroy the nation's compartmentalized subcultures and to turn large segments of its proletariat into a middle class—without, however, the contributions of Marxism.

Pasolini's second novel, *Una vita violenta* is in part an answer to the more justified objections raised against *Ragazzi di vita*. Pasolini, a convinced and avowed Marxist, was especially sensitive to the critics who took him to task for ideological inadequacy, for having escaped into the private world of a kind of eternal adolescence and primitiveness instead of attempting to represent the awakening social consciousness of the masses on their way to claim their place in the sun. Thus Tommaso Puzzilli, the protagonist of *Una vita violenta*, is seen as more fully rounded than Riccetto and is made to undergo a political education which changes his initial heedless spontaneity into a sense of responsibility toward others. Whether the book for all its orthodox intentions is as successful as its predecessor is questionable. My own feeling is that the first part of *Una vita violenta* is more effective than the second and that the episodes most strongly reminiscent of *Ragazzi di vita* are what saves it from being a completely pedestrian and unimaginative illustration of a thesis.

Tommaso is at the beginning just another Riccetto. He too lives in a Hooverville on the outskirts of Rome. He too is involved with the other boys of his district in a number of wild exploits, such as stealing a car and holding up a hapless gas station attendant one night. He too meets a girl to whom he becomes engaged and with whom he plays the role of the proper young fiancé: the descriptions of their Sunday outings are peculiarly and unexpectedly condescending, but I believe unwittingly so. There are other episodes in the first part of the book which mark a departure from *Ragazzi di vita*: Tommasino's participation in a "rumble" staged by a group of Fascist sympathizers, and the revolt of the women of Pietralata against the police, who are rounding up their suspect husbands and sons. But the most striking innovation has to do with technique. It is in a flashback at the beginning of Part Two that we are told of the Puzzillis' coming to Rome as refugees during the war, of how they were forced to leave the country, where their land and animals and the father's job as caretaker in the public schools had permitted them to live quite comfortably, much better than they now live in Rome. Still, in the long run they turn out to be more fortunate than many of their new neighbors, for they are assigned an apartment in the complex of public housing being built in the no-man's-land of Pietralata. It is to this apartment that Tommaso returns after his stint in jail for having stabbed a heckler during a street fight, and it is at this point that the thrust of the narrative changes.

Tommaso appears to have left his adolescence behind him. He finds work and becomes a respectable member of society— so much so that he averts his eyes when he happens upon an ex-companion who has not succeeded as he has, but has become a crippled beggar huddling on a street in Rome. At the beginning of this turning point, however, Pasolini introduces the theme of death. First there is the brief report of the sudden death of Tommasino's two baby brothers, an episode which makes a strong appeal for sympathy from the reader by bringing into view the injustices and deprivations which reduce human life to the level of animal, or even insect, life. Then there are the first symptoms of Tommasino's tuberculosis, which eventually leads him to a long stay in a city hospital. There he meets and learns to admire and respect a group of Communists who are organizing and supporting the hospital attendants in a strike. Tommasino joins the party upon his release. But the story is now rapidly approaching the end. Tommasino dies in a new tubercular attack, brought on by his trying to save a prostitute during a flood.

As can be seen, Pasolini's intention in *Una vita violenta* was to write a novel which would follow the classical pattern by being the complete and exemplary story of a central character. In this respect *Una vita violenta* is not different from the social novels of the nineteenth century, from Zola, for instance. But while Pasolini is excellent at catching the "feeling" of the life of his protagonists, he is less successful with the concreteness of historical background. He leaves the reader with strong sense impressions: unpleasant odors, rough and dirty textures, deformed limbs, blemished skins, rotting clothing, mud, heaps of garbage. But there is little or nothing in the book which will help a future reader to reconstruct the complexity of an epoch. Pasolini's talent is lyrical and sentimental, not narrative and historical. That is why the episode of the "talking" dogs, tucked away in the flow of euphoric slang, is the real clue to the quality of his art.

As I pointed out at the beginning of this essay, Gadda, rather than Pasolini, is the writer recognized by the novelists of the latest avant-garde as their forerunner. But actually, if we compare Gadda's work with that of Sanguineti or Leonetti, for instance, both antinovelists are experimental novelists with a vengeance, we must conclude that the kinship is more symbolic than real. Sanguineti in *Il gioco dell'oca,* 1967 (The Goose Game) and Leonetti in *Tappeto volante,* 1967 (Flying Carpet) have written novels which have nothing in common with the genre in its familiar forms, except perhaps the colorful book jackets and the fictitiousness of the world represented. In attempting to speak of works such as these, it becomes at once painfully evident that the terms commonly used in connection with the novel of realism, the novel *par excellence,* are no longer adequate. Their authors declare *Il gioco dell'oca* and *Tappeto volante* to be novels. Leonetti even adds the usual postscript disavowing any responsibility should his characters happen to resemble persons living or dead. He claims, in other words, the same privileges for the imagination that storytellers and fabulists have done at all times. But I believe that novels like Sanguineti's and Leonetti's, if they are novels at all, are so only by a process of elimination. They are obviously not plays, nor poems, nor essays, nor news reports, nor philosophic treatises, nor driving manuals. At best, they may be called constructions, shapes, with the same relation to the novel proper that a mobile in a museum has to a classical statue of antiquity. This means that in the concept of construction or shape, as applied to them, there is not the slightest residue of the idea that art is an imitation, however free and personal, of nature. In the novels of both Gadda and Pasolini, instead, the connection between art and nature is still solid, even though Pasolini's narrative is almost exclusively mimetic, while in Gadda there is an added metaphorical dimension, the work serving not only to depict reality, however apparently deformed, but also to epitomize the process of knowledge.

The "goose game" which gives its name to *Il gioco dell'oca* is an old table game in which the players, casting dice, move their wooden geese from square to square, incurring hazards or gaining advantages. Sanguineti has made up his own squares, one hundred and eleven of them, each one with its illustration: newspaper cuttings; advertisements; pictures of mermaids, of monsters, of Salvador Dali's girl with mustache; scenes from music halls; fantasies from comic strips; and so on. A reproduction of the cardboard on which the game is played appears on each of the endpapers of the book. Paralleling the squares—also referred to as slots or coffins—are the one hundred and eleven short chapters which constitute the so-called novel. They tell no coherent story; each chapter consists of an anecdote, a comment, a reflection on life, or an explosion of publicity slogans, well known mottos, and references to the latest gossip. The book is to be read in the same way as the game is played, by moving from chapter to chapter as the throw of the dice indicates. In fact, as the dedication at the beginning states, the book is to be played with rather than read. "Ce n'est que superpositions d'images de catalogue," Sanguineti concludes.

Tappeto volante represents a different kind of experiment. The first-person narrator seems at the outset to be really telling a story: he wakes up from a nightmare and his day begins. After a few sentences, however, the reader is aware that if story there be, it is a very strange story, told in an even stranger way. The narrator, whose name is Shelley, has a wife whose name is Mary. He is by profession a clockmaker, but instead of repairing clocks, he wrecks them in order to resell them to a particularly sophisticated class of Swiss collectors. Shelley is in love with Olivia, an elusive woman who has set up a whole series of signals by which she communicates, or gives the illusion of communicating, with him. Thus, for instance, Shelley and Olivia may be telephoning to one another when they are seized with the desire to meet. She promises to send a taxi to get him. He goes downstairs and picks out the right one from among the many taxis passing by because he discovers an 18 (part of Olivia's telephone number) in the taxi's license plate. But before taking the taxi he must decipher the meaning of the other numbers: does the coded message mean that he is to take the taxi, that he is to telephone Olivia, or that he is to wait for a call from her? The possibilities are almost infinite, and so are the possibilities of error, given the multiplicity of meanings that each gesture, each word, each signal has. The whole novel proceeds with this rhythm. Olivia, the etymology of whose Shakespearean name is at one point given as Oli-via, she who makes the (salad) oil disappear (there is a maid in the Shelley household who has this detestable habit: is she another spy of Olivia's?), is also supposed to stand for a kind of new Beatrice in this new *Vita nuova*. In the postscript Leonetti promises to set forth elsewhere the theory of the type of novel he has just written.

It does not take much to see how these two experimental novels of the late sixties support my statement that the narrative intents and procedures of Gadda and Pasolini have very little in common with the new experimentalism, which is essentially structural rather than linguistic. In a second meeting of *Gruppo 63*, which took place in Palermo in 1965, Renato Barilli spoke of a second generation of experimentalists, who have gone beyond the instrumental use of a *vision autre*. They have recognized, that is, that Robbe-Grillet and Butor, for instance, in their antinovels may not at all have intended primarily to analyze man's psychological reaction to objects as a comment on his reaction to society, but that they may have been concerned instead "with inventing a mechanism which proceeds at a particular pace, at a rhythm consisting of continual advances and retreats and of vast circular trajectories."[14] Similarly Sanguineti and Günter Grass, Barilli continues, may not at all have chosen to rely on dreams (in Sanguineti's other novel *Capriccio italiano*) and dwarfs in order to fight ethical and social taboos, but more simply to effect "an ingenious renewal of the picaresque."

Now, while for Gadda one could certainly speak of *vision autre*, the deformation and excess of a disordered psyche which gives his expression such virulence, there can be no question that for neither Gadda nor Pasolini has writing a novel ever been equivalent to constructing a game. They are both fundamentally earnest and moralistic in their approach to art. They have a message to transmit, easily recognizable in Pasolini, less so in Gadda. The themes they treat undoubtedly present

only divergences if we examine them in the context of one another's work. But when we look at Gadda and Pasolini from
a certain distance, from the perspective of the new new experimentalism, for instance, we can only conclude that the themes
they treat are the old ones—crime, guilt, death—and that the
feeling of revulsion for the fault in nature that both writers
experience derives from the traditional, classic view of man in
his relation to other men and to the world about him.

NOTES

All translations are mine, with the exception of the passage on page
248, which is quoted from William Weaver's translation of *Quer
pasticciaccio* (*That Awful Mess on Via Merulana*, New York,
George Braziller, 1965).

1. Gianfranco Contini, "Preliminari sulla lingua del Petrarca," *Pa-
ragone-Letteratura*, 1951, pp. 3–26.

2. Angelo Guglielmi, "Avanguardia e sperimentalismo," in *Gruppo
63* (Milan, Feltrinelli, 1964), p. 19.

3. P. P. Pasolini, "Il neo-sperimentalismo, *Officina*, February 1956;
now in *Passione e ideologia* (Milan, Garzanti, 1960), pp. 470–83.

4. Renato Barilli, " 'Cahier de doléance' sull'ultima narrativa italiana," *Il Verri*, 1960; now in *La barriera del naturalismo* (Milan,
Mursia, 1964), p. 171.

5. Elio Filippo Accrocca, *Ritratti su misura di scrittori italiani*
(Venice, Sodalizio del Libro, 1960), p. 205.

6. Ibid., p. 321.

7. Italo Calvino, "Main Currents in Italian Fiction Today," *Italian
Quarterly*, IV, 13–14 (1960), p. 12.

8. C. E. Gadda, "Un'opinione sul neorealismo," can now be read in
I viaggi la morte (Milan, Garzanti, 1958), pp. 252–53.

9. C. E. Gadda, *La cognizione del dolore* (Turin, Einaudi, 1963),
p. 48.

10. This review can now be read in *Passione e ideologia*, pp.
318–24.

11. Ibid., pp. 313–18.

12. "La poesia dialettale del '900," now in *Passione e ideologia,* especially pp. 61–62.

13. "Nove domande sul romanzo," *Nuovi argomenti,* 38–39 (May-August 1959), p. 48.

14. Renato Barilli, in Gruppo 63, *Il romanzo sperimentale* (Milan, Feltrinelli, 1966), p. 23.

Bibliographical Notes

NOTE: The bibliographical notes for each essay of this volume were prepared by the authors, except for the essays on Svevo, Tozzi, Silone, and Moravia, for which the notes were prepared by the editor. Whenever possible, preference has been given to items that have appeared in English. In the case of articles, as a rule only those published in readily available periodicals (either English or Italian) have been included.

Giovanni Verga

The best biographical account of the Sicilian writer is the volume written a quarter of a century ago by Nino Cappellani, *Vita di Giovanni Verga* (Florence, Le Monnier, 1940). Recently, Giulio Cattaneo has produced a valuable though far from satisfactory book, *Giovanni Verga* (Turin, UTET, 1963). From the more critical angle there is Luigi Russo's important, frequently penetrating, if at times rhetorical, *Giovanni Verga*, 6th ed. (Bari, Laterza, 1959), and Thomas G. Bergin's *Giovanni Verga* (New Haven, Yale University Press, 1931). On Verga's style there are two excellent essays, Leo Spitzer's "L'originalità della narrazione nei *Malavoglia*," *Belfagor*, xi (1956), 37–53, and Vittorio Lugli's "Lo stile indiretto libero in Flaubert e Verga," *Dante e Balzac* (Naples, E. S. I., 1952), pp. 221–39. Ines Scaramucci's *Introduzione a Verga* (Brescia, La Scuola, 1959) is a sympathetic treatment of its subject, and Giorgio Luti's essay on Verga (composed of five chapters, originally published in various periodicals as articles) in *Italo Svevo e altri studi sulla letteratura italiana del primo Novecento* (Milan, Lerici, 1961) offers many insights into the style of the Sicilian novelist, the structure of his masterwork, and its position in modern Italian literature. Among the early commentators there is A. Momigliano, *Dante, Manzoni, Verga* (Messina, D'Anna, 1944), pp. 201–59, and Giulio Marzot's *L'arte del Verga* (Vicenza, R. Istituto Magistrale, "D. G. Fogazzaro," 1930). The finest piece on "Nedda" and its importance in Verga's development is a short essay by Adriano Seroni, published separately with the same title (Lucca, Lucentia, 1950) and in *Nuove ragioni critiche* (Florence, Sansoni, 1961). Leone Piccioni's essay, "Per una storia dell'arte del Verga," *Letture leopardiane* (Florence, Vallecchi, 1952) is of special interest for its precise stylistic examination of Verga's prose.

Italo Svevo

The bibliography on Svevo, while numerically impressive, tends to be qualitatively uneven. There are two monographs on Svevo's life and work: A. Leone De Castris, *Italo Svevo* (Pisa, Nistri-Lischi, 1959), an exhaustive, but seldom clear and direct, analysis of Svevo's literary production; and Bruno Maier, *La personalità e l'opera di Italo Svevo* (Milan, Ugo Mursia, 1961), a disappointing, superficial analysis of the subject. Carlo Bo, in his *Riflessioni critiche* (Florence, Sansoni, 1953), has written an interesting profile of Svevo, "Per un ritratto di Svevo," pp. 443–64. Giorgio Luti, in *Italo Svevo e altri studi sulla letteratura del primo Novecento* (Milan, Lerici, 1961), has made several central observations about Svevo's life, cultural background, and themes. One of the most brilliant essays written in Italian is Giacomo Debenedetti's "Svevo e Schmitz," *Scritti critici*, 2nd ed. (Milan, Mondadori, 1955), pp. 50–116; Giuseppe Pontizzia's article "La tecnica narrativa di Italo Svevo," *Il Verri*, IV, 5 (1963) 150–166, is a careful study of Svevo's technique within the framework of other important European novels.

In English there are several commendable essays on Svevo: Russell Pholf's pages on "Imagery as Disease in *Senilità*," *Modern Language Notes*, LXXVI, 2 (1961), 143–50, are exceedingly pertinent, as are the essays by Edouard Roditi and Renato Poggioli (the latter collected in *The Spirit of the Letter*, Cambridge, Harvard University Press, 1963). Both pieces serve as respective introductions to the original American translations of *Senilità* (*As a Man Grows Older*) and *La coscienza di Zeno* (*The Confessions of Zeno*). Lowry Nelson, Jr.'s, "A Survey of Svevo," *Italian Quarterly*, III, 10 (1959), 3–33, is a competent piece of work whose value is impaired by the numerous (and frequently unnecessary or questionable) comparisons with other European writers. By contrast, Richard Gilman's review-article, "Svevo: News from the Past," *New Republic*, CXLIX, 18 (1963), 19–23, is an incisively written and unusually revealing study of the quality of *A Life* and of Svevo's relevance to the contemporary reader. Of particular interest are also the essays by Jean Murray, "The Progress of the Hero in Italo Svevo," in *Italian Studies*, XXI (1966), 91–100, and François Bondy, "Italo Svevo and Ripe Old Age," in *Hudson Review*, XX, (1967–68), 575–98.

The first and only monograph published by an English critic, *Italo Svevo, The Man and the Writer* by P. N. Furbank (Berkeley, University of California Press, 1968), contains an excellent account of Svevo's life as well as a penetrating, though brief, analysis of his novels.

Luigi Pirandello

The authoritative edition of Pirandello's novels is the two-volume work edited by Corrado Alvaro, *Tutti i romanzi di Pirandello* (Milan, Mondadori, 1957). The following are translations of Pirandello's novels:

* With the exception of a few lines from *Il Turno* (*The Merry-Go-Round of Love*), passages quoted from the novels are from the translations listed above.

Late Mattia Pascal, The, trans. William Weaver. Garden City, Doubleday, 1964.

Merry-Go-Round of Love, The, trans. Frances Keene, and *Selected Short Stories,* trans. Lily Duplaix, with a Foreword by Irving Howe. New York, The New American Library, 1964.

Old and the Young, The, trans. C. K. Scott-Moncrieff. New York, Dutton, 1928.

One, None and a Hundred-Thousand, trans. Samuel Putnam. New York, Dutton, 1933.

Outcast, The, trans. Leo Ongley. New York, Dutton, 1925.

Shoot! The Notebooks of Serafino Gubbio, Cinematograph Operator, trans. C. K. Scott-Moncrieff. New York, Dutton, 1926.

Criticism of Pirandello's work, as can be readily imagined, is rather vast. The reader will find the following particularly interesting and valuable in his further study of the author:

Acrosso, Maria. *La critica letteraria*. Rome, Palumbo, 1967.

Angioletti, G. B. *Luigi Pirandello, narratore e drammaturgo*. Turin, ERI, 1964.

Bartocci, G. "Pirandello as a Novelist," in *AULIA Proceedings*, I (1965), 71–74.

Budel, Oscar. *Pirandello: Studies in Modern European Thought and Literature*. New York, Hillary House, 1966.

Cambon, Glauco, ed. *Pirandello: A Collection of Critical Essays*. Englewood Cliffs, Prentice-Hall, 1967.

Cambon, Glauco. "Pirandello as a Novelist," in *Cesare Barbieri Courier*, IX (1967), 16–19.

Ferrante, Luigi. *Pirandello*. Florence, Parenti, 1958.

"Homage to Pirandello, A." *Forum Italicum*, 1 (1967).

Hughes, M. Y. "Pirandello's Humor," in *Sewanee Review*, XXXV (1927), 175–86.

Janner, Arminio. *Luigi Pirandello*. Florence, La Nuova Italia, 1967.

Leo, Ulrich. "Pirandello: Kunsttheorie and Maskensymbol," in *Deutsche Vierteljahrschrift*, XI (1933), 94–129.

MacClintock, L. *The Age of Pirandello*. Bloomington, Indiana Univ. Press, 1951.

May, Frederick, ed. *Luigi Pirandello: Short Stories*. London, Oxford Univ. Press, 1965.

Ragusa, Olga. *Pirandello*. New York, Columbia Series of Modern Writers, 1968.

Rizzo, Gino. "Pirandello versus Pirandellism," in *Cesare Barbieri Courier*, IX (1967), 4–7.

Starkie, Walter. *Luigi Pirandello (1867–1936)*. 3d rev. ed. Berkeley, University of California Press, 1965.

Vittorini, Domenico. *The Drama of Luigi Pirandello*. Philadelphia, Univ. of Penn. Press, 1935.

Weiss, Auréliu. *Le Théatre de Luigi Pirandello dans le mouvement dramatique contemporain*. Paris, Librairie 73, 1964.

Whitfield, J. H. *A Short History of Italian Literature*. London, Cassell, 1960 and 1962.

Aldo Palazzeschi

Ever since his début, shortly after the turn of this century, Pallaz-
zeschi has enjoyed much popularity with the critics and the readers
of his native country. Little is available in English about his work,
despite the fact that a great deal of his poetry and fiction has been
available in translation. Among the numerous items in Italian, the
most comprehensive is the study by Giorgio Pullini, *Palazzeschi*
(Milan, Mursia, 1965), which contains a complete bibliography. In
addition, the reader may wish to consult one of Palazzeschi's earliest critics, Renato Serra (*Le lettere*, Rome, "La Voce," 1920), and
Francesco Flora's *Dal romanticismo al futurismo* (Milan, Mondadori, 1925). Pietro Pancrazi's graceful review-articles on Palazzeschi are collected in *Scrittori d'oggi* (Bari, Laterza, 1946). In
addition, see also Alfredo Gargiulo's *La letteratura italiana del
Novecento* (Florence, Le Monnier, 1940); Luigi Russo's *I Narratori,
1850–1957* (Milan, Principato, 1958); Sergio Solmi's *Scrittori negli
anni* (Milan, Il Saggiatore, 1963); Emilio Cecchi's *Di giorno in
giorno* (Milan, Garzanti, 1954); and the perceptive essay by
Eugenio Montale, "Palazzeschi ieri e oggi," in *L'immagine*, II, 1948.
   Palazzeschi's poetry has recently been studied by Alberto Gozzi
("Palazzeschi e la poetica della leggerezza") in *Il Verri*, 20 (1965),
82–92; Claudio Marabini has surveyed the author's production in
his long article, "A.P.," in *Nuova Antologia*, 501 (1967), 58–80.
   Le sorelle Materassi, in the English translation by Angus David-
son *(The Sisters Materassi)* was published by Doubleday & Co. in
1953.

Federigo Tozzi

Federigo Tozzi has traditionally been studied by a relatively small,
but intelligent number of critics. His reputation has steadily been
growing in recent years, a fact evidenced by the publication, on the
one hand, of the first volumes of what is to be the complete and
definitive edition of his *opera omnia*, and, on the other hand, by the
announced publication by Cornell University Press of the first

English translation of *Con gli occhi chiusi*—a project undertaken with the assistance of the Translation Center in Texas. For the time being, the only sustained treatment in English of Tozzi's fiction is to be found in Domenico Vittorini's *The Modern Italian Novel* (Philadelphia, University of Pennsylvania Press, 1930, reprinted by Hillary House Publs., 1966). Both Ben Johnson and William Arrowsmith devote a few excellent, but all too brief, lines to Tozzi in *Stories of Modern Italy* (New York, Random House, 1960) and *Six Italian Novellas* (New York, Pocketbooks, 1964) respectively. The monograph by Ferruccio Ulivi (*Federigo Tozzi*, Milan, Mursia, 1962) contains an exhaustive bibliography of articles, reviews, and studies that have appeared in Italy and elsewhere; among these, Eurialo De Michelis' *Saggio su Tozzi* (Florence, La Nuova Italia, 1936) is particularly interesting for its appraisals. Another recent study on Tozzi has been written by F. N. Cimmino, *Il mondo e l'arte di Federigo Tozzi* (Rome, Volpe, 1966); Giose Rimanelli, in his polemical book *Il mestiere del furbo* (published under the pseudonym of A. Solari by Sugar, 1960), presents a persuasive assessment of Tozzi and addresses himself to the influence Tozzi has had on the younger generation of novelists.

Ignazio Silone

The longest and most complete interpretative essay in English is R. W. B. Lewis' "Ignazio Silone: The Politics of Charity," in *The Picaresque Saint*, New York, L. J. Lippincott, 1958, pp. 109–78. The human side of Silone has been studied with much insight by Iris Origo, "Ignazio Silone: A Study in Integrity," in *Atlantic Monthly*, 219 (1967), 86–93. Special facets of Silone's narrative have been analyzed by Robert A. Georges, "Silone's Use of Folk Beliefs," in *Midwest Folklore*, XII (1962), 197–203; Kenneth Lefley, "Ignazio Silone," in *Encounter*, XXIII, ii (1964), 49–51; Franz Schneider, "Scriptural Symbolism in Silone's Bread and Wine," in *Italica*, 44 (1967), 388–400; and A. Kingsley Weatherhead, "Ignazio Silone: Community and the Failure of Language, in *Modern Fiction Studies*, VII (1961), 157–68. The anonymous article in the *Times Literary Supplement*, Aug. 18, 1961, p. 548, "Moralist with a

Cause," is both informative and sympathetic to Silone's political and moral position. In Italian, Ferdinando Virdia's short, low-keyed monograph, *Silone* (Florence, La Nuova Italia, 1967), may be consulted with profit. The long essay by Arnaldo Bocelli, "Itinerario di Ignazio Silone," in *Nuova Antologia*, 497 (1966), 25–33, is valuable, as are the two pieces by Alessandro Scurani, each with its special focus, "La lunga confessione di Silone," in *Letture*, XXI (1966), 3–26, and "La religiosità di Ignazio Silone," in *Letture*, XXI (1966), 485–504.

Alberto Moravia

Moravia's popularity in the English-speaking world has made him one of the most widely studied writers of contemporary Italy. In book form, perceptive analyses of his work may be read in Donald Heiney's *Three Italian Novelists: Moravia, Pavese, Vittorini* (Ann Arbor, University of Michigan Press, 1968) and in the more generic monograph by Giuliano Dego, *Moravia* (New York, Barnes and Noble, Inc., 1967). For a broad survey of Moravia's literary production, see Sergio Pacifici's "Alberto Moravia," in *A Guide to Contemporary Italian Literature: From Futurism to Neorealism*, New York, World Publishing Co., 1962, pp. 29–56.

In addition, the reader will find the following essays useful and illuminating for their points of view and insights:

Baldanza, Frank. "The Classicism of Alberto Moravia." *Modern Fiction Studies*, III (1958), 309–20.

Bergin, Thomas G. "The Moravian Muse." *Virginia Quarterly Review*, XXIX (1953), 215–25.

Foster, Kenelm. "Alberto Moravia." *Blackfriars*, XLIII (1962), 221–30.

Heiney, Donald. "Alberto Moravia." *Three Italian Novelists*. Ann Arbor, University of Michigan Press, 1968, pp. 49–82.

————. "Moravia's America." *America in Modern Italian Literature*. New Brunswick, Rutgers University Press, 1964, pp. 202–20.

Ragusa, Olga. "Alberto Moravia: Voyeurism and Storytelling." *Southern Review*, IV (1968), 127–41.

Rimanelli, Giose. "Moravia and the Philosophy of Personal Existence." *Italian Quarterly,* No. 41 (1967), 39–68.

In Italian, the study by Edoardo Sanguineti, *Alberto Moravia* (Milan, Mursia, 1962) is both carefully documented and well written; Alberto Limentani's monographic work, *Alberto Moravia tra esistenza e realtà* (Venice, Neri Pozza, 1962) is original and particularly persuasive in its analysis of the existentialist undercurrent in Moravia's fiction. Both volumes are complemented by full bibliographies.

Elio Vittorini

The sudden death of Elio Vittorini in 1966 generated a new wave of interest in his own work and in his place in Italian literature. In this connection, see the special issue of *Il menabò* (No. 10, 1967) devoted to brief pieces by Vittorini and criticism of his work by others.

In English one may begin with Sergio Pacifici's "Elio Vittorini," in *A Guide to Contemporary Italian Literature* (New York, World Publishing Co., 1962), 87–113; also "Understanding Vittorini 'Whole.'" *Italian Quarterly,* I (1958), 95–98; and my studies, *Three Italian Novelists: Moravia, Pavese, Vittorini* (Ann Arbor, University of Michigan Press, 1968), pp. 147–213, and "Vittorini, the Opera, and the Fifth Dimension," in *College English,* 17 (May, 1966), 451–56.

Other useful essays are R. W. B. Lewis' "Elio Vittorini," *Italian Quarterly,* IV, 15 (1960) 55–61; C. A. McCormick's "Elio Vittorini" in *Italian Quarterly,* No. 39–40 (1967), 39–61; and Glauco Cambon, "Elio Vittorini: Between Poverty and Wealth," *Wisconsin Studies in Contemporary Literature,* III (1962), 20–24.

In Italian, the most interesting pieces are:

Bocelli, Arnaldo. "L'arte di Vittorini." *Il Mondo,* XVIII, (1966), 9.
Forti, Marco. "Vittorini e *Le donne di Messina.*" *Letteratura,* LXXIV–LXXV (1965), 70–80.
Pampaloni, Geno. "I nomi e le lacrime di Elio Vittorini." *Il Ponte,* XI (1949), 1534–41.

Pautasso, Sergio. *Elio Vittorini.* Milan, Borla Editore, 1967.
Piccioni, Leone. "Coerenza di Vittorini." *Sui contemporanei,* (Rome, Fabbri, 1953), pp. 99–154.
Tommaso, Piero De. "Elio Vittorini." *Belfagor,* XX (1965), 552–78.

Cesare Pavese

Articles in English dealing with Pavese are very few; among them the following should be mentioned: Leslie A. Fiedler, "Introducing Cesare Pavese," *The Kenyon Review,* XVI, 4, Autumn 1954; Susan Sontag, "The Artist as Exemplary Sufferer," in *Against Interpretation* (New York, Farrar, Straus and Giroux, 1966), pp. 39–48; Stuart Hood, "A Protestant Without God," *Encounter,* XXVI, 5 (May 1966), 41–48; Giose Rimanelli, "The Conception of Time and Language in the Poetry of Cesare Pavese," *Italian Quarterly,* VIII, 30, 14–34; Paolo Milano, "Pavese's Experiments in the Novel," *The New Republic,* CXXVIII, 18 (May 4, 1953), 18 ff.; R. W. Flint's "Introduction" to *The Selected Works of Cesare Pavese* (New York, Farrar, Straus and Giroux, 1968); and Donald Heiney, *Three Italian Novelists: Moravia, Pavese, Vittorini* (Ann Arbor, University of Michigan Press, 1968), pp. 83–146. From the biographical point of view, Natalia Ginzburg's essay "Portrait of a Friend: Cesare Pavese," in *Atlantic Monthly* (Supplement: *Perspectives of Italy,* 1959), CCIII, 75–77, is both sensitive and beautifully written.

In Italian, in addition to the monographs listed, the following essays recommend themselves as being particularly useful to understanding Pavese more completely: Guido Guglielmi, "Mito e Logos in Pavese," in *Convivium,* CCVI, pp. 93–98; and Maria Luisa Premuda, "I *Dialoghi con Leucò* e il realismo simbolico di Pavese," in *Annali della Scuola Normale Superiore* di Pisa, XXVII (1957), III–IV, 222–49.

I should also recall the critical works mentioned in the chapter, and suggest the fundamental monographs: Franco Mollia, *Cesare Pavese* (Padua, Rebellato, 1960, then Florence, La Nuova Italia, 1963); Lorenzo Mondo, *Cesare Pavese* (Milan, Mursia, 1962); and the recent psychoanalytical interpretation: Dominique Fernandez, *L'échec de Pavese* (Paris, Grasset, 1968).

Finally, for an extended treatment of the themes of Pavese's works, the reader is referred to my study *The Smile of the Gods* (Ithaca, Cornell University Press, 1968).

The Italian Resistance Novel

For additional information and insights into the works of the writers discussed in my essay, the reader may wish to consult the following:

Accrocca, Elio Filippo. *Ritratti su misura*. Venice, Sodalizio del Libro, 1960.

Fernandez, Dominique. *Il romanzo italiano e la crisi della coscienza moderna*. Milan, Lerici, 1960.

Gallo, Niccolò. "La narrativa italiana del dopoguerra." *Società*. II (June, 1950).

Heiney, Donald. *Three Italian Novelists*. Ann Arbor, University of Michigan Press, 1968.

Longobardi, Fulvio. *Vasco Pratolini*. Milan, Mursia, 1964.

Manacorda, Giuliano. *Storia della letteratura italiana contemporanea (1940–1965)*. Rome, Editori Riuniti, 1965.

Pacifici, Sergio. *A Guide to Contemporary Italian Literature: From Futurism to Neorealism*. (New York, World Publ. Co., 1962), pp. 143–49.

Paoluzi, Angelo. *La letteratura della resistenza*. Florence, Cinque Lune, 1956.

Rosa, Alberto Asor. *Vasco Pratolini*. Rome, Università di Roma, 1958.

Rosengarten, Frank, *Vasco Pratolini: the Development of a Social Novelist*. Carbondale, Southern Illinois University Press, 1965.

Russo, Luigi. *I narratori*. Milan, Principato, 1958.

Gadda, Pasolini, and Experimentalism

For bibliography in English, see, in addition to reviews of *Quer pasticciaccio* and *Ragazzi di vita*: Dante Della Terza, "Italian Fiction from Pavese to Pasolini," *Italian Quarterly*, X (1966), 3–20, and "The Neorealists and the Form of the Novel," *Italian Quarterly*, III (1959), 29–41; and Sergio Pacifici, "From Engagement to Alienation: A View of Contemporary Italian Literature," *Italica*, XL (1964), 236–58. On *Gruppo 63*, see my own "Italian Criticism: 1964," *Books Abroad*, XXXIX (1965), 283–87.

For bibliography in Italian, see Angelo Guglielmi, "Carlo Emilio Gadda," in *I contemporanei* (Milan, Marzorati, 1963), II, 1051–70; Giorgio Bàrberi Squarotti, *La narrativa italiana del dopoguerra* (Bologna, Cappelli, 1966), pp. 42–50, 191–93, and *Poesia e narrativa del secondo novecento* (Milan, Mursia, 1967), pp. 133–48, 327–31; Gaetano Mariani, *La giovane narrativa italiana tra documento e poesia* (Florence, Le Monnier, 1962), pp. 140–44, 164–72; and Gian Carlo Ferretti, *Letteratura e ideologia* (Rome, Editori Riuniti, 1964), pp. 163–356.